Cloud-Based Intelligent Informative Engineering for Society 5.0

Cloud-based Intelligent Informative Engineering for Society 5.0 is a model for the dissemination of cutting-edge technological innovation and assistive devices for people with physical impairments. This book showcases cloud-based, high-performance information systems and informatics-based solutions for the verification of the information support requirements of the modern engineering, healthcare, modern business, organization, and academic communities.

Features:

- Includes broad variety of methodologies and technical developments to improve research in informative engineering.
- Explores the Internet of things (IoT), blockchain technology, deep learning, data analytics, and cloud.
- Highlights cloud-based high-performance information systems and informatics-based solutions.

This book is beneficial for graduate students and researchers in computer sciences, cloud computing, and related subject areas.

Chapman & Hall/CRC Cloud Computing for Society 5.0

Series Editor:
Vishal Bhatnagar and Vikram Bali

Digitalization of Higher Education using Cloud Computing
S.L. Gupta, Nawal Kishor, Niraj Mishra, Sonali Mathur, Utkarsh Gupta

Cloud Computing Technologies for Smart Agriculture and Healthcare
Urmila Shrawankar, Latesh Malik, Sandhya Arora

Cloud and Fog Computing Platforms for Internet of Things
Pankaj Bhambri, Sita Rani, Gaurav Gupta and Alex Khang

Cloud based Intelligent Informative Engineering for Society 5.0
Kaushal Kishor, Neetesh Saxena and Dilkeshwar Pandey

Cloud based Multi-Modal Information Analytics: A Hands-on Approach
Srinidhi Hiriyannaiah, Siddesh G M, Srinivasa K G

Integration of IoT with Cloud Computing for Smart Applications
Rohit Anand, Sapna Juneja, Abhinav Juneja, Vishal Jain, Ramani Kannan

For more information about this series, please visit: https://www.routledge.com/ Chapman–HallCRC-Cloud-Computing-for-Society-50/book-series/CRCCCS

Cloud-Based Intelligent Informative Engineering for Society 5.0

Edited by
Kaushal Kishor
Neetesh Saxena
Dilkeshwar Pandey

CRC Press
Taylor & Francis Group
Boca Raton London New York

CRC Press is an imprint of the
Taylor & Francis Group, an **informa** business

A CHAPMAN & HALL BOOK

First edition published 2023
by CRC Press
6000 Broken Sound Parkway NW, Suite 300, Boca Raton, FL 33487-2742

and by CRC Press
4 Park Square, Milton Park, Abingdon, Oxon, OX14 4RN

CRC Press is an imprint of Taylor & Francis Group, LLC

ISBN: 9781032101514 (hbk)
ISBN: 9781032461328 (pbk)
ISBN: 9781003213895 (ebk)

DOI: 10.1201/9781003213895

Typeset in Palatino
by codeMantra

Contents

Preface

In every human civilization, including rural, urban, smart city, and future societies ("Society 5.0" a future society of Japan), the Internet and cloud technologies are crucial. It is also necessary for future human civilizations to have a study book on Cloud-based Intelligent Informative Engineering for Society 5.0. Cloud-based intelligent informative engineering is experiencing fast transformation as human society and human ideals become more dominant in many aspects of our daily lives. It's becoming more difficult for us to maintain a healthy balance between technology and society. It's too early to tell which should take precedence right now: technology or society? As a result, society and technology are at odds with one another. For those who are interested in learning about the convergence of cloud computing and Industry 4.0 with Society 5.0, machine-to-machine communication, and machine-to-person communication, this book serves as a text/research/reference book. We hope that this book will serve as a guide for those who want to learn more about these topics. This book explains these principles in an easy-to-understand manner. As a prerequisite, we expect readers to be acquainted with the fundamentals of intelligent computing, cloud computing, the Internet of things (IoT), machine learning, and the Python programming language. A fundamental grasp of rural/urban cultures and human psychologies is required for issues like socio-technological perspectives on Society 5.0 and sentiment analysis of smart digital societies. Though prerequisite knowledge is not required, readers can still follow along and understand the approaches described in psychological models of technophobia, social data processing, sentiment data analysis and sentiment evaluation methods, multi-access edge computing and video surveillance technology as well as multiple disease prediction and societal opinion mining algorithms. The principles in this book are explained in a way that is easy to understand. But formal proofs/source codes of these theoretical ideas are generally missing from this book. At the conclusion of each chapter, the references include citations to research publications in which the findings were initially presented and proven, as well as references to more current information. Figures and examples are used instead of proofs in this text to explain why we should believe the conclusion in issue. Chapter 10 ends with appendices that provide the source code for the algorithms and tables that have been explained and discussed in the results and discussion portions of each chapter. There are many similarities between the ideas, models, and algorithms in this book and those utilized in commercial and open-source digital environments. There will be a focus on the future of society (including "Society 5.0"), as well as a broad overview of the ideas, model designs, hardware designs, and algorithms presented. In a cloud-IoT integrated distributed computing environment, these tools, models, and algorithms may be effectively leveraged to get insights into rural and urban civilizations. In this text and pictures, we've organized our many years of teaching and research expertise in cloud-IoT technologies and intelligent machine learning, deep learning, multi-access distributed edge computing, and video surveillance technologies based on unmanned aerial vehicles. As readers of this book (first version) provide feedback and recommendations, we will include them into the future edition.

Editors

Dr. Kaushal Kishor received his Ph.D. in Computer Science and Engineering from AKTU Lucknow, in the domain of Mobile Ad hoc Network, and his M.Tech and B.Tech in Computer Science and Engineering from UPTU Lucknow. Currently, he is working at ABES Institute of Technology, Ghaziabad, as an associate professor in the Department of Information Technology. He has supervised more than 50 projects for graduate and post-graduate students. He has more than 18 years of experience in teaching. He is Gate Qualified 2003 score 94.5 percentile. He has book published: (1) *Design and Analysis Algorithms* (**ISBN no. 978-93-81695-20-3**), (2) *Computer Networks* (**ISBN no. 978-93-81695-27-2**), (3) *Compiler Design* (**ISBN no. 938169530 x and 13 9789381695302**), (4) *Design and Analysis of Algorithms: Techniques and Control Management* (**ISBN no. 978-81-8220-516-1**), (5) *Computer Networks: A System Approach* (**ISBN no. 978-81-8220-516-3**), and (6) *Compiler Design Principles, Techniques, and Tools* (ISBN no. 978-81-8220-626-7) for various engineering fields such as B.Tech and MCA students. He has published 25 papers in peer-reviewed international/national journals and conferences. His research interest includes Artificial Intelligence, Computer Networks, Algorithm, Compiler Design Wireless, and Sensor Networking.

Dr. Neetesh Saxena is currently an Assistant Professor (Lecturer) at the School of Computer Science and Informatics at Cardiff University, UK, with more than 14 years of teaching/research experience in academia. Before joining CU, he was an Assistant Professor at Bournemouth University, UK. Prior to this, he was a Post-Doctoral Researcher in the School of Electrical and Computer Engineering at the Georgia Institute of Technology, USA. He was also with the Department of Computer Science, The State University of New York (SUNY) Korea, South Korea, as a Post-Doctoral Researcher and a Visiting Scholar at the Department of Computer Science, Stony Brook University, USA. He earned his PhD in Computer Science and Engineering from the Indian Institute of Technology (IIT) Indore, India. He was a DAAD Scholar at Bonn-Aachen International Center for Information Technology (B-IT), Rheinische-Friedrich-Wilhelms-Universität, Bonn, Germany, and was also a TCS Research Scholar. His current research interests include cyber security and critical infrastructure security, including cyber-physical system security: smart grid, V2G, and cellular communication networks. He has published several high-quality publications in IEEE/ACM transactions, IEEE, Elsevier, and Springer journals, as well as in ACM CCS workshop, IEEE ICC, IEEE TrustCom, IEEE SMC, ACSAC, and IEEE CCNC. He is a Recipient of the ComSoc YP and WICE Best Paper Award at

IEEE ICC 2017. He has organized several conferences and workshops including an IEEE SMC Society sponsored summer school "Human Factors in System Safety and Security" at Bournemouth University, UK. He has also served as a Reviewer for many prestigious IEEE journals, such as TIFS, TVT, COMST, TSG, TII, TSC, TC, TMC, TEM, and SJ. He has served as a Session Chair for IEEE SMC 2013 and 2018, and a Track Chair: Information Technology and the Internet for IEEE TEMSCON 2018. He has also been a TPC Member for many international conferences such as IEEE ICC, IEEE MILCOM, IEEE TrustCom, IEEE SmartGridComm, IEEE WiMob, IEEE PIMRC, and IEEE ICCC, and an Independent Reviewer for ESORICS, ECIS, IEEE VTC, HICSS, IEEE ICUFN, and TEMSCON. He is a Senior Member of IEEE and a Member of IEEE SMC, IEEE ComSoc, ACM, and Eta Kappa Nu.

 **Prof. (Dr.) Dilkeshwar Pandey,** Ph.D. (DCRUST, Haryana), M.E. (Delhi College of Engineering, DU), B.E. (BIT, Sindri) Professor, CSE, KIET Group of Institutions, NCR, Ghaziabad, possessing over 30 years of experience in teaching and software development, Dr. Dilkeshwar Pandey is an avid researcher and has immensely contributed in transforming computer education in the institution. Spearheading Innovation and R&D in areas such as computer vision and data science. He has been pivotal in conceiving and organizing faculty development programs to stay abreast with the latest developments. He has guided not only students but also research scholars across the country, especially in the area of image processing. He has also contributed by publishing numerous papers in journals of international repute. He has published 6 patents and one has been granted.

Contributors

Shivani Agarwal
Ajay Kumar Garg Engineering College
Ghaziabad, India

Shashank Awashthi
GL Bajaj Institute of Technology and
  Management
Greater Noida, India

Sansar Singh Chauhan
GL Bajaj Institute of Technology and
  Management
Greater Noida, India

Manish Chhabra
ABES Institute of Technology
Ghaziabad, India

Megha Gupta
IMS Engineering College
Ghaziabad, India

Kaushal Kishor
ABES Institute of Technology
Ghaziabad, India

Aditya Sam Koshy
IMS Engineering College
Ghaziabad, India

Amit Kumar
IMS Engineering College
Ghaziabad, India

Arvind Kumar
Raj Kumar Goel Institute of Technology
Ghaziabad, India

Parma Nand
Sharda University
Greater Noida, India

Mahaveer Singh Naruka
GL Bajaj Institute of Technology and
  Management
Greater Noida, India

Rupa Rani
ABES Institute of Technology
Ghaziabad, India

Amit Kumar Singh Sanger
KIET Group of Institutions
Ghaziabad, India

Akanksha Shukla
Ajay Kumar Garg Engineering College
Ghaziabad, India

Abhilasha Singh
SRM Institute of Science and Technology
Ghaziabad, India

Atul Kumar Singh
Galgotias University
Greater Noida, India

Raj Kishor Verma
ABES Institute of Technology
Ghaziabad, India

Satya Prakash Yadav
GL Bajaj Institute of Technology and
  Management
Greater Noida, India

1

Managing Information System with the Help of Cloud Computing

Akanksha Shukla and Shivani Agarwal

Ajay Kumar Garg Engineering College

CONTENTS

DOI: 10.1201/9781003213895-1

1.1 Introduction

In the present time of digitalization, digital data plays a primary role in making our lives more comfortable and secure. The success of an organization lies in various plans/strategies and decisions adopted by the management. Adopting a strategy that can fulfill the organization's goal or aim is extremely difficult after having analysis of various data. That's why an effective management information system (MIS) must be used to save, store, and analyze the voluminous amount of data, which helps the managers to adopt the right strategy [1]. The process of collecting information is not of any use if it is not able to serve the correct purpose or right goal of the organization. MIS count in the use of various sets of protocols when applied to the data/information can generate quick business solutions. Since cloud computing is the future of the Internet so cloud computing along with MIS is developing new business ideas and ensuring business growth too.

1.1.1 What is Cloud Computing?

Cloud generally refers to something which is present at remote locations. It can provide various services over private and public networks like WAN, LAN, or VPN. Most of the applications like customer relationship management and emails run on the cloud. A distributed system consists of autonomous computers linked by a network and distribution middleware to coordinate activities and share system resources so users perceive it as a single, integrated computing facility [2,3]. A Wi-Fi access point, base station, or satellite connects mobile nodes to the Internet. Mobile cloud computing is limited to infrastructure-based communication technologies and cannot be used ad hoc. Mobile ad hoc cloud computing employs mobile devices to build a virtual supercomputer. Mobile nodes interact over a mobile ad hoc network that enables discovery, monitoring, and routing. Cloud middleware handles failures, mobility, communications, and tasks. It conceals complexity and gives users and apps a single system view [4–6].

1.1.2 History of Cloud Computing

In the early 1960s, an American Computer Scientist and Psychologist J.C.R. Likelier invented the cloud computing. In the 1990s, few telecommunication giants started offering virtual private network services at affordable prices. By 1994, the cloud metaphor was started to be used for virtualized services. The beauty of this technology went on running throughout the era of the twenty-first century; probably, in 2006, Amazon created Amazon Web Services (AWS) and also noted its Elastic Computing Cloud (EC2); the beta version of Google is too introduced. In 2012, Google compute engine was released; Oracle too introduced Oracle cloud with three basic services for business (IaaS, PaaS, and SaaS). Currently, Linux and Microsoft Azure share most of their work parallel.

1.1.3 Basics of Cloud Computing

There are some services and models available to make cloud computing feasible and accessible to end users.

1.1.4 Deployment Models

There are only four types of access in the cloud: public, private, hybrid, and community.
   The public cloud can be accessible to each and every person. In public cloud, applications and data are stored and managed by third parties whereas private cloud is operated by the organization it serves; there is no involvement of Iaas or Paas. Hybrid cloud is a combination of both public and private cloud, and it's best for heavy workload. Community cloud allows the facility of sharing the resources between the several organizations over the same platform.

1.1.4.1 Service Models

There are basically three types of service models (Figure 1.1):

   Infrastructure as a service: In this service model, the responsibility of managing data and application lies on the users. Example: AWS.

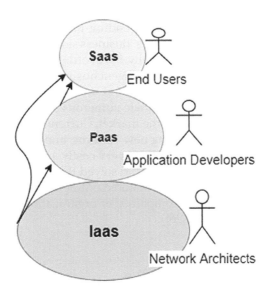

FIGURE 1.1
Service models.

Platform as a service: It is primarily responsible for development and deployment of applications. Example: Apprenda.

Software as a service: In this service model, cloud provider delivers complete software to the client or it allows access to the software only. Example: Google Apps

1.2 What is Cloud Computing in the Management Information System?

A MIS is a tool or a device that facilitates in illustrating a differentiation between their common performance and their set goals as it helps the organization in measuring their growth [7–10]. It extracts the data from the various sources, accesses it, and then produces the result, which helps the decision-makers in making the crucial decision. It consists of information related to each field which helps the personnel of the organization at the time of need [11–15].

Implementation of MIS is an expensive occurrence as it includes the installation and maintenance of IT infrastructure. The hardware consists of expensive storage devices, while the compatible software system helps in coordination and analysis of the stored data. Now, the introduction of cloud computing has totally transformed the traditional high rated MIS by substituting hardware storage devices with effective on-demand cloud storage that can store voluminous information and can be easily reachable through any Internet-connected devices from any geographical location [16–21].

1.3 Need for MIS

The number of customers and their corresponding needs are exponentially increasing, keeping business organizations on their toes. Business startups and competition with rival companies also tend to increase exponentially. So, in order to keep in queue with this competition, it becomes necessary to acquire intelligent business decorum as well new modern steps for ensuring the flow of business [22–24].

Cloud computing and MIS together facilitate numerous efficient solutions to help a business grow and obtain a driving edge in the market. Currently, MIS with cloud computing is leading to amazing patterns, designing new patterns, and assuring the growth of businesses. The traditional old structure of MIS is very costly and also involves IT experts for permanent maintenance. Cloud computing has solved this problem by offering many virtual data storage solutions. As all the data is stored online so cloud computing has brought down the expenses. In this manner, companies or organizations can save a lot of money and can use it ever needed more [25,26].

1.3.1 Cloud Storage

Cloud storage is a kind of virtual memory that allows an individual or users to create, update, delete, and perform all unscrupulous operations on the data with the help of the Internet. In this kind of storage procedure files and data can be saved in the Internet-based cloud memory proposed by the cloud service providers. This quality provides the users a chance to access the information from any geographical location at any time from any device and also can share the data with anyone across the network.

1.3.2 Why Use Cloud Storage

- It was common to see people carrying storage devices containing important data related to them in earlier days. File backup is also not easy because another device also must have the same capacity. In order to transfer data from one user to another, one must need a system that requires a long time to complete the task if file is long.
- If any virus or bug enters the device, the possibility of data loss would be high and all the hard work will be wasted. So, cloud storage here comes as a champion having less money and more power. One can access the data from anywhere at the time of need without carrying physical storage devices. Backups for the data are easily made.
- Data has been increasing day by day in an exponential manner so proper storage of data without any hassle is being provided by the cloud service providers.
- Cloud provides the flexibility which is appreciable as one can log in from anywhere and can access the information when needed.

1.3.3 Working of Cloud Storage

- Servers placed in remote locations store the data of the user, who is connected to the server, and user uploads the data into the Internet and sends to the server connected. Then, that data is sent to different servers stored remotely. Users can access this data when needed via the Internet [27,28].
- Data is stored in different servers so if one fails to provide the facility because of any reason then no need to worry as the same data is available to another server also [29].
- Cloud storage can be public, private, and hybrid.
- Communication with the data can be done easily as automatic sharing is done by giving a link just like Google drive.
- Organizations need not worry about the maintenance of storage devices as it is done by service provider.
- Scaling can be done easier according to the use of storage space.
- Cloud services are used by simply paying a fixed amount set by service provider based on storage and usage of end user. A service provider can also add the servers dynamically.

1.3.4 Review on Management Information System with the Help of Cloud Computing

Cloud computing is actually a model which enables easy, favorable, on-demand network access to a shared pool of devices. It is treated as a model and service rather than a product or computing device [30]. In the domain of information and content procedure, cloud computing model provide simple and user-oriented information and resources to the entire information sector. Due to various elevations, cloud computing model is used in several places like e-commerce, e-governance, Web-based document management, and in the field of Web storage.

Let us take an example of usage of cloud computing in e-governance that how governments have adopted the strategies to implement and manage e-governance [31]. Due to the lack of proper utilization of resources day by day success rate has been declined so this biasing can be burned out by proper management opted by the government. So, for this particular purpose, an effective framework [32] has been designed based on cloud computing hypothesis which is more intellectual likewise also accessible to all. This framework is having three layers: knowledge base, inference engine, and user interface.

Knowledge base comprises rules and facts about the particular problem area from where the system extracts its expertise. In order to accomplish, the knowledge base system must have an element, i.e., **inference engine**, which can further scan the facts and can be able to provide the solution to the problems provided by the user. **User interface** is the median through which user can interact with the system by the mean of human-understandable language.

MIS is a summation of individuals, methodology, information that supports managers to take quick informed decisions. MIS system is a contraption used for making decisions and in turn can strengthen the high performance of the organizations [33]. Cloud computing technology with MIS is a new concept that enhances the efficiency of the technology and diminishes the entanglement in data to user management. A Thai qualification framework has been implemented in accordance with cloud computing MIS which is the applied information technology used to assemble, explore, and precede data in systematic manner and adjust the faults which conformed to saying that cloud computing technology can aid user to approach database resource through the Internet from any geographical location [34] (Figure 1.2).

The introduction of cloud computing pattern in healthcare system also influences today's society a lot. For this purpose, electronic healthcare and electronic billing system has been put forward as an appliance as in traditional healthcare system, patient's information is manipulated and disclosed and various types of misconception have occurred. This procedure uses the concept of open-source public cloud computing technologies and mobile plus cloud paradigm [35]. A **Medbook** platform is preferred, a kind of cloud solution which in turn provides patients, professionals, and healthcare payers a platform to interchange electronic information about billing-related tasks and electronic health records operations like insert, delete, and update records using cloud services [36] (Figure 1.3).

How Does Cloud Computing Change Management?

Cloud computing offers very positive effects like virtualization, scalability, and easy collaboration, which help the management in turning the business more productive, remunerative, and coherent. Cloud computing has given some of the vital tools to managers to manage their business in an easy manner and they can connect with their employees at the time of need and can share the resources or information of each and every project without any time delay. So, it's surprising to see how **cloud computing** is changing management for the better.

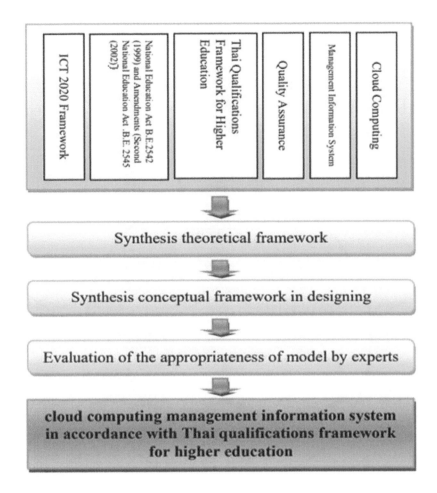

FIGURE 1.2
Cloud computing management information system.

Both **cloud computing** and **MIS** create a great chance for businesses to grow at a splendid rhythm. Cloud computing makes MIS productive and provides tools that help it to achieve the highest expertise as MIS holds key to the overall business performance (Figure 1.4).

1.4 Data Management in Cloud Computing

Cloud computing plays a primary/key role and has become a major influence in data management. In a cloud-based data management schema, organizations rent bins and evaluate power in order to make the data management applications work preferably than making considerable capital in-house investment for infrastructure. Cloud-based data management is in turn helping to realize the perspective of large-scale data management solutions by giving efficacious amount of resources [37]. Data management is one of the most

FIGURE 1.3
MIS with cloud computing.

important research areas in cloud computing prevailing today. Many cloud-based data management systems are functioning now like Bigtable in Google, HBase in stream, and PNUTS in Yahoo.

1.5 Data Security in Cloud

The cloud security is very important as more and more organizations are moving their data to the cloud. The major challenge is that the owner of the data may not have control over where the data is placed [38]. So a secure data secure storage system to ensure the data availability at the time of need is a must [36]. The main primary problems regarding data security emphasize:

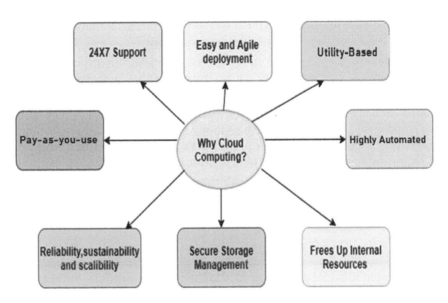

FIGURE 1.4
Need of cloud computing.

- How fast users get aware of the data over the cloud is safe.
- How to regain data if data is lost or not in proper format.
- How to implement key technology to solve problems related to cloud environment.

A data secure storage scheme was proposed based on Tornado codes [36] by using the technique of symmetric encryption and erasure codes and Proof of Relevance (POR) algorithm with trusted logs, which provide users the test results. The computational efficiency of POR when involved with data security scheme based on Tornado (DSBT) will get more relevant.

1.6 Cloud-Based E-Learning Systems

A cloud-based e-learning system is assumed to be a submodule of cloud computing in the field related to education [37]. With the help of servers, applications, and services, cloud computing has overcome the various challenges of high cost related to e-learning [38]. Implementing e-learning with the help of cloud computing has given so many benefits:

- **Lower cost:** As the cloud environment provided by cell phones, laptops, and personal computers enabled the users to run all the associated application with minimum ordering of internet connectivity.
- **Increase performance:** No performance-related issues arise as proper functioning is performed by client machines. Many of the applications and process of e-learning system applications are reserved in the cloud.

- **Immediate software updates:** All the software is updated automatically in cloud; as a result, e-learners will always get updated timely.
- **Pros for teachers:** Many benefits can be gained by teachers/instructors from cloud-based e-learning as preparing test papers, assessing tests, homework, and sending feedback and communicating with them in online manner when appropriate, etc.
- **Benefits for learners:** Same as teachers, learners can also get very much benefitted from cloud-based e-learning system as they can also do all their assignments and projects via online medium and can also get and receive feedback from teachers and share any problem related to field of education easily [39].
- **Enhanced compatibility regarding document's format:** e-learning application running over cloud possesses more compatibility with various file formats, which cannot be read easily on personal computers or mobile phones.

1.6.1 Cloud-Based College-Enterprise Classroom Training Method

Due to enhancement in social competition, student-centric, resource-sharing, or mutually developed training patterns have been adopted by most of the educational organizations. That's the main reason why an innovative college-enterprise classroom has been a primary part of cooperation between schools and enterprises. Hence, a cloud computing-based college-enterprise framework has been proposed due to its high compatibility, unlimited storage space, reliable computational facilities, and flexible data exchange and knowledge coordination. Due to several drawbacks in traditional enterprise classroom, a new powerful pattern of cloud-based college-enterprise classroom is needed. The traditional classrooms cannot be able to meet the requirements of increasing learners' strength as inappropriate computer rooms, especially those colleges that are engaged in information engineering. Based on the various beneficial aspects of cloud computing, a cloud has been introduced to design an applicable pattern/layout of the college-enterprise classroom.

A cloud-based college-enterprise classroom comprises mainly three parts: a cloud platform, a virtual reality teaching platform, and virtualization-assisted teaching system (Figure 1.5).

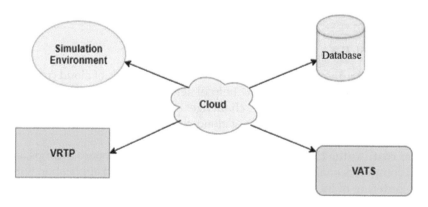

FIGURE 1.5
Cloud-based college-enterprise classroom framework.

- **Virtualization-assisted teaching system:** In accordance with specific teaching objectives and business procedures, a peculiar teaching system for a specific area should be developed as VATS is an important component.

- **VR teaching platform:** In this platform, various visualization methods are used to make a teaching-learning process more interactive and more understandable as visual effects impose a great impact on someone's mind.

- **Cloud platform:** This platform is introduced to better design an information-based college-enterprise classroom. In cloud, resources from both the teachers and students are kept and can be shared as per their requirement and need. The resources contain e-textbooks and informative videos.

So, this framework enables the students to perform enterprise practice inside the campus and can upraise their theoretical as well as practical ability.

1.7 Cloud-Based Employee Management System

One of the primary challenges of small and medium enterprises is human resource management and to manage the employee information. So, to overcome this challenge, employee management system with cloud computing is introduced. It emphasizes authentic cloud platform and providers to provide four main modules, which are record management, payroll management, staff assessment, and leave management.

Cloud-based data management system stores employee's information both personal and professional and can be accessed on demand instantly with proper authentication check.

1.7.1 Employee Management System

It is a kind of software that stores employees' data in a more secure manner and can be accessed with few clicks at the time of requirement. It also helps the employees to give their best efforts in the right direction as each and every information is available or in reach of every employee so decision-making ability or right decision can be easily taken at right time so in turn this activity will also enhance the growth of the organization itself. The pocket human resource management system provides a very simple and easy way to manage user interface and helps in tracking the performance of the employees. It provides an overview of the entire staff management.

1.7.2 Cloud-Based Human Resource Management System

Human resource management system can be defined as an ordering of systems and processes required for efficiently managing the human resource department of an organization. The HRMS cloud solution permits one to properly manage the attendance and leaves of every single employee. Its automated system has the ability to stack the record of every employee. Zing HR Cloud-Based Human Resource Management System is basically designed for small and medium enterprises. It has enhanced features that can track or keep record of travel and other outlays which are work-related. The cloud management system builds an indiscriminate platform that is beneficial and easily accessible too.

It unifies data for a centric platform to offer the best and quicker HR management. Modern HR demands are increasing rapidly day to day as workforce and external and legal requirements go on changing usually. The utility of cloud-based HR management system is:

- Strain selection process and learn from past mistakes or success to confirm that you are receiving the best talent each time.

- Employees are given remote access to each and every information that is needed for them to perform best at all time.

- Fill open positions frequently and monitor skill gaps using federated online applications.

- To identify your hard-working and best employee and reward them to keep growing their performance further.

- Support employees in their progressive roles with proper guidance and also provide tools to them which can help others by creating training materials and other contents too.

In short, we can say that cloud-based HR management system provides so many advantages like portability, greater customization, easy to use, efficient reporting, self-administration, having integrated solution, and cost-effective.

1.8 Cloud-Based Health Management System

Cloud-based software as a service (SAAS) is famous in healthcare spotting for documenting patient activity and managing information. Cloud-based health information system operates as SAAS applications and is approachable through any Web browser or desktop application. It provides common cloud computing benefits (like high accessibility, minimized operation expenditure, and reduced hardware maintenance) and imparts benefits, especially for larger organizations.

- **Assistance to data security, network**

    IT departments can clearly view and observe the activity through cloud-based health management system and easily identify the abnormal activity. It can easily prevent the apps (compromised) to share the information with other apps over the network and easily detect the unauthorized activity.

- **Benefits to resource management**

    Consolidating isolated information systems onto cloud-based systems saves time on administrative tasks; equates data between applications; and updates files and records available in multiple applications. Users don't have to contact any specific IT department for special permissions as all the healthcare departments are stabilized onto one platform.

- **Welfare to specific practice types**

    Cloud-based health information systems can particularly benefit rural practices and healthcare organizations with lower estimate. A health information management system stretches an entire health IT infrastructure. Cloud-based health information systems are adjustable and can easily be revised as organizations designed more applications.

1.9 Supply Chain Management

As we all are aware that millions of products are transported on daily basis making it hard to maintain the voluminous amount of data, cloud technology has helped a lot in solving such type of global supply chain issues. The aim of any business is to get its products to the target customers. The supply chain generally refers to the system, collection, and connection of resources that are used in a product or service to customers from producers. Cloud computing introduces access and use of remote servers in contrast to in-house servers to handle data. There are various ways by which cloud computing can affect supply chain. Companies are using cloud computing to bring transformation to the management of their supply chain. SaaS has been proven one of the best ways to craft cloud computing into the supply chain management market. Cloud computing in the form of SaaS in supply chain is extrapolated to have a swift rise in the coming years. There are some specific activities of organization that are commonly focused on in supply chain. These activities include logistics, future prediction, planning, service, and spare parts management including sourcing and procurement. Many of these activities have been proficiently improved by supply chain managers with the use of cloud computing.

The information storage becomes easy, less costly, and more accessible with the supply chain automation. Also, it helps in inventory level, transportation information, and so on. The analytics and intellectual intelligence provided by cloud computing can totally mutate the supply chain. Cloud computing helps in ease of scaling the supply chain operations. Thus, if essential data is given, there are far less chances for a company to get downfall and deny supplies to their customers and also cloud computing provides expansion by giving infrastructure, platform, or a base and software solutions for the supply chain network and leads to benefits either in finance or in operational perspective. Cloud-based supply management can also be capable to significantly cut down on lost product as it can track down a shipment during any phase of transport.

1.9.1 Cloud Computing Paradigms

Cloud computing paradigm is the assigned solution when it comes to the interconnectivity of devices and sharing of data via the Internet. With the advancement and emergence of IoT, the cloud computing has proved to be the most effective to date. Cloud computing provides a much larger room for the trade-off between performance and cost. It not only provides the perspective to solve the large-scale business problems but also gives the chance to revamp the performance/cost ratio. Hence, cloud computing is turning up as a new instance that aims to deliver computing as beneficial. The cloud computing paradigm arises as a result of maturity and junction of several of its supporting models and technologies (Figure 1.6).

Many of the organizations have enacted this latest technology; one is Hartford that dispatches information technology services to its users. With the use of cloud computing in the technological system, the IT infrastructure has totally changed. This organization mainly focuses on property business and mutual funds.

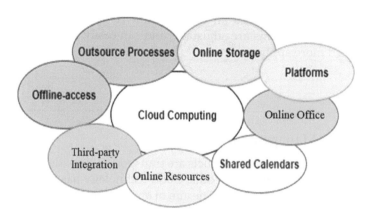

FIGURE 1.6
Cloud computing paradigms.

The other one is Delhaize America; this organization is also implementing cloud computing; basically, this organization works on grocery chains, which has a huge amount of data to manage since cloud computing helps in studying the impact of weather on sales and different product categories in stores. So, with the help of cloud computing, organization can diagnose the weather and can be able to take the right decision at right time.

Another one is Pearson Company which is also employing the cloud computing services and providing high-quality education across the world. This technology helps the organization in enhancing the online education and also helps in improving the concepts and performance of the learners.

1.10 Conceptual Framework in Designing Cloud Computing Management Information System in Academic Area

The development of this framework comprises four junctures [40]:

- Integrate the peculiarity of cloud computing MIS in academic area from related works and researches.
- Integrate the segments of cloud computing MIS in academic area.
- Design miniatures of cloud computing MIS in academic area.
- Estimate the facsimile of cloud computing MIS in academic area.

MIS is consistently a computer system used for tackling five main components: (1) hardware, (2) software, (3) data (information for decision-making), (4) strategy (design, evolution, and deed/documentation), and (5) people (individuals, group, or organization). The miniature of cloud computing management information system in academic work relies on six main elements: consumer, client, connectivity, center, curriculum, and cloud computing Technology is commonly known as C6 (Figure 1.7).

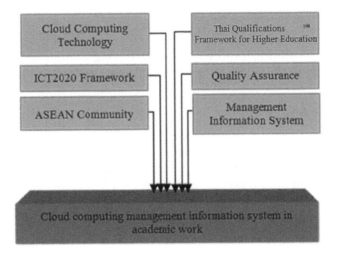

FIGURE 1.7
Conceptual frameworks in designing.

1.11 Cloud Computing and Its Amalgamation with Information Science

The information technology foundations are growing speedily with the help of cloud computing. Due to transfiguration and superseding of information, the easy access and availability of information help to shift an information society from traditional society [30]. The cloud computing facsimile also helps to create knowledge-based economy. In real terms, the information science is an area that consists of fields of many subjects that focus on properties and behavior of information. The Cloud Computing Outlook may be carried out in multiple academic field of information science and institutional areas, which are as follows:

1.11.1 Information Networks

It is a set of two or more computers that are connected to share resources or information. It uses two technologies that are computing and telecommunications.

1.11.2 Information System

It is a well-ordered system for collection, storage, processing, and communication of information. It uses a series of equipment that are responsible for the effective distribution of information.

1.11.3 Knowledge Lattice and Networks

Knowledge grid is a kind of enactment of attachment of multiple computers which are distributed topographically but connected via networks and can work together to execute the joint tasks.

1.11.4 Information Center and Data Center

It is a kind of library where one can go and get any information. It is a kind of repository that is responsible for storing, processing, and retrieving information for propagation at finite intervals on demand according to selectively expressed needs by the users.

1.11.5 Information Analysis Center

It is the standardized process of discovering and interpreting information. Information analysis intimates the application of human talent including basic abilities like complete interpretation of natural language. India is having thousands of information network for the purpose of institutes, universities, and academics like National Information System for Science and Technology, National Information Center Network, and Education and Research Network. Now, we will see some traditional areas of information science where cloud is applicable:

- In GUI-based search engines
- In collection, selection, and organization of knowledge
- In document delivery services
- To entertain and outline website of information science and information network.
- For preparing auto-indexing and fuzzy-based IRS.

1.12 Cloud Computing: Challenges

There are numerous challenges that are faced by the organization, which are moving to the public cloud. Let us discuss some of the challenges.

1.12.1 Security

While using cloud computing, you have to heavily depend on service providers; as there are so many providers in the market, this is the most challenging part: how to trust those players and how to know their service policies.

1.12.2 Data Possession

It is very important to perceive who is accessing the data and for what purpose because moving to the cloud organizations will not totally lose track of their data but they lose some level of ownership of data in some particular control.

1.12.3 Standard Architecture

There is no specific standard architecture being used for cloud services. Most of the cloud service providers like Microsoft Azure, AWS, and Google App Engine all impose different architectures so this lack of standard has an adverse impact on customers' ability to relocate from one service provider to another.

1.12.4 Need for Internet Connectivity

A proper Internet connection is required to work with cloud computing. With slow/dead Internet connection, you cannot perform task reliably and this could be a problem.

1.12.5 Compatibility

It would be difficult to use different dealers and to flawlessly integrate legacy and cloud services.

In order to vanquish these challenges, organizations need to overview their business needs in a more systemic manner and access the potential gains and opportunities against the risks so that transition from traditional services to cloud services is properly planned and understood.

1.13 Cloud Computing Life Cycle

In order to deliver the advantages and to overcome the challenges, a cloud life cycle applies proven and documented project management principles that are known by most IT and business managers. This life cycle has **four** phases, namely **Architect, Engage, Operate, and Refresh**. The use of cloud life cycle has been proven a good mechanism for the organizations to control and manage not only their migration but also day-to-day management of their public cloud environment.

The cloud life cycle provides an organization a management structure to assess the following:

- The puberty of an organization to move to the public cloud.
- After getting migrated how the organization is managing the new environment on daily basis.
- What new services can be moved to a public cloud environment?

1.13.1 Methodology

In line with all well-managed information system, this structure maintains restraint and allows a company to halt at any step if stuck and can restart when internal or external conditions allow without losing any work or tasks done in the previous step. In the proposed methodology, we used to perform each of the six steps: examine, collect, transform, cleaning, security, and communicate at every level of MIS.

- **Examine**
  This step provides an insight into what an organization needs at what time so that the right decision can be taken at right time. Also, work is to be done to select the right supplier and get internal approval also.
- **Collect**
  This step involves the collection of the right data from the right source so that the primary aim of the target audience can be fulfilled.

- **Transform**
  This step synchronizes the data and converts it into rich information data so that the smooth transitions of proper data and full usage of users can be fulfilled as per the requirement of the organization.

- **Cleaning**
  This step manages the new cloud service as efficiently as possible. The organization will be in need of opting for the new setup, especially at the IT management level, so the requirement is to manage the cloud supplier and particularly clean the supply chain relationship.

- **Security**
  Here, for security purposes, we use a new substitution block cipher algorithm [41]. The algorithm uses a matrix key, which when multiplied with ternary vector and applied a sign function on the product generates a sequence.
  Algorithm for generating the sequence:
  1. Consider the sequence for 0-n values (n is a positive integer).
  2. Convert each element of the given sequence into ternary form of a given digit number.
  3. Now, represent the values of Step 2 in the form of $(n+1)$ * (digit number).
  4. Subtract 1 from each element of matrix given in Step 3.
  5. Assume a random matrix key of size (digit number*digit number).
  6. Multiply the output of Step 4 by the output of Step 5.
  7. Convert positive values of the matrix by 1, negative values by –1, and 0 by 0.
  8. Add 1 to each element of the output of Step 7.
  9. Convert ternary values of Step 8 into decimal form. A desired sequence is generated.
  10. A subkey is added to the individual numerical values of the message to generate cipher text.

- **Communicate**
  This step involves the cloud service offerings to the target audience of each level of organization, which is as per the desired requirement of itself (Figure 1.8).

1.14 Future Scope

As in the given chapter, so many aspects related to cloud computing are discussed, but still, so many things are remained uncovered over which more research work can be required. Future research on cloud life cycle will focus on the development of a cloud vendor assessment to help the consumer to determine the correct cloud computing service that offers and meets their needs. Further study can also be proposed on applying different data mining methods to analyze the teaching methods and e-learning methods and also construct a reinforced learning environment of enterprise practical teaching based on cloud platform [42–44]. A new field can also be introduced, i.e., information system and management in media industries with the help of cloud computing [45].

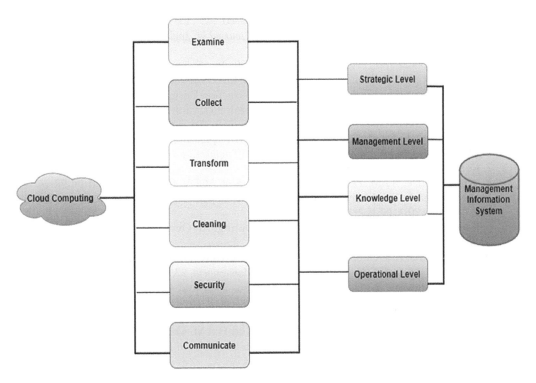

FIGURE 1.8
Model of cloud computing with MIS.

1.15 Conclusion

In this part, we summarized that no doubt cloud computing is offering many facilities and an efficient atmosphere from where one can access the resources or information in less span of time and can take appropriate decision at each level of management. In spite of the fact that many undeveloped countries are not using this service as it involves the foreign service provider, in future era of globalization, either country should pay confidence on foreign service provider or try to build their own cloud services and rely on it itself. So, MIS with the help of cloud computing can create a toned cloud-based knowledge economy/wealth and healthy informatics implementation along with technological advancement of information science. Finally, we proposed a range of open topics and research paths that should be pursued further.

References

1. C. Kavitha, Prevention of Vulnerable Virtual Machines against DDOS Attacks in the Cloud, *IJREAT International Journal of Research in Engineering & Advanced Technology*, 2, 2, 1–6, April–May 2014.

2. K. Kishor, P. Nand and P. Agarwal, Subnet Based Ad Hoc Network Algorithm Reducing Energy Consumption in MANET. *International Journal of Applied Engineering Research*, 12, 22, 11796–11802, 2017.

3. K. Kishor, P. Nand and P. Agarwal, Secure and Efficient Subnet Routing Protocol for MANET, *Indian Journal of Public Health*, 9, 12, 200, 2018. doi: 10.5958/0976-5506.2018.01830.2.

4. K. Kishor, P. Nand and P. Agarwal, Notice of Retraction Design Adaptive Subnetting Hybrid Gateway MANET Protocol on the basis of Dynamic TTL value adjustment. *Aptikom Journal on Computer Science and Information Technologies*, 3, 2, 59–65, 2018. doi: 10.11591/APTIKOM.J.CSIT.115.

5. K. Kishor and P. Nand, Review Performance Analysis and Challenges Wireless MANET Routing Protocols, *International Journal of Science, Engineering and Technology Research (IJSETR)*, 2, 10, 1854–185, October 2013, ISSN 2278-7798.

6. K. Kishor and P. Nand, Performance Evaluation of AODV, DSR, TORA and OLSR in with Respect to End-to-End Delay in MANET, *International Journal of Science and Research (IJSR)*, 3, 6, 633–636, June 2014, ISSN 2319-7064.

7. S. Raov, N. Raonk and E. Kumari, Cloud Computing: An Overview, *Journal of Theoretical and Applied Information Technology*, 9, 1, 71–76, 2009.

8. A.L. Bento and R. Bento, Cloud Computing. A New Phase in Information Technology Management, *Journal of Information Technology Management*, 22, 1, 39–46, 2011.

9. C. Yang, Q. Huang, Z. Li, K. Liu & F. Hu, Big Data and Cloud Computing: Innovation Opportunities and Challenges, *International Journal of Digital Earth*, 10, 1, 13–53, 2017. doi: 10.1080/17538947.2016.1239771.

10. A. Mohiuddin, S.M. Abu, C. Raju, A. Mustaq and H.R.M. Mahmudul, Advanced Survey on Cloud Computing and State-of-the-Art Research Issues, *IJCSI International Journal of Computer Science Issues*, 9, 1, 201–207, 2012.

11. B. Iyer and J. C. Henderson, Preparing for the Future: Understanding the Seven Capabilities of Cloud Computing, *MIS Quarterly Executive*, 9, 2, 117–131, 2010.

12. P. Mell and T. Grance, *The NIST Definition of Cloud Computing*, Tech Report National Institute of Standards and Technology, USA, August 2009.

13. H. Erdogmus, Cloud Computing: Does Nirvana Hide behind the Nebula?, *IEEE Software*, 26, 2, 4–6, 2009.

14. Y. Chen, X. Li and F. Chen, Overview and Analysis of Cloud Computing Research and Application, in *Proceedings of IEEE International Conference on E-Business and E-Government*, 1–4, 2011.

15. L. Li and Z. Tao, The Development of Cloud Computing, *Information Technology*, 86–93, 2010.

16. N. Sultan, Cloud Computing for Education: A New Dawn?, *International Journal of Information Management*, 30, 2, 109–116, 2010.

17. D. Kasi Viswanath, S. Kusuma and S.K. Gupta, Cloud Computing Issues and Benefits Modern Education. *Global Journal of Computer Science and Technology*, 12, 10, 1–7, July 2012. ISSN 0975-4172.

18. T.N. Vanitha, M.S. Narasimha Murthy and B. Chaitra, E-Healthcare Billing and Record Management Information System using Android with Cloud, *IOSR Journal of Computer Engineering (IOSR-JCE)*, 11, 4, 13–19, May–June 2013. e-ISSN: 2278-0661, p-ISSN: 2278-8727. https://www.iosrjournals.org/iosr-jce/papers/Vol11-issue4/C01141319.pdf

19. P. Mell and T. Grance, "The NIST Definition of Cloud Computing," NIST Special Publication 800-145, 2011. http://csrc.nist.gov/publications/nistpubs/800-145/SP800-145.pdf.

20. T. Dillon, C. Wu and E. hang, Cloud Computing; Issues and Challenges, AINA, 20–23 April 2010, *24th IEEE International Conference, Perth, WA*, 27–33.

21. S.M. Thompson and M.D. Dean, Advancing Information Technology in Health Care, *Communications of the ACM*, 52, 6, 118–121, 2009.

22. L. Peiyua and L. Dong, The New Risk Assessment Model for Information System in Cloud Computing Environment, *Procedia Engineering*, 15, 3200–3204, 2011.

23. Z.J. Xun and G. ZhiMin, Survey of Research Progress on Cloud Computing. *Application Research of Computers*, 27, 2, 429–433, 2010.

24. F. DengGuo, Z. Min, Z. Yan and X. Zhen, Study on Cloud Computing Security. *Journal of Software*, 22, 1, 71–83, 2011.

25. S. Qiang, H. Youtao and D. Yuxin, Research on a Quantitative Information Security Risk Assessment Model. *Journal of Computer Research and Development*, 43, 594–598, 2006.

26. F. Deng-guo, Z. Yang and Z. Yu-qing, Survey of Information Security Risk Assessment. *Journal of China Institute of Communications*, 7, 25, 10–18, 2004.

27. P. Ruxandra-Ştefania, Data Mining in Cloud Computing, *Database Systems Journal*, III, 3, 2012.

28. J. Voas and J. Zhang, Cloud Computing: New Wine or Just a New Bottle? *Database Systems Journal. IEEE Internet Computing Magazine*, III, 3/2012, 2009.

29. B. Ambulkar and V. Borkar, Data Mining in Cloud Computing, *MPGI National Multi Conference 2012 (MPGINMC-2012)*, 7–8 April 2012.

30. P.K. Paul and M.K. Ghose, Cloud Computing: Possibilities, Challenges and Opportunities with Special Reference to Its Emerging Need in the Academic and Working Area of Information Science, *International Conference on Modelling Optimization and Computing, Procedia Engineering*, 38, 2222–2227, 2012.

31. K. Mukherjee, Cloud Computing: Future Framework for e-Governance, *International Journal of Computer Applications*, 7, 7, 31–34, October 2010.

32. G. Grant and D. Chau, Developing a Generic Framework for E-Government, *Journal of Global Information Management*, 13, 1, 1–30, 2005.

33. T. Rodmunkong and P. Wannapiroon, The Design of Cloud Computing Management Information System Accordance with Thai Qualifications Framework for Higher Education, *International Journal of e-Education, e-Business, e-Management and e-Learning*, 3, 3, 214–218, June 2013.

34. A.M. Rodriguez, et.al. Open911: Experiences with the Mobile Plus Cloud Paradigm, in *Proceedings of 2011 IEEE Cloud Computing Conference, Washington, DC, USA*, 4–9 July 2011.

35. A.A. Vankudre, Data Management in the Cloud Computing, *IJSRD – International Journal for Scientific Research & Development*, 5, 12, 2018, ISSN (online): 2321-0613.

36. R. Wang, Research on Data Security Technology Based on Cloud Storage, *13th Global Congress on Manufacturing and Management, Procedia Engineering*, 174, 1340–1355, 2017.

37. T.D. Nguyen, T.M. Nguyen, Q.T. Pham and S. Misra, Acceptance and Use of E-Learning Based on Cloud Computing: The Role of Consumer Innovativeness, In Murgante, B., et al. (eds.) *Computational Science and Its Applications – ICCSA*, Springer International Publishing, Switzerland, 159–174, 2014.

38. L. Wang, G.V. Laszewski, A. Younge, X. He, M. Kunze, J. Tao and C. Fu, Cloud Computing: A Perspective Study, *New Generation Computing*, 28, 2, 137–146, 2010.

39. G. Riahi, E-Learning Systems Based on Cloud Computing: A Review, *Procedia Computer Science*, 62, 352–359, 2015.

40. T. Rodmunkong, P. Wannapiroon and P. Nilsook, The Challenges of Cloud Computing Management Information System in Academic Work, *International Journal of Signal Processing Systems*, 2, 2, 160–165, December 2014.

41. A. Shukla and P. Shukla, A New Substitution Block Cipher Algorithm with Its Efficiency Valuation, *IRJET*, 3, 12, 1105–1109, 2016.

42. M. Kayali, N. Safie and M. Mukhtar, The Effect of Individual Factors Mediated by Trust and Moderated by IT Knowledge on Students' Adoption of Cloud Based E-Learning, *International Journal of Innovative Technology and Exploring Engineering (IJITEE)*, 9, 2, December 2019, ISSN: 2278-3075.

43. N. Zhao, M. Xia, Z. Xu, W. Mi and Y. Shen, A Cloud Computing-Based College-Enterprise Classroom Training Method, *World Transactions on Engineering and Technology Education 2015*, WIETE, 13, 1, 2015.

44. K. Kishor, R. Sharma and M. Chhabra. Student Performance Prediction Using Technology of Machine Learning, *Micro-Electronics and Telecommunication Engineering*. Springer, Singapore, 541–551, 2022.

45. A. Lugmayr, Brief Introduction into Information Systems & Management Research in Media Industries, in *2013 IEEE International Conference on Multimedia and Expo Workshops (ICMEW)*, 2013.

2

Wireless Networks Based in the Cloud That Support 5G

Kaushal Kishor

ABES Institute of Technology

Parma Nand

Sharda University

CONTENTS

2.1 Introduction

In recent years, information transmission and computing technologies have been profoundly merging, and different wireless access technologies have been successfully deployed. This has led to a proliferation of wireless access technologies. One may reasonably anticipate that the next mobile communication technology of the fifth generation, known as 5G, will no longer be able to be characterized by a solitary business model or a representative technological feature. 5G is a multi-service and multi-technology integrated network that will satisfy the future demands of a broad variety of big data and the fast expansion of a large number of enterprises. Additionally, it will improve the user experience by offering intelligent and tailored services.

Cloud computing provides ubiquitous on-demand access to a shared pool of programmable computer resources with little administrative work. It is gaining popularity in the area of communication technology (CT) as a flexible, economical, and powerful mobile network enabler. For efficient resource utilization and advanced multicell algorithms, centralized baseband pools for the radio access network (RAN) are being studied, but they require dedicated hardware and do not offer the same characteristics as cloud computing platforms, such as on-demand deployment and virtualization, resource pooling, and elastic service meters that are common in cloud computing platforms. For future mobile communication systems with dense RAP installations and severe multicell interference, a significant increase in access nodes, and huge rate fluctuations, these cloud computing properties are essential enablers. Using cloud computing for 5G mobile networks and signal processing methods is examined in this article.

2.1.1 The Emergence of Wireless Networking Technology

Over the last 20 years, there has been a dramatic increase in the development of wireless networks. They have had a significant influence on people's lives in many spheres, including their economic, social, and working environments. With the assistance of large amounts of data, modern human civilization has reached the information age. The need for cutting-edge technology to underpin upcoming apps and services in every facet of people's lives is constantly growing, and this trend is expected to continue. As the Internet of Things (IoT), connected vehicles (IoV), and wearable gadgets continue to advance at breakneck speed, the quantity and diversity of smart devices that connect to wireless networks will grow exponentially, far outstripping the present network capacity [1,2].

The following difficulties are being presented to wireless networks as a result of the proliferation of mobile data:

2.1.1.1 Capacity for Connectivity

Conventional methods of communication focus primarily on human-to-human interaction as their primary mode of communication. The IoT and other associated technologies are growing in popularity, which means that more gadgets will soon be able to connect to networks. As a result, the ever-increasing need for human-to-device and device-to-device communication should be able to be met. Therefore, the fifth-generation mobile communication technology, also known as 5G, is anticipated to give a solution that can link anything, anytime, and everywhere [2].

2.1.1.2 Performance of the Network

As more innovative apps get access to mobile networks, consumers have come to expect to be able to quickly and easily access a wide range of information [3]. This is due to the fact that more unique applications are being developed. By using 5G networks, users are able to have quick access in any setting to real-time multimedia resources in addition to other types of information that may be of benefit to them.

2.1.1.3 Resource Optimization

The quality of service (QoS) of classic communication technologies may often be enhanced by improving the hardware and other infrastructures. This can be accomplished in a number of different ways. Nevertheless, this strategy incurs additional costs and often results in a waste of resources. It is anticipated that 5G networks would automatically recognize the communication situations, dynamically assign network resources, offer substantial connectivity and network performance on demand, and increase the effectiveness of resources that are already in use [4,5].

2.1.2 Wireless Networks Capable of 5G

5G is increasingly becoming the new focus of attention in both the academic world and the business world [6]. It is anticipated that by the year 2020, 5G will have established itself as the dominant mobile communication technology and will be able to satisfy the information needs of human civilization via unhindered interconnection of the wireless globe [7]. The IoT and mobile wireless networks for personal consumption and business will advance with basic ecological changes as bandwidth and capacity of wireless mobile communication systems are increased, and as mobile network applications are rapidly developed. In order to support the growth of the 5G sectors, unique hardware and software will be upgraded at a quick pace, and wireless communication technology, computer technology, and information technology will all be tightly and profoundly interworked [8].

Even though 5G has been conceptualized and a prototype has been developed, the technology still faces a number of significant technological hurdles as well as enormous problems. It is difficult to reconcile the rising needs of mobile networks with the expanding complexity of the network environment, which necessitates more usage of resources and energy to increase network capacity [9]. These two aspects, in particular, are in stark opposition to one another. Since the beginning of the twentieth century, the creation of a low-carbon economy has been the consensus of the human community due to the rising prominence of global warming, climatic anomalies, the energy crisis, and other associated challenges. A green communication technology and network architecture must be developed in order to meet the needs of a sustainable, resource-optimized, and energy-efficient communications technology. As can be seen in Figure 2.1, it is able to cut down on the amount of resources and energy that are used, as well as enhance the efficiency with which resources and energy are used. This is done in line with the principles that govern the design of future wireless communication networks. As a result, 5G represents a significant research and innovation, and the development of technologies based on 5G standards is the only path forward for the advancement of wireless networks.

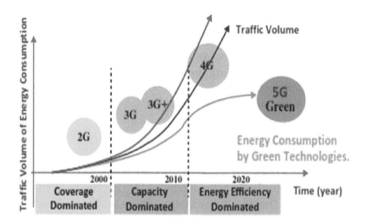

FIGURE 2.1
In order to achieve 5G by 2020, we need a transition to greener communications.

2.1.2.1 The Cost of Using the Internet (Energy Consumption by Existing Technologies)

Shannon channel capacity theory indicates a linear connection between capacity and bandwidth, but a logarithmic relationship with power. It is possible to minimize energy consumption by increasing effective bandwidth within a certain capacity, or vice versa, according to the fundamental theorem. For example, mobile operators may save over 50% of energy by using modern wireless access technologies to dynamically manage their licenses' spectrum and completely use spectrum resources. A further potential limitation for heterogeneous wireless network development is the rapid increase in energy consumption and spectrum resource use, as shown by a number of data points. It is possible to increase network energy consumption and delay or hinder the development of future heterogeneous wireless communication networks by using present technology. It is just a matter of time until we see a rise in mobile apps for individuals and businesses, as well as a rise in the mobile communication-related industrial ecology. Not only does 5G provide users with blazing-fast download speeds, it is also an intelligent network for business applications and a superior user experience, making it more than just another air interface technology. The following are expected outcomes from 5G:

2.1.2.2 Sufficient Speed and Capacity

Next-generation wireless networks are needed for mobile applications. In order to handle full HD video, mobile terminals need a data transmission rate of at least 10 Mbps, 100 Mbps, and 10 Gbps. Wireless network traffic should increase if the network has sufficient speed and capacity, because each user's daily traffic is predicted to exceed 1 GB, and high-traffic terminals need 10 GB.

2.1.2.3 Friendliness

Communication systems need ubiquitous coverage and steady quality. Existing mobile communication networks cover practically the whole population, although there are coverage gaps in wilderness, ocean, Antarctica, and aviation. In high-speed train and tunnels, mobile communication systems may be inaccessible. Future mobile communication systems must provide ubiquitous coverage and stable communication quality. 5G wireless networks should deliver always-online service with undetectable connection and transmission delays. Functionally, more sophisticated apps give working and living convenience and efficiency beyond basic communication and multimedia.

2.1.2.4 Accessibility

Although 5G uses complicated processes, from the user's perspective, it is straightforward and convenient. It is simple to connect a wide range of wireless devices, especially wearable ones, and applications and services may be accessed via a single interface; this makes it easier for users to transition between networks and devices.

2.1.2.5 Economy

Two aspects: (1) Despite increasing network traffic, the tariff per bit is falling and will fall more. (2) Dynamic network resource allocation reduces infrastructure investment and improves QoS.

2.1.2.6 Personality

Future communication is a user-experience-centric, people-oriented technology that may be personalized by users. Providers may give optimum network access and customized recommendations based on user desire, network, and physical location.

2.1.3 5G and Mobile Cloud Computing

One of the most exciting developments in cloud computing is the arrival of 5G. Data creation, storage, use, and exchange will be impacted by 5G in most industries, notably those that use IoT, AI, and machine learning. A new generation of 5G mobile networks will change cloud computing's and networks' roles in data storage, transport, and access. In the last decade, cloud computing has been essential to sustaining healthy IT infrastructures, as businesses want their scattered workforce to collaborate and produce more quickly and efficiently. In the event of a cyber attack or natural disaster, the cloud provides backup and recovery services to ensure that massive amounts of data may be quickly sent and shared across many devices. On its own 5G networks, the cloud will be reborn in 2021. 5G will allow mobile devices to transport enormous amounts of data. In order to keep up with the avalanche of data that will be generated by these gadgets, the cloud will be required. Cloud service companies are forced to grow storage capacity and alter pricing as a result of this. Smart cities, driverless cars, telemedicine care, and better data analytics are all possible because of Industry 4.0's twin engines: edge computing and the IoT. It is almost impossible to avoid network congestion with the world's 20 billion IoT devices and other forward-looking technologies all needing ultra-low latency. By bringing processing and storage closer to the user, 5G and edge computing will usher in a new era of innovation. Many industries, particularly cloud-based ones, would benefit from increased capacity, functionality, and adaptability brought on by 5G and cloud technology. Mobile network providers may now offer competitive services that non-cellular IoT companies cannot. Due to these developments, there will be more possibilities to invest in the cloud. Many technologies will benefit from 5G's improved cloud technology.

Analytics and streaming data employ cloud infrastructure for storage. Streaming analytics on big data still suffer latency issues with today's cellular networks. Real-time streaming concerns will be lessened due to 5G's speed. Industrial Internet of Things (IIoT): Processing and interpreting sensor data in real time is crucial for significant insights to control cost and efficiency in supply chain management and process manufacturing. 5G might reduce the cost and increase the efficacy of big data research given its distant and variable nature [10].

Edge computing: 5G affects mobile and remote device performance. 5G will transfer ten times more data than 4G to sensor-based remote systems like location tracking applications, home automation systems, and voice assistants.

AI and NLP: As more companies employ AI and NLP, they will need to handle vast volumes of data. Most cloud computing service providers have CPUs and storage, but they need to increase real-time data input. 5G will provide sufficient data transfer for AI and NLP applications.

5G will boost VR and AR applications, bringing new concepts to retail, travel, and health care [11].

2.1.4 Mobile Cloud Computing Issues MCC Applications Encounter These Issues

2.1.4.1 Availability

Availability is whether we can utilize something. In MCC, availability means accessing the communication channel when needed. Unavailability is user network access failure. MCC does not ensure network access. Response time, cost, usage, error rate, and network correctness affect availability. Reduced reaction time may raise costs. Interference reduces network accuracy. This reduces throughput. Network management must account for these aspects. Mobiles were not as accurate as other gadgets. Accuracy affects throughput. Some new technologies give customers with reduced mistake rates and accurate networks. Radio interference reduces accuracy and increases demand for radio channels. Radio interference disrupts channel availability. Utilization affects availability. Users' biggest issue is availability [12].

2.1.4.2 Bandwidth

Bandwidth is when parallel signals from various resources move quickly. Mobile communications need bandwidth. Low bandwidth slows transmissions. We can enhance channel usage by compressing data before delivering it. Bandwidth use depends on supplied data. Large data transfers increase delay and reduce efficiency. 3G and 4G have bandwidth issues. Wireless networks have less bandwidth than cable systems because network capacity is defined by bandwidth per cubic meter. As mobile users expand, they desire more apps. The insufficient bandwidth impacts the functioning of these services. In past network generations, reduced bandwidth hindered user services. This issue was fixed in prior generations, yet still persists [13].

2.1.4.3 Heterogeneity

Heterogeneity describes how mobile cells and access technologies work together. Heterogeneous networks (HetNets) link computers and devices with different protocols and operating systems to share resources.

2.2 Networking That Are Hosted on the Cloud

An entirely new technique to build and run private networks via the Internet using cloud computing architecture has emerged. Virtual private networking (VPN) is another name for cloud networking (VPN). As a result of cloud networking, conventional network operations and services such as connection and security, as well as administration and control, are published as services. Virtualization of the network foundation, radio access cloud networks, and mobile cloud networking are a few examples of this sort of service (MCN).

2.2.1 The Virtualization of the Network Foundation

Network visualization (NVF) migrates telecom equipment from specialized to universal x86-based COTS servers. Current telecom networking equipment uses proprietary platforms, where all network pieces are locked boxes that cannot share hardware resources. Capacity growth depends on more hardware, whereas idle hardware resources lay dormant after capacity decrease, which is time-consuming, inflexible, and expensive. NFV transforms network parts into separate programs that can be deployed flexibly on a single server, storage, and exchange platform. As demonstrated in Figure 2.2 with decoupled software and

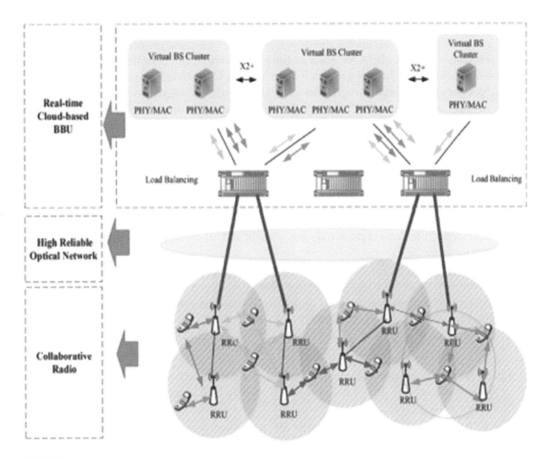

FIGURE 2.2
C-RAN architecture.

hardware, the capacity of any application may be enlarged fast by boosting virtual resources, which has substantially increased network flexibility. NFV's IT base is cloud computing and virtualization. COSTS' ubiquitous computing, storage, and networking capabilities may be virtualized and used by higher programs. Virtualization decouples application and hardware while reducing resource supply time from days to minutes. Cloud computing allows for the flexible growth and decrease of applications, which improves resource usage and system response time. NFV implementation benefits include the following:

- Operators spend less on purchases, operations, maintenance, and energy.
- Business deployment is sped up while innovation is slowed. Improved testing and integration, lower development costs, and rapid software installation replace traditional hardware deployment.
- Network apps allow multi-version and multi-tenant so diverse applications, users, and tenants may share a unified platform.
- Different physical domains and user groups may get individualized care, and service modules can be added quickly.
- The network is open, and company innovation may boost profits.

2.2.2 Radio Access Networks Hosted in the Cloud

There are a number of reasons for the development of cloud radio access networks, sometimes referred to as Cloud-RANs, such as the general trend of current network conditions and the evolution of technical growth. Clean system C-RAN is composed of three parts: central processing, collaborative radio, and cloud infrastructure in real time. Primary objectives are to reduce base station usage and energy consumption, to implement technologies that enable collaboration and virtualization in order to realize resource sharing as well as dynamic scheduling, to increase the efficiency of spectrum utilization, and to achieve low costs, high bandwidths, and flexibility in operation. As mobile networks continue to evolve at breakneck speed, C-main RAN's goal is to meet these new difficulties. These challenges include issues related to energy consumption, the costs of construction, operation, and maintenance, and spectrum resources. The end result of this endeavor is to pursue a sustainable increase in both business and profit in the future [14].

The C-RAN architecture is primarily made up of the following three components, as can be seen in Figure 2.2:

- Distributed network that consists of an antenna and a remote radio unit (RRU).
- A high-bandwidth, low-latency optical transmission network that links the RRU to the bandwidth-based unit (BBU).
- All the benefits of a centralized baseband processing pool consisting of high-performance general processors and real-time virtual technology RAN architecture.
- The centralized method has the potential to significantly cut down on the amount of base stations as well as the amount of energy that is used by the air conditioning systems.
- The high-density RRU reduces the distance between the RRU and the users, reducing emission power while maintaining network coverage. Low transmission power extends the terminal's battery life and reduces wireless access network power usage.

C-RAN is an alternative to the conventionally dispersed base station in that it disrupts the fixed connection link that exists between RRUs and BBUs, meaning that each RRU is independent of any particular BBU. RRU sends and receives signals in a virtual BBU, while the real-time virtual allocation baseband pool supplies the virtual base station's processing power.

The number of BBU sites may be reduced by up to two orders of magnitude inside the C-RAN architecture. Some important central machine room may be used as the central baseband pool, and the accompanying auxiliary equipment, so that operations and administration can be made easier. When it comes to C-RAN, there is no reduction of RRUs; however, because of their low power consumption, they can be simply installed in a restricted area with the power supply and without the need for regular maintenance. This is made possible by the fact that the number of RRU is not reduced. As a consequence of this, it has the potential to quicken the pace at which the operational network is built.

2.2.3 Cloud Networking on Mobile Devices

European Commission EP7 project Mobile Cloud Networking uses cloud computing and virtualization of network functions to establish a cellular network. It is a cloud-based mobile app and communication platform. It investigates, implements, and evaluates LTE's technical foundation. This mobile communication system supports atomic services and flexible payment using the mobile network, decentralized computing, and intelligent storage.

2.2.4 MCN's Aims

- It will enable for on-demand payment, self-service, flexible consumption, remote access, and other services by providing the basic infrastructure and platform software of a traditional network in a service model.

- The framework of cloud computing does not permit the integration of mobile devices. From data centers to mobile terminals, MCN increases the reach of cloud computing. MCN services are now available, with the new virtualization layer and monitoring mechanism in place.

- MCN centers its attention on two primary tenets: (1) The cloud computing service has to demonstrate the resource pool, and (2) the architecture should be service-oriented. The work that is associated with MCN primarily consists of the following components: mobile platform services, wireless cloud, mobile core network cloud, and cloud computing infrastructure.

- The MCN design is service-oriented, and its functional components may be modularized into a variety of different services. MCN derives the services it offers from resources that may be either physically present or virtualized. These resources can also be both. The MCN service may be broken down into two categories: the composite service and the atomic-level service.

The following significant individuals and connections in the MCN architecture:

- Service manager (SM): SM supports multi-tenant services and offers a user-friendly external visual interface.
- The real services are provided by the service orchestrator (SO).
- Cloud controller (CC): CC facilitates SO configuration and deployment.

2.3 Networking Platforms on the Cloud

Cloud computing is a kind of Internet-based computing that offers computers and other devices with pooled processing resources and data on demand. It is a way to make a flexible pool of computer resources available to anybody, anywhere, at any time. NFV, SDN, and other sophisticated networking technologies have led to the widespread usage of cloud platforms to manage virtual network resources and services, allowing for additional connection options, greater performance, and reduced pricing.

2.3.1 OpenNebule

The general architecture of OpenNebule, an open source toolkit for cloud computing, is seen in Figure 2.3. With the use of Xen [15], Kernel-based Virtual Machine (KVM) [16], or VMware ESX [6], it facilitates the creation and management of private clouds. It also offers a Deltacloud adapter that works in collaboration with Amazon Elastic Compute Cloud (Amazon EC2) [17] to manage hybrid clouds. As an alternative to traditional cloud service providers like Amazon, Amazon partners that operate their own private clouds on various OpenNebula instances may also serve as remote cloud service providers. OpenNebula's most recent version supports XEN, KVM, and VMware in addition to providing real-time access to EC2 and ElasticHosts. Additionally, it facilitates managing virtual networks as well as copying and transmitting picture files.

The functions that OpenNebula offers the business in order to deploy the private cloud, hybrid cloud, and public cloud are as follows:

1. Multi-tenant operations that are very secure;
2. High availability;
3. On-demand preparation and monitoring of compute, storage, and network resources;
4. Optimizing distributed resources to improve workload performance;

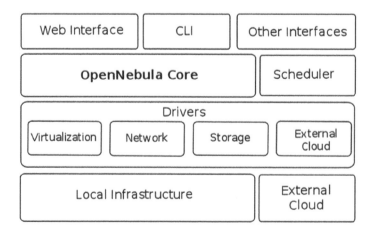

FIGURE 2.3
OpenNebula architecture.

5. Management that is centralized across various areas and makes use of all accessible interfaces; and

6. A high capacity for expansion.

For local users and administrators, this means providing an adaptable and flexible private cloud architecture that allows them to execute virtual services inside their own controllable domain (Figure 2.4). The OpenNebula virtual infrastructure offers the APIs for virtualization, networking, image and physical resource setup, administration, monitoring, and accounting via its Application Programming Interfaces (APIs). In order to keep up with the ever-changing needs of its customers, an OpenNebula private cloud offers a highly available and scalable architecture. When submitting, monitoring, and controlling OpenNebula cloud services through the OpenNebula operations center or cloud-based interfaces, the services are housed on virtual machines.

In order to administer the hybrid cloud, OpenNebula uses Amazon EC2 and the Deltacloud adaptor (see Figure 2.5). OpenNebula's public cloud extends the private cloud's REST interface. If you allow partners or other users to use your infrastructure or offer your services, implement a cloud interface. Local cloud is the obvious backend for public cloud.

According to Figure 2.6, third-party drivers, core, and tools are all part of OpenNebula's infrastructure. Create, launch, and shut down VMs; assign storage for VMs; and monitor real and virtual machine statuses directly with the operating system. The VMs, storage devices, and virtual networks are all managed by the core layer. Using the command line or a browser, the user may interact with the APIs.

OpenNebula relies on shared storage devices to provide virtual machine pictures. This allows any computing node to have access to the same pool of available VM images. OpenNebula will log into the compute node and immediately perform the instructions that correspond to the virtualization management tasks whenever a user requests that a virtual machine be started or shut down. This model is also known as the agentless model [18], since it does not need the installation of any extra software (or service) on the compute nodes. As a result, the complexity of the system is reduced to a significant degree.

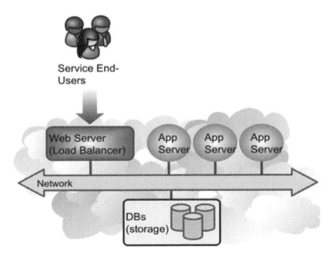

FIGURE 2.4
OpenNebula private cloud. (Source: OpenNebula project.)

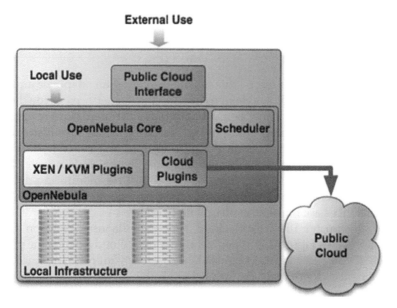

FIGURE 2.5
OpenNebula hybrid cloud. (Source: OpenNebula project.)

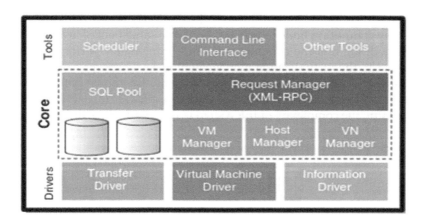

FIGURE 2.6
OpenNebula tri-layer architecture. (Source: CloudUser, 2010.)

In addition, OpenNebula uses a bridge to connect the virtual network, and the IP address and MAC address of each node are created randomly within a defined range. The network will be linked to a particular bridge, while each bridge will have its own network owner who may choose whether or not the network will be open to the public. The virtual network is completely separate from the other networks, and it makes use of ebtables.

2.3.2 OpenStack

OpenStack is a cloud operating system that can be used to construct both public and private clouds [19]. It is designed to manage several aspects of data center computing, including storage and networking. It is anticipated that it would provide an open standard for cloud computing platforms in order to give businesses with a solution that is known as infrastructure as a service (IAAS). Management, design, and development processes are all available to the public in the open source community. There is no need for a separate underlying application since the underlying provides the top application with all of the compute, storage, and networking resources it needs. Currently, hundreds of organizations are contributing to its source code. As a result, OpenStack has an excellent degree of both openness and compatibility resources accessible via public API.

The following is a list of the five components that make up OpenStack:

1. The Keystone company offers an authentication service.
2. Nova delivers computing service.
3. Swift offers a service for storing things.
4. Glance offers image service.
5. Horizon offers a function called the dashboard.

On particular, Horizon is a Web framework written in Python that was built by Django for graphically administering the OpenStack infrastructure. It manages the virtual computing resource allocation and scheduling, which is the component for managing the allocation and scheduling of VM. Nova is the computing controller of OpenStack, and it is responsible for allocating on-demand VM in response to user requests. It also manages the virtual computing resource allocation and scheduling. Nova is the component of OpenStack that manages scheduling from the beginning of the VM life cycle to its conclusion. In point of fact, the virtual machine is not managed by Nova directly; rather, it is handled by the Hypervisors of the underlying operating system using the libvirt API [20]. As seen in Figure 2.7, Nova, which is composed of the following modules, gives user's

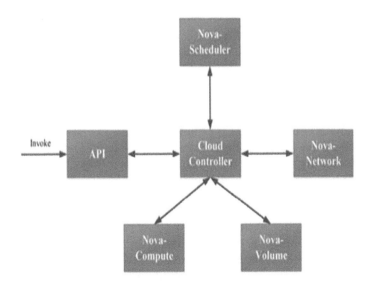

FIGURE 2.7
NOVA.

access to APIs that allow them to run and maintain virtual machines (VMs), while the cloud infrastructure itself must be handled using Nova-API.

- The Message Queue is OpenStack's communication module between each node. It is mostly based on Advanced Message Queue Protocol (AMQP). The primary activities of Nova take a significant amount of time; hence, in order to shorten the amount of time it takes for Nova to respond to a user's request, the company uses an asynchronous method known as callbacks.
- The life cycle of the instance, which is most often a virtual machine (VM), is managed by Nova-Compute. Nova-Compute will handle the request to construct or terminate a virtual machine (VM) using the libvirt API after it has been received. The results will then be returned through the message queue.
- Nova-Network is responsible for providing the VM with network connection services, and this module handles the VMs' intra- and inter-network connections. To be more specific, Nova-primary Network's responsibilities include the configuration of things like security groups, virtual local area networks (VLANs), and IP addresses for virtual machines (VMs).
- Outages, downtime, and system-level failure are not an issue for the VM since Nova-Volume offers persistent storage for it.
- Nova-Scheduler is a daemon that is started when the cloud platform is first created. This is particularly crucial for the computer equipment and has the potential to significantly decrease the losses brought on by power outages, downtime, and system-level failure. Nova-Scheduler is a daemon that is started when the cloud platform is first created. Nova-Scheduler is responsible for determining which computational node should be utilized to build a virtual machine (VM) when it has received a request to do so from Nova. Nova-Scheduler is responsible for managing the migration of virtual machines (VMs) and the redistribution of resources whenever migration of VMs is required. VM migration is a very complicated process, and Nova-Scheduler must handle it in order to prevent the waste of computing resources and guarantee that the overall performance of the cloud platform does not suffer while VM migration is taking place (e.g., by putting to sleep hosts that are not in use to reduce the amount of energy they use).

Keystone manages authentication and service tokens. OpenStack identifies and grants access to cloud computing resources and services. Keystone verifies OpenStack users based on their user name and password when they log in. If valid, Keystone returns a Token that may be used as OpenStack authentication. Swift offers OpenStack with distributed virtual object storage for a scalable and redundant object store. Each Swift storage node offers strong data permanence and is symmetrical. Due to the symmetrical design, adding nodes increases capacity without master–slave configuration dependency or single node failure. Swift is unlike Nova-Volume, which offers persistent VM storage. Nova-Volume is analogous to a hard drive, but Swift offers huge object storage and provides VM and cloud applications with data containers, encrypted storage, data backup, etc. Glance stores and retrieves VM images. When OpenStack produces a VM, the image may be retrieved by Glance and used to renew the original VM. Glance offers the standard REST interface to query device images.

2.4 5G Wireless Mobile Network Adopts Deep Learning Architecture

The taxonomy of 5G wireless mobile network deployment of deep learning architectures is described in this section [21,22]. In 5G wireless mobile networks, the taxonomy classified papers that used deep learning approaches. The 5G wireless mobile network researches were used to develop deep learning architectures and challenges. A 5G wireless mobile network architecture based on deep learning might be built using the taxonomy [23]. Using the taxonomy, deep learning architectures for 5G wireless mobile networks may be extracted and sorted according to various criteria. When it comes to 5G mobile networks, you will see a variety of different deep learning algorithms in use. Before diving into the details of 5G wireless mobile networks, let us take a look at the core principles of each deep learning framework. The fundamental concepts describe how deep learning architectures achieve their objectives [24–26].

2.4.1 Convolution Neural Network

This section provides history on CNN and research that used it to build 5G wireless mobile network solutions. CNNs are used for image processing and pattern identification: simple structure, flexibility, and minimal training parameters [27–29]. CNNs have input, convolution, pooling, and output layers. Convolution layer accepts input picture and applies filter to extract feature map. Bega et al. [30] created 3D CNN-based DeepCog for 5G resource management. 5G infrastructure is sliced. DeepCog allocates each slice's resources. DeepCog is successful in real-world scenarios. Gante et al. [31] presented temporal CNN for 5G mmWave outdoor location. The temporal CNN obtained 1.78 m of average error for non-line-of-sight mmWave outdoor sites with modest bandwidth, binary data, and a single anchor. Huang et al. [32] used deep learning to allocate cooperative resources depending on 5G channel conditions. CNN was created using channel data and optimized resource allocation. CNN may replace conventional resource optimization with full-scale channel information in a dynamic channel context [33,34]. The approach reduces optimization complexity and computational time and improves performance.

ML, a subset of AI, attempts to build systems/machines that can automatically learn from data patterns and experience and improve their predictions. Machine learning involves algorithms and self-training computer systems [35–37]. Applying ML approaches (decision tree, logistic regression, linear regression, SVM, KNN) to large data sets may be tricky. Traditional ML libraries cannot handle large datasets; hence, new methods are required [38]. ML technology and solutions were too pricey for SMBs. Cloud computing boosts machine learning. "Intelligent cloud" is cloud-based machine learning. Cloud ML improves both cloud and ML algorithms [39].

2.5 Conclusion

A few papers on 5G's technical standards have already appeared, even if the field of 5G research is still in its early phases. Although some researchers have discussed how to build the 5G network from multiple perspectives, such as air interface, millimeter wave, and energy consumption, the majority of these studies focus on technical particulars and rarely build the entire system from the perspective of the global perspective, despite the fact that some researchers have discussed this topic. We may reasonably expect that 5G will not be defined by a single service or one kind of technology. 5G is expected to be the future architecture of wireless networks in order to create virtual, customizable, and intelligent mobile communication systems in the future of computer, network, and communication technologies. That is because 5G is slated to be the next-generation wireless network infrastructure. These industries are evolving into a more diverse ecosystem because of constant advances in wireless communication networks' bandwidth and capacity as well as the rapid development of mobile Internet apps for personal and business usage. More than just an air interface technology, 5G can enable a wide range of business-oriented applications because to its faster data transfer rates, greater bandwidth, and higher capacity.

References

1. Kishor, K., Pandey, D. Study and development of efficient air quality prediction system embedded with machine learning and IoT, in Deepak G. et al. (eds), *Proceeding International Conference on Innovative Computing and Communications. Lecture Notes in Networks and Systems*, vol. 471 (Springer, Singapore, 2022). https://doi.org/10.1007/978-981-19-2535-1.
2. Kishor, K., Saxena, S., Yadav, S., Yadav, S. Study and development of air monitoring and purification system. *Vivechan International Journal of Research*, 10(2) (2019), ISSN 0976-8211.
3. Kishor, K., Nand, P., Agarwal, P. Secure and efficient subnet routing protocol for MANET. *Indian Journal of Public Health*, 9(12), 200 (2018). https://doi.org/10.5958/0976-5506.2018.01830.2.
4. Kishor, K., Nand, P., Agarwal, P. Notice of retraction design adaptive subnetting hybrid gateway MANET protocol on the basis of dynamic TTL value adjustment. *Aptikom Journal on Computer Science and Information Technologies*, 3(2), 59–65 (2018). https://doi.org/10.11591/APTIKOM.J.CSIT.115.
5. Kishor, K., Nand, P., Agarwal, P. Subnet based ad hoc network algorithm reducing energy consumption in MANET. *International Journal of Applied Engineering Research*, 12(22), 11796–11802 (2017).
6. Li, Q.C., Niu, H., Papathanassiou, A.T., Wu, G. 5G Network capacity: Key elements and technologies. *IEEE Vehicular Technology Magazine*, 9(1), 71–78 (2014).
7. Wang, L.-C., Rangapillai, S. A survey on green 5G cellular networks, in *2012 International Conference on Signal Processing and Communications (SPCOM)* (IEEE, Bangalore, 2012), pp. 1–5.
8. MacCartney, G.R., Zhang, J., Nie, S., Rappaport, T.S. Path loss models for 5G millimeter wave propagation channels in urban microcells, in *2013 IEEE Global Communications Conference (GLOBECOM)* (IEEE, Atlanta, 2013), pp. 3948–3953.
9. Rappaport, T.S., Sun, S., Mayzus, R., Zhao, H., Azar, Y., Wang, K., Wong, G.N., Schulz, J.K., Samimi, M., Gutierrez, F. Millimeter wave mobile communications for 5G cellular: It will work! *IEEE Access* 1, 335–349 (2013).
10. https://www.itbusinessedge.com/mobile/the-impact-of-5g-on-cloudcomputing/.
11. http://paper.ijcsns.org/07_book/201708/20170832.pdf.
12. https://ieeexplore.ieee.org/document/7064896.
13. https://www.comparethecloud.net/articles/how-5g-will-accelerate-cloudbusiness-investment/.
14. Checko, A., Christiansen, H.L., Yan, Y., Scolari, L., Kardaras, G., Berger, M.S., Dittmann, L. Cloud ran for mobile networks – A technology overview. *IEEE Communications Surveys and Tutorials*, 17(1), 405–426 (2015).

15. Barham, P., Dragovic, B., Fraser, K., Hand, S., Harris, T., Ho, A., Neugebauer, R., Pratt, I., Warfield, A. Xen and the art of virtualization, in *Proceedings of the Nineteenth ACM Symposium on Operating Systems Principles, SOSP '03* (ACM, New York, NY, 2003), pp. 164–177. ISBN 1-58113-757-5. http://doi.acm.org/10.1145/945445.945462.
16. Kivity, A., Kamay, Y., Laor, D., Lublin, U., Liguori, A. KVM: The Linux virtual machine monitor, in *Proceedings of the Linux Symposium*, vol. 1 (2007), pp. 225–230.
17. Wang, G., Ng, T.E. The impact of virtualization on network performance of Amazon EC2 data center, in *INFOCOM, 2010 Proceedings IEEE* (IEEE, San Diego, 2010), pp. 1–9.
18. Rose, M., Broussard, F.W. *Agent Less Application Virtualization: Enabling the Evolution of the Desktop.* White Paper, IDC, and Sponsored by VMware (2008).
19. Sefraoui, O., Aissaoui, M., Eleuldj, M. Openstack: Toward an open source solution for cloud computing. *IJCA – International Journal of Computer Applications*, 55(3), 38–42 (2012).
20. Bolte, M., Sievers, M., Birkenheuer, G., Niehörster, O., Brinkmann, A. Non-intrusive virtualization management using libvirt, in *Proceedings of the Conference on Design, Automation and Test in Europe* (European Design and Automation Association, Dresden, 2010), pp. 574–579.
21. Gohil, A., Modi, H., Patel, S.K. 5G technology of mobile communication: A survey, in *2013 International Conference on Intelligent Systems and Signal Processing (ISSP)* (IEEE, Gujarat, 2013), pp. 288–292.
22. Li, Q.C., Niu, H., Papathanassiou, A.T., Wu, G. 5G network capacity: Key elements and technologies. *IEEE Vehicular Technology Magazine*, 9(1), 71–78 (2014).
23. Tudzarov, A., Janevski, T. Functional architecture for 5G mobile networks. *International Journal of Advanced Science and Technology*, 32, 65–78 (2011).
24. Larew, S.G., Thomas, T.A., Cudak, M., Ghosh, A. Air interface design and ray tracing study for 5G millimeter wave communications, in *2013 IEEE Globecom Workshops (GC Wkshps)* (IEEE, Atlanta, 2013), pp. 117–122.
25. MacCartney, G.R., Zhang, J., Nie, S., Rappaport, T.S. Path loss models for 5G millimeter wave propagation channels in urban microcells, in *2013 IEEE Global Communications Conference (GLOBECOM)* (IEEE, Atlanta, 2013), pp. 3948–3953.
26. Olsson, M., Cavdar, C., Frenger, P., Tombaz, S., Sabella, D., Jäntti, R. 5GrEEn: Towards green 5G mobile networks, in *2013 IEEE 9th International Conference on Wireless and Mobile Computing, Networking and Communications (WiMob)* (Lyon, 2013), pp. 212–216.
27. Liu, T., Fang, S., Zhao, Y., Wang, P., Zhang, J. Implementation of training convolutional neural networks, *Computer Vision and Pattern Recognition* (2015). https://arxiv.org/abs/1506.01195.
28. Gupta, S., Tyagi, S., Kishor, K. Study and development of self sanitizing smart elevator, in Gupta D., Polkowski Z., Khanna A., Bhattacharyya S., Castillo O. (eds) *Proceedings of Data Analytics and Management. Lecture Notes on Data Engineering and Communications Technologies*, vol 90 (Springer, Singapore, 2022). https://doi.org/10.1007/978-981-16-6289-8_15.
29. Sharma, A., Jha, N., Kishor, K. Predict COVID-19 with chest X-ray, in Gupta D., Polkowski Z., Khanna A., Bhattacharyya S., Castillo O. (eds) *Proceedings of Data Analytics and Management. Lecture Notes on Data Engineering and Communications Technologies*, vol 90 (Springer, Singapore, 2022). https://doi.org/10.1007/978-981-16-6289-8_16.
30. Bega, D., Gramaglia, M., Fiore, M., Banchs, A., Costa-Perez, X. DeepCog: Cognitive network management in sliced 5G networks with deep learning, in *Proceedings of the IEEE INFOCOM 2019-IEEE Conference on Computer Communications* (IEEE, Paris, France, July 2019), pp. 280–288.
31. Gante, J., Falcão, G., Sousa, L. Deep learning architectures for accurate millimeter wave positioning in 5G. *Neural Processing Letters*, 51(1), 487–514 (2020).
32. Huang, D., Gao, Y., Li, Y. et al., Deep learning based cooperative resource allocation in 5G wireless networks. *Mobile Networks and Applications*, 1–8 (2018).
33. Sharma, R., Maurya, S., Kishor, K. Student performance prediction using technology of machine learning, in *Proceedings of the International Conference on Innovative Computing & Communication (ICICC) 2021* (July 3, 2021). Available at SSRN: https://ssrn.com/abstract=3879645 or http://dx.doi.org/10.2139/ssrn.3879645.

34. Jain, A., Sharma, Y., Kishor, K. Prediction and analysis of financial trends using ML algorithm, in *Proceedings of the International Conference on Innovative Computing & Communication (ICICC) 2021* (July 11, 2021). Available at SSRN: https://ssrn.com/abstract=3884458 or http://dx.doi.org/10.2139/ssrn.3884458.

35. Kishor, K., Sharma, R., Chhabra, M. Student performance prediction using technology of machine learning, in Sharma D.K., Peng SL., Sharma R., Zaitsev D.A. (eds.) *Micro-Electronics and Telecommunication Engineering. Lecture Notes in Networks and Systems*, vol 373 (Springer, Cham, 2022). https://doi.org/10.1007/978-981-16-8721-1_53.

36. Kishor, K. Communication-efficient federated learning, in Yadav S.P., Bhati B.S., Mahato D.P., Kumar S. (eds) *Federated Learning for IoT Applications. EAI/Springer Innovations in Communication and Computing* (Springer, Cham, 2022). https://doi.org/10.1007/978-3-030-85559-8_9.

37. Kishor, K. Personalized federated learning. in Yadav S.P., Bhati B.S., Mahato D.P., Kumar S. (eds) *Federated Learning for IoT Applications. EAI/Springer Innovations in Communication and Computing* (Springer, Cham, 2022). https://doi.org/10.1007/978-3-030-85559-8_3.

38. Rai, B. K., Sharma, S., Kumar, G., Kishor, K. Recognition of different bird category using image processing. *International Journal of Online and Biomedical Engineering (iJOBE)*, 18(07), 101–114 (2022). https://doi.org/10.3991/ijoe.v18i07.29639.

39. Tyagi, D., Sharma, D., Singh, R., Kishor, K. Real time 'driver drowsiness'& monitoring & detection techniques. *International Journal of Innovative Technology and Exploring Engineering*, 9(8), 280–284 (2020). https://doi.org/10.35940/ijitee.H6273.069820.

3

Implications of Cloud Computing for Health Care

Manish Chhabra

ABES Institute of Technology

CONTENTS

DOI: 10.1201/9781003213895-3

3.1 Introduction

Any business model that includes providing hosted services through the Internet might be considered a kind of CC in the modern era. The National Institute of Standards and Technology defines CC as a model for facilitating on-demand, anywhere, anytime network access to a shared pool of configurable computing resources (such as networks, applications, servers, storage, and services) that can be quickly provisioned and released with minimal management effort or interaction from the service provider.

Any sort of computer system architecture is required for the CC, whether hardware or software.

In computer science, we do things like

- Designing;
- Developing construction of hardware and software;
- Processing, planning, organizing, and overseeing many moving parts;
- Categories of data; and
- Utilizing computers for academic study.

3.1.1 Definition of Cloud

In IT, cloud means network or Internet. Cloud is anything located far. CC may provide services through public or private networks, such as WANs, LANs, or virtual private connections (VPCs) in Amazon Web Services (AWS). Email, online conferencing, and Customer Relationship Management (CRM) are all cloud-based applications.

3.1.2 What Is Cloud Computing?

CC refers to altering, customizing, and accessing Internet programs. Online data storage, IT infrastructure, and IT apps are offered. CC eliminates platform dependence issues by not requiring software installation on local workstations. CC makes our business app mobile, productive, and collaborative [1].

National Institute of Standards and Technology's (NIST's) cloud definitions: CC enables simple, on-demand network access to customizable computing resources (such as servers, storage, applications, networks, and services) that may be instantly supplied and released with minimum (management) effort or service provider contact. CC model supports availability with five fundamental qualities, three service models, and four deployment types (Figure 3.1).

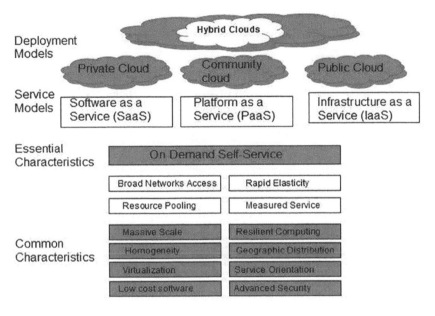

FIGURE 3.1
Hybrid Cloud.

3.2 Important Aspects of Cloud Computing

- Self-service: A user may unilaterally supply computer capabilities, such as server time and network storage, as needed without contacting each service provider. CC lets consumers utilize web services and resources on demand. Anyone may utilize them using a web browser.

- Broad network access is offered through common techniques that thin or thick client systems may employ (e.g., android phones, palmtop, tablets, laptops, and workstations). A CC is web-based and accessible from anywhere at any time.

- Service resource pooling: Multiple customers use givers' computational resources. Inimically allocate and reassign resources as needed. Consumers may not care where resources are located, but they should be mindful of distant hazards. CC lets you renter shared adjustable resources. Shared hardware, database, and basic infrastructure are possible.

- Flexibility to the consumer: This seems faultless, inexhaustible, and responsive to their changing needs. Increasing or decreasing resources is straightforward. Automatically monitored are consumer-used or allocated resources.

- Metrics: Consumers pay for the services they consume; metering reports, monitoring and controlling users' resource consumption per unit of time, and enabling transparency for both the service provider and consumer [2].

3.2.1 Benefits of Cloud Computing (CC)

- CC provides self-service on demand. Without cloud service, the resources may be utilized.
- Cloud resources that are networked to provide platform-independent client access.
- CC is cost-effective; thus, it has high utilization and efficiency.
- CC's load balancing is realistic and reliable.
- Behind-the-scenes services and CC techniques make CC practical and accessible to customers.

3.2.2 Below Are the Working Models for CC

Cloud-deployment models, cloud models, and CC deployment models describe cloud access and placement, and CC has four access types.

3.2.3 Public Cloud

Public cloud definition – The cloud infrastructure is available to the public or a large industrial group and is owned by companies offering cloud services. This concept illustrates a publicly available, external cloud environment [2].

3.2.4 Private Cloud

Private cloud definition: A company or organization owns cloud infrastructure. It might be handled by the organization or a third party, on- or off-site. A private cloud, often called an internal or on-premise cloud, is meant to serve only customers of the cloud's owner.

3.2.5 Hybrid Cloud

The cloud infra is a collection of two or more clouds (private, public, or community) connected together by proprietary or standardized technologies to facilitate data and application mobility (e.g., cloud bursting for load balancing between clouds).

3.2.6 Community Cloud

The cloud infrastructure is shared by several enterprises and serves a community with common purpose, security, policy, and conformance issues.

3.3 Service Models

CC is built on service models. Below are three basic service models [3].

3.3.1 Infrastructure as a Service (IaaS)

This service paradigm redistributes operations-related storage, hardware, servers, and networking components. The service provider owns and maintains the infra equipment.

Per-use pricing is common. Consumers utilize their own platform (Window/Unix) and apps Amazon EC2 or OpenNebula.

3.3.2 Platform as a Service (PaaS)

Platform as a service redistributes the fundamental infrastructure and platform (Windows/Linux/Unix), making application deployment simple without the expense and complexity of purchasing and maintaining hidden hardware and software. For example, App Engine and Azure consumers utilize own apps Windows Azure, Google App Engine, and Hadoop.

3.3.3 Software as a Service (SaaS)

This service paradigm, sometimes called "software on demand," redistributes infrastructure, platform, and software/applications. These services are pay-per-use for customers. Consumers utilize online software, for example, Gmail, Google documents, and Google drives.

3.3.4 Advantages of Cloud Computing in Healthcare System

Modern healthcare organizations prioritize "quality" above other commercial duties. Future healthcare practitioners should consider CC technology. From rising operational costs and infrastructure to stringent government oversight, security challenges, and real-time data to easy communications, 24/7 access, and solid backups, the medical profession is battling [4].

CC's on-demand, Internet-based services and high-data availability have transformed health care into Health Tech.

3.4 Collaboration

Sharing enhances teamwork. CC simplifies data exchange. The cloud lets you securely exchange health data in real time with physicians, nurses, and caregivers.

You may remotely access health-related information and records at any time, wherever in the world. The cloud is also a great tool for healthcare practitioners, enabling remote conferencing and fast updates on patient status [5].

3.4.1 Security

Medical data must be confidential. The wealth of data maintained by this domain is the focus of attracting malicious attackers, causing security and data breaches. Cloud networks are secure because they have special security tools which are able to alerts you of suspicious attacks [6].

Because the cloud acts as a data repository, cloud service providers like Amazon Web Services and Microsoft Azure pay special attention to privacy standards, such as HIPAA. HIPAA is a federal law that required the creation of national standards to safeguard sensitive patient health information from being disclosed. GDPR-2 regulates data privacy and protection in the EU and EEA. GDPR intends to give people control over their personal data and simplify the legal environment for international business [7].

These service providers feature firewalls and consumer-controlled encryption. This makes it your most secure and dedicated data-centric solution.

3.4.2 Cost

The cloud can contain large amounts of information at a very low cost. CC works with a prepaid subscription model. This indicates that one can only need to pay for the services which one is using. By doing necessarily shifting IT budgets from Capex to Opex, CC can significantly trim internal infrastructure and other operating costs. Ultimately, even smaller hospitals with limited budgets will be able to adopt a cloud-supported model [8].

3.4.3 Speed

Speed is an important benchmark before deciding on a technological choice. The tools based upon CC can update resources at a good speed with less to very less intervention and obtain real-time updates for all relevant information. The advantages of CC in health care include unparalleled speed plus having faster access to information, overcoming obstacles faced by industry shareholders and patients. This type of technology will also change the area of clinical research, and the CC can facilitate clinical trial management as well as knowledge sharing easy [9].

3.4.4 Scalability and Flexibility

Health sectors operate in a dynamic environment. The cloud will drive technologies used in health sectors, such as electronic medical records, android-based apps, patient portals, Internet of Things (IoT) devices, and big data analytics. It gives uncomplicated scalability and flexibility to improve the final decision-making process. In addition to 24*7 availability, health sector givers need to significantly increase their data and network storage requirements in response to service requirements. The technology based upon clouds can easily well-balanced the storage needs according to the needs of healthcare professionals [10].

3.5 Applications of Cloud Computing in Health care

The health ecosystem is huge, differing, and highly complex and includes insurers, networks of hospitals and doctors, laboratories, pharmacies, patients, and other organizations. The collectively all of this ought to work within the framework of various government regulations. For this environs to function efficiently plus quickly, it is very important that sensitive information is transferred between them promptly and precisely, confidentially, and securely in between these organizations. The protection of patient information is considered to be a very sensitive and confidential health issue and due to this reason which is probable one too that negatively affected the growth of the transition from the healthcare system to the cloud. When it comes to the cloud, sharing them requires the use of innovative technologies and tools. However, there are many data fields, services, and info that can certainly useful to the cloud collaboration, as they can spread across several countries, states, and among cities. In the present scenario, it seems to be that private clouds will be positioned firstly for security reasons and then migrated to public infrastructure.

Distributed systems are made up of autonomous computers that are linked together by a network and distribution middleware, allowing them to coordinate their activities and share system resources so that users see it as a single, integrated computing facility [11,12], for example, Wi-Fi, base stations, or satellite link mobile nodes like a robot or smartphone to the Internet. Mobile CC is limited to infrastructure-based connections and cannot be employed in ad hoc mobile settings. Ad hoc CC on mobile devices combines mobile devices into a virtual supercomputer node. For network discovery, monitoring, and routing, mobile nodes interact through a mobile ad hoc network. Resources, failures, mobility, communications, and tasks are all handled by the cloud. It conceals complexity and provides a single system picture to users and programs [13–15].

ML aims to create systems/machines that can learn from data patterns and experience on their own and improve their predictions without being explicitly programmed. Machine learning is the study of algorithms and the creation of self-training machines [16–18]. Large datasets may make it difficult to use ML algorithms (decision tree, logistic regression, linear regression, SVM, KNN, and so on). Because traditional ML libraries cannot handle huge datasets, we needed alternative techniques [19–20]. Small- and medium-sized businesses were unable to afford ML technology and solutions. Machine learning applications benefit from the cloud. Machine learning is used in the "intelligent cloud." Cloud and ML algorithms benefit from machine learning [21,22].

It appears to be a good idea to first outline the uppermost priorities for the healthcare industry and then assess which aspects of CC can be applied effectively to benefit those areas In current world, rising healthcare costs epically we have also seen in COVID-19 outbreaks in first phase to the second phase, and maybe in future phases, quality of patient and client care, privacy, security and data righteousness, and misfortune situation recovery appear to be topmost priorities. Some of the distinctive features, such as scalable infra, data centers to give persistent data, security models, speedy access to information, etc., can be used to locate the some of these priorities [23].

3.5.1 Dynamic Scalability of Infrastructure

As the customer bottoms up in the health sector industries grows, so do the healthcare solution givers, and so does the business. As businesses grow, organizations are investing heavily in computing power and information technology resources to meet their thriving needs. Those computing infrastructures act as resources which are arranged to serve a rather complicated but strenuous environment [24]. With CC, institutions now have options to address these issues. The cloud gives IaaS as a service and PaaS as a business model where companies can grease of the existing infrastructure or change it to suit their business and requirements plus their demand. Additional servers can be increased or decreased as needed for a short period of time [25,26].

Instead of storing information like hospital information, network of doctors, pharmacies, their location, etc., on private servers (local), they can move them to data centers for storage. The vendor is primarily responsible for updating the software. Ultimately, this will relaxed up some resources and decreased the cost of maintaining them for healthcare solution givers. Since the CC gives a scalable infrastructure, organizations can better tailor and optimize resource scheduling. In some small- and medium-sized clinics that cannot afford to make large investments in IT, staff members able to take leverage of CC with a cost-effective payment structure and trim maintenance costs. An example of this is Amazon S3, which offers scalable storage architecture [27]. Health cloud is being developed by Telstra and the Royal Australian College of General Practitioners and is likely to contain applications of healthcare industries such as "clinical software, support tools, decisions for disease prevention and management, healthcare plans, preferred tools, and prescribing, training, and other policy-making and clinical services" [28].

3.5.2 Information Sharing

Health sectors are not stored. Mergers with other healthcare industries are needed. Information is delivered and received to handle complaints, offer customer service desk and support, accept new members, and process provider requests. Providers store EMRs in their own databases [29]. If some of this information can be transported to the cloud and shared among healthcare sectors and platforms, it may lead to better and faster service coordination and higher customer satisfaction. With 100% compliance, patient information such as Electronic Health Record System (EHRs), EMRs, Personal Health Records (PHRs), and Payer-based Health Records (PBHRs) may be uploaded to the cloud and shared with physicians and hospitals in other states or countries. Sharing information reduces mistakes. It might provide quicker, higher-quality services at lower cost. MS HealthVault provides some of these benefits. HealthVault is a centralized location to store health information including medical imaging, medication records, etc. This allows pharmacies, laboratories, hospitals, polyclinics, etc., to retrieve and mean health info for their essentiality, giving patients better and faster services. Customers may use the HealthVault Connection Center to add fitness gadgets, such as heart rate monitors, to their health records. Oracle's Exalogic Elastic Cloud and Amazon Web Services both provide cloud health data storage [30]. HealthImaging's insight "The Office of the National Coordinator of Health Information Technology in the US Department of Health and Human Services" recently picked Acumen Solutions' CRM and cloud-based project management solution for selecting and implementing EHR systems throughout the United States. Software helps regional extension centers to handle communications with medical providers about EHR selection and installation. Accenture and AT&T created a cloud-based medical imaging service [31]. This program, which allows doctors to evaluate X-rays, medical reasoning imaging, and CT scans, lets them see more patients. This program enables healthcare providers to examine, exchange, and share photographs.

3.5.3 Availability in CC

Cloud services' "high" availability may allow healthcare enterprises to provide bundled services with minimum downtime. CC may be programmed for near-real-time scheduling. Multiple nodes will be used to construct clusters [32]. At the start of a computation, resources are fixed, but applications may be raised or decreased to balance the demand. Managing medical apps via the cloud will make them more available and accessible, say experts. This might cut expenses. Understanding health security and privacy is the first step for CC healthcare applications. Several third-party firms are creating technologies to monitor cloud service providers. Medical industries are collaborating with suppliers to design this equipment with enhanced security measures for their company and clients. An increasing number of third-party vendors gives cloud monitoring and management tools, such as Cloud kick, Logic Monitor [33], etc. Most importantly, several service providers give tools that only monitor server or service uptime [34]. AWS gives native monitoring tools for the customer's EC2 instances.

3.5.4 Benefits of Adopting CC for Healthcare Organizations

CC has brought a new business model that gives many benefits that will benefit the entire medical community. By using the cloud for health care, patients and healthcare organizations will benefit greatly from patient experience, collaboration between healthcare organizations, and trim IT costs for healthcare companies. This collaborative approach allows healthcare givers to communicate with each other to give faster and more effective responses, thereby helping to improve patient care by sharing information among healthcare organizations, such as healthcare clinics, hospitals, diagnostics centers, pharmacies, and insurance [35].

Companies can effectively share medical records of patients, registered medical prescription information, digital X-rays, examination results, medical records, doctors' working conditions, etc. This information can be accessed anytime, anywhere authorized personnel. All this information will be used to make decisions, get more accurate diagnoses and treatments for better results, schedule medical appointments, speed up insurance approvals, etc., thereby greatly improving patient care. IT expenses are a more significant benefit for healthcare firms when switching to cloud services. By affiliate the cloud model, all IT works will be moved to the offshore CC infrastructure, where all the processes will be executed and stored. The new pay-per-use model allows companies to pay only for what they use; therefore, there is no extra requirements to purchase heavy and costly hardware infrastructure, licensed software, or local staff for maintenance, security, and replication, as the cloud givers will take care of them. Human life is priceless, and medical resources are limited [36]. The medical services taken care by cloud givers conform to the concept of low cost. Patients and medical organizations can use this new technology to improve the quality of patients. The combined high-performance platform performs nursing care, coordinates medical processes, and trims investment in IT infrastructure or maintenance costs, thereby improving health.

3.5.5 Impacts of Cloud Computing on Healthcare Sector

There have been major changes in the propagation, exhaustion, and sharing plus storage of medical records. From traditional storage to digitizing medical records, the health sector has certainly come a long way in providing best data management techniques.

For sectors that are historically lagging contemporary sectors, the health sector segment is leading the adoption of the cloud. As per West Monroe Partner's report, 35% of healthcare institutions observed greater than 50% of their infrastructure and data in the cloud [23]. Therefore, the health sector has shown itself to be the most advanced with the adoption of the cloud in comparison with other sectors. The proliferation of CC in health sector goes one step further in data storing in cloud architectures. Healthcare givers are now taking advantage of that technology to customize their healthcare plans to increase efficiency, optimize workflows, and trim costs associated with providing health care and improve results [37].

There are two benefits to migrating to the cloud. The cloud has proven to be beneficial for both health sector professionals and patients. CC has end up to be beneficial in discounting operational costs, while giving access to givers to give high-quality in-personal service. Patients asking to provide immediate care will have access to the same agility as the health service. The cloud also increases patient undertakings their health plans, giving patients access rights to the given health records, which in turn improves patient outcomes [38].

The democratization of health data and its remote access frees healthcare givers and patients and removes barriers to places that restrict access to health care.

In the following ways CC is bang on health care: reduction in cost

The fundamental of CC is the availability on demand of computing resources, such as data storage and computing power. Hospitals and healthcare givers no longer need to purchase hardware or workstations together. In this, no prepaid fees joined with cloud data storage. One can only pay for the computational assets one actually uses, which can save you a lot of money.

CC also offers an ideal comfortable atmosphere for scaling. This is the parameter desired in our time. Cloud-based environments are ideal for conducting scale and capacity reviews at a low cost, as patient data flow not only from EMR format records but also through various health applications and health wearable's [39].

3.5.6 Ease of Interoperability

The easiness of cloud operation helps to establish data integration across the healthcare entities, regardless of original point or cloud storage location. As a result of easiness of cloud operability facilitated by the support of the cloud, consumer information is very handy and accessible for assessment and perspicacity to ease the health devising and rendition.

CC gives access to health sector givers to easily accessible consumers' (patient) data collected through various sources, to be share with key collaborator and gives prescription and other treatable protocols in a time frame manner. It also trims the gaps between experts, allowing you to view and comment on cases, regardless of geographic restrictions [40].

3.5.7 Access to Powerful Analytics

Medical data, structured and nonstructural, are a great credit. Admissible patient records from a variety of origins can be grouped plus calculated in the cloud. Enhance medical research by applying big data analysis and AI/ML algorithms to patient data reside in the cloud. The advancement of CC power of the cloud makes it more feasible to process large datasets. Carrying out analysis of customer records can also surface the way for the development of a more exemplify caring plan for patients at the personal level. In addition, details of all relevant patients are recorded and will not be overlooked when prescribing treatment. CC information analysis is useful when obtaining useful patient records.

3.6 Ownership of Consumer (Patient) Information

CC emulates info and gives patients to manage their own status of their health. It leads to informed decisions, encouraging patient participation in their own health decisions and working as a tool for patient educational status and seriousness of involvement. Consumer records and images from scans can be easily archived and retrieved by storing info in the cloud. The security of cloud remains a concern, but the cloud's soundness for info storage is undoubtedly high. Redundancy of info is decreases as the system runs for longer. Backups are automated, and there are no points of contact where data are stored, making data recovery much easier.

3.6.1 Telemedicine Function

Remote data access can be the biggest benefit that cloud data storage offers. The summation of CC and health has the gravity to optimize many health-related reserves, such as telemedicine, post-hospital care plans, and virtual drug compliance. This also improves usability of medical services via telemedicine. Telemedicine applications increase the convenience to health sector delivery while improving the patient overall experience. CC-related telemedicine architectures and apps give easiness of the sharing of medical information, improve receptiveness, and give health insurance to patients on time while giving overall prevention, medication, and recovery stages [41].

3.7 Barriers in Using CC in Healthcare Systems Sectors

3.7.1 Security Concerns

The main problem in cloud adoption in health sector is the potential security risks linked with it. Consumers' data are fully confidential, and medical info residing in the cloud must be protected from external threats. Encrypting info, using security paired keys for uses, and using blockchain are one or another ways in health sector to protect responsive patient info stored in the cloud.

3.7.2 Complaisance with Safety Standards

Medical data and related apps must comply with many data laws such as HIPAA, HITECH, and GDPR. It also applies to data uploaded in the cloud. Establishing compliance with info stored in the cloud is something that health sector professionals might be aware of when going toward the cloud [17].

3.7.3 System Downtime

CC gives more reliability, but downtime is a truth from time to time. Having a contingency plan ahead of time and preparing for potential obstacles can help you overcome any downtime. Bias design is recommended as the best practice when building cloud applications. It has no secret that advances in CC in health care are revolutionizing the industry. Healthcare givers can now rely on the cloud for improved connectivity, flexible storage, and wider coverage. This means that the position of CC in health sector can affect the quality of life of patients around the world [42].

You have a powerful opportunity to trim business margins and increased the overall value of care for all patients. CC solutions enable healthcare givers to control hardware, software, and personnel. When healthcare professionals are faced with life-threatening situations, they need a solution that is as swift as they do.

3.7.4 World Market for CC in Health Sectors

CC is everywhere, because more and more IT giants such as Amazon, Google, Microsoft, etc., are actively moving and participating in the cloud, making large data centers to establish the cloud and help enterprises to benefit from it [35]. They are working with medical partners to create records of all medical services [43]. MS worked with Kaiser Permanente to develop the MS HealthVault apps. For example, its ultimate aim is to keep all fitness and health data in one place so that it can be easily arranged and shared with the several medical organizations including patients. Google Health is using CC services to obtain medical data from the My Chart Cleveland Clinic program. For too many health sectors, the cost-effective cloud model has forced them to reconsider their current operational profitable practices and including risks and benefits to test how they are able to use the CC [44]. The sooner those companies deploy the cloud, the sooner they are able to do so higher efficiency and give uncommon info sharing between medical institutions and patients. According to a research and survey conducted by marketandmarkets.com (M&M), approximately 32% of health sectors are able to use certain cloud-based applications. Approximately 75% of healthcare companies that currently do not use any cloud-based apps are responded that they are planning to adopt cloud technology in the coming 3–5 years [45]. By their researches, strategic enterprises are likely to adopt the public cloud model than the hybrid model and finally the private cloud model. These results going to be steady with a survey done by Accenture in starting of 2010. It also showed that early users of CC in the medicinal world will have overall advantages over lagging companies in terms of money and efficiency evolves.

When healthcare organizations consider migrating their services to the cloud, they need to conduct strategic planning to understand the benefits and risks of the new model assess its ability to achieve its goals, and determine the strategies developed to implement it. There are some reference materials that you can use to build your CC defined plan; for example, Marx and Lozano [46] described a nine-stage cloud lifecycle approach to help users start cloud projects. It is evidence of pilot projects, strategies and roadmaps, modeling and architecture, implementing ideas, expansion, integration, collaboration, and maturity.

The Project Management Institute is a nonprofit association specializing in project management. They have published a CC whitepaper that can be used as a reference for any cloud project manager. Stanoevskaya-Slabeva et al. [47] also presented a pragmatic guide for changing old-fashioned IT infra to the cloud: preliminary analysis of the requirements and readiness of CC, strategic decisions for the implementation of CC, pilot implementation, and internal communication, including outer resources and ongoing monitoring and evaluation.

The US Federal IT Healthcare Strategic Plan [48], released in June 2008, can be used by big federal agencies to implement cloud-based healthcare projects. The agenda requires the Office of the National Coordinator for Health Information Technology to take the lead in developing and deploying interoperable health information technology infrastructure across the country to improve the quality index and care of patients. The key plan has two objectives: patient-focused health care and community health sector. Each objective comprises four goals. The goals of both goals are confidentiality and security, interoperability, implementation, and co-management. The path of plan achieving each goal is detailed in 43 strategies that outline the work required to achieve each goal. All of the planning is governed with a milestone against which growth can be measured, as well as a series of descriptive steps taken to achieve each strategy.

In addition to the aforementioned strategic planning methods, this document also gives a health CC planning model (HC2SP) based on research [49] that can be used by medical organizations to determine its direction, course of action, and resource distribution. Moving from traditional health care to the cloud, the model has four stages: identification, assessment, follow-ups, and action; for elaboration, see Figure 3.2.

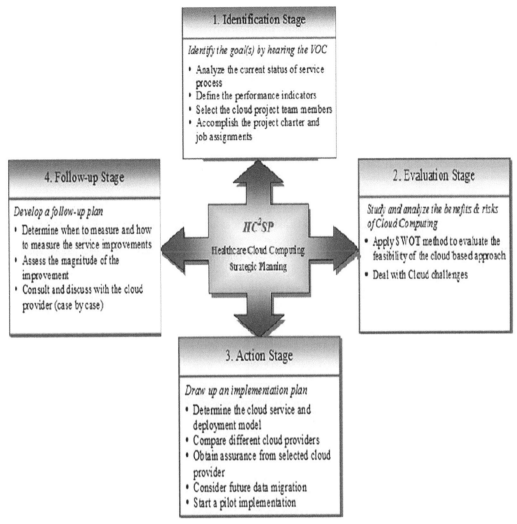

FIGURE 3.2
HC2SP model. SWOT, strengths, weaknesses, opportunities, and threats; VOC, voice of customer).

Given HC2SP model, the foremost step is to analyze the present state of the existing service process in the healthcare organization and determine the main goal of improving service by listening to the requirements of clients or patients. Root cause analysis can be used to get detailed assessment of problems in the ongoing maintenance program. A typical level of cause would be expressed as follows [50]:

Stage 1: Assessment
 Problem 1: The system of hospitalizing or discharging a patient is time taking lengthy. What for? Too many repetitive graphs. What for? The paper chart system is ineffective. What for? Lack of systems such as EHR/EMR. What for? This necessitates a large upfront investment in IT and support infrastructure.

Objective identification and its scope must be clearly defined in order to give services to end patients more efficiently. In addition, the critical planning team should also identify medical service quality parameters and explain their purpose and the purpose of each indicator. This part of the model gives the key planning team with a well-defined framework for addressing emerging problems in the services.

Stage 2: Assessment

The second part of the model is to assess the convenience and challenges of implementing CC. ENISA [51], Cloud Security Alliance [52], and NIST [53] have organized complete set of guidelines for assessing the advantages and risks of CC. Potential users can also use of strengths, weaknesses, opportunities, and threats (SWOT) breakdown to evaluate the feasibility of cloud-based methods [].

In addition, users need to evaluate how the identified problems can be resolved. There are many links available for this (see Table 3.1 [34,52,53,55,56]). For example, Armbrast et al. [57] reported ten major barriers to CC. From simple product development to large-scale research projects, every obstacle is combined with an opportunity (solution). Buya and Ranjan [55] discussed several co-management issues in the cloud, such as data hindrance, co-logging, and shared cluster aggregation. They also give additional links to address the issues discussed. In addition, Kuo et al. [56] have proposed an XML-type mediation program to solve the info blocking problem.

For example, Buya and Ranjan [55] discussed several co-management issues in the cloud, such as data hindrances, co-logging, and distributed cluster aggregation. It also gives additional links to address the issues discussed. In addition, Kuo et al. [56] have proposed an XML-type mediation program to solve the info blocking problem.

The Cloud Security Alliance [52] describes 12 areas in which CC is focused. These areas fall into two major categories: management and conveyance. With explanations, suggestions are also given for each domain. The NIST Guidelines for Security and Privacy in Public Cloud Computing [53] lists many of the prime key security and privacy concerns of CC and givers guidance on appropriate preventive measures that organizations should follow when devising or initiating public cloud outsourcing agreements. Ward and Sipier [34] are concerned with the issue of jurisdiction. They supported five strategies for cloud clients to address jurisdictional issues.

Step 3: Action

Once the new computational model evaluation is being carried out, the medical or pharmaceutical companies or institutions will be able to determine whether to use the service. If its answer is being yes, you need to develop an application plan. This article proposes a five-step plan as shown below.

TABLE 3.1

Capable Solutions to the CC Challenges

Challenges	Resources	Solution Summary
Management and technical issues	Buyya and Ranjan [55]	Cloud-federated management references
	Kuo et al. [56]	XML-based data interoperability mediator
Security and legal issues	Cloud Security Alliance [52]	Cloud governance and operations solutions (12 domains)
	NIST guidelines [53]	Security and privacy precautions
	Ward and Sipior [34]	Five data jurisdiction strategies

Step A: Define Cloud Service and Deployment Model

CC may refer to several service types (IaaS, PaaS, and SaaS) and deployment methodologies (private, public, community, and hybrid cloud). Each service or deployment approach offers benefits and dangers [58]. Distinct services or deployment methods should have different contractual priorities.

Step B. Compare different cloud givers

Getting the right cloud providers is the most fundamental part of your implementation plan. Different givers may give more than one type service models, service plans, auditing methods, and privacy and security policies. The medical institutions must compare different products. In addition, before signing a contract, it is necessary to assess the reputation and performance of the givers.

Step C. Get guarantees from selected cloud givers

The medical or pharmaceutical institutions ensure that the selected givers give quality services and maintain strong confidentiality, security, legal practices, and regulations. Service quality assurance includes on-demand access, pay-as-you-go, fast flexibility, timely troubleshooting support, and operational transparency [51]. Confidentiality and security guarantees cover confidentiality, integrity, availability, authenticity, authorization, and nondenial of data. In addition, the vendor must ensure that info (including all its backups) is only located in geological locations permitted by contracts, service level agreements, and regulations.

Step D: Consider future data migration

As the giver has discontinued business or service operations (such as the recently closed Google Health [59]), service quality has dropped to an unacceptable level, and the health sectors may have to move info and services to another givers or internal IT department. Environmental issues and potential contract disputes are possible. Information portability should be considered in advance as part of the plan [60].

Step E: Start pilot implementation

The different critical planning techniques indicate that an health sector companies or instructions with no cloud experience should first pilot its implementation [46,47]. The test must be justifiable for providing sector companies or institutions with evidence of the benefits of CC.

Stage 4

The final point is the deployment of the CC infrastructure and the drawing up of subsequent plans. The plan specifies when and how to calculate improvement. Reasonable goals are determined in advance, and the results of new services are measured against specified goals or performance indicators to assess the degree of improvement [61]. If the new conditions of service are not met, WHO needs to consider what factors are affecting performance targets. If the primary reason for noncompliance is the cloud givers, the organization will negotiate and discuss with the givers how to improve the service, or it may consider transferring info and services to another givers or returning to its internal IT environment.

Risks of Cloud Computing in Health Care

The lack of security and privacy are the two main concerns that healthcare givers face when choosing a cloud solution [42].

To overcome these concerns, healthcare companies looking for alternatives (Health Insurance Portability and Accountability Act (HIPAA) of 1996) [27].

Large-scale data breaches have been reported more and more in recent years, raising concerns among patients who fear that hospitals and doctors using cloud service givers' could complicate data privacy. There are also concerns about allowing multiple users to share EHRs between installations.

3.7.5 Availability and Control

CC can sometimes fall due to some probabilities. There will be situations where healthcare givers will need data, cloud platforms will be inactive, and productivity will be adversely affected. Even the company's physical equipment faces these problems that require restoration of service [62].

3.7.6 Security Threats

The main threat to security is hacking, which accounts for 47% of the 416 cyber cases. Cloud networks give security tools to search, alert, and deal with suspicious behavior. However, they are not perfect. The Department of Health and Human Rights is investigating 416 cases, including breaches of health information security [63].

3.7.7 Legal and Compliance Risks

Many data security regulations aim to protect certain types of data. For example, HIPAA requires healthcare givers to protect patient data. Companies protected by these regulations do not just need to protect their data; they usually need to know.

3.8 Conclusion

The adoption of CC technologies has significant proliferation on pre-existing healthcare infrastructure and the growth of IT especially cloud-based technologies and IoT-based technologies. Both of these proven more beneficial in terms of response time of patient's data collected but also the disease diagnosis. The patient's overall recovery time and over-burden healthcare infrastructure get benefitted with CC techniques. The roles and responsibilities of CC in healthcare areas will be proven more rewarding with the help of artificial intelligence/IoT/ML in coming era. But the patients' data security and data thefts will be simultaneously challenging issues which will be surfaced out once full dependency established on cloud-based technologies. This is to be focused more as challenges and solutions over CC roles in healthcare sector.

References

1. Kumar, A. World of cloud computing & security, *International Journal of Cloud Computing and Services Science (IJ-CLOSER)*, 1(2), 44–58, 2012.
2. Buyya, R. Introduction to the IEEE transactions on cloud computing, *IEEE Transactions on Cloud Computing*, 1(1), 3-21, 2013. DOI: 10.1109/TCC.2013.13.

3. Pal, S. et al. Efficient architectural framework for cloud computing, *International Journal of Cloud Computing and Services Science (IJ-CLOSER)*, 1(2), 66–73, 2012.

4. Buyya, R. et al. Cloud computing and emerging IT platforms: Vision, hype, and reality for delivering computing as the 5th utility, *Future Generation Computer Systems*, 25, 599–616, 2009.

5. Vijindra et al. Survey on scheduling issues in cloud computing, *International Conference on Modeling Optimization and Computing (ICMOG-2012), Procedia Engineering*, vol. 38, 2881–2888, 2012.

6. Rathor, V. S. et al. Survey on load balancing through virtual machine scheduling in cloud computing environment, *International Journal of Cloud Computing and Services Science (IJ-CLOSER)*, 3(1), 37–43, 2014.

7. Rai, B. K., Sharma, S., Kumar, G., Kishor, K. Recognition of different bird category using image processing. *International Journal of Online and Biomedical Engineering (IJOE)*, 18(07), 101–114, 2022. DOI: 10.3991/ijoe.v18i07.29639.

8. Xiaoshan, H. E. et al. QoS Guided min-min heuristic for grid task scheduling, *Journal of Computer Science and Technology*, 18(4), 442–451, 2003.

9. Chauhan, S. S. et al. QoS Guided heuristic algorithms for grid task scheduling, *International Journal of Computer Applications*, 2(9), 24–31, 2010.

10. Xu, B. et al. Job scheduling algorithm based on Berger model in cloud environment, *Advances in Engineering Software*, 42, 419–425, 2011.

11. Kishor, K., Nand, P., Agarwal, P. Subnet based ad hoc network algorithm reducing energy consumption in MANET. *International Journal of Applied Engineering Research*, 12(22), 11796–11802, 2017.

12. Kishor, K., Nand, P., Agarwal, P. Secure and efficient subnet routing protocol for MANET, *Indian Journal of Public Health*, 9(12), 200, 2018. DOI: 10.5958/0976-5506.2018.01830.2.

13. Kishor, K., Nand, P., Agarwal, P. Notice of retraction design adaptive subnetting hybrid gateway MANET protocol on the basis of dynamic TTL value adjustment. *Aptikom Journal on Computer Science and Information Technologies*, 3(2), 59–65, 2018. DOI: 10.11591/APTIKOM.J.CSIT.115.

14. Kishor, K., Nand, P. Review performance analysis and challenges wireless MANET routing protocols. *International Journal of Science, Engineering and Technology Research (IJSETR)*, 2(10), 1854–1855, 2013, ISSN 2278-7798.

15. Kishor, K., Nand, P. Performance evaluation of AODV, DSR, TORA and OLSR in with respect to end-to-end delay in MANET. *International Journal of Science and Research (IJSR)*, 3(6), 633–636, 2014, ISSN 2319-7064.

16. Kishor, K., Sharma, R., Chhabra, M. Student performance prediction using technology of machine learning. In: Sharma D.K., Peng S.L., Sharma R., Zaitsev D.A. (eds) *Micro-Electronics and Telecommunication Engineering. Lecture Notes in Networks and Systems*, vol. 373. Springer, Singapore. 2022. DOI: 10.1007/978-981-16-8721-1_53.

17. Kishor, K. Communication-efficient federated learning. In: Yadav S.P., Bhati B.S., Mahato D.P., Kumar S. (eds) *Federated Learning for IoT Applications. EAI/Springer Innovations in Communication and Computing*. Springer, Cham, 2022. DOI: 10.1007/978-3-030-85559-8_9.

18. Kishor, K. Personalized federated learning. In: Yadav S.P., Bhati B.S., Mahato D.P., Kumar S. (eds) *Federated Learning for IoT Applications. EAI/Springer Innovations in Communication and Computing*. Springer, Cham, 2022. DOI: 10.1007/978-3-030-85559-8_3.

19. Gupta, S., Tyagi, S., Kishor, K. Study and development of self sanitizing smart elevator. In: Gupta D., Polkowski Z., Khanna A., Bhattacharyya S., Castillo O. (eds) *Proceedings of Data Analytics and Management. Lecture Notes on Data Engineering and Communications Technologies*, vol. 90. Springer, Singapore, 2022. DOI: 10.1007/978-981-16-6289-8_15.

20. Kishor, K., Pandey, D. Study and development of efficient air quality prediction system embedded with machine learning and IoT. In: Gupta D. et al. (eds) *Proceeding International Conference on Innovative Computing and Communications. Lecture Notes in Networks and Systems*, vol. 471, Springer, Singapore, 2022. DOI: 10.1007/978-981-19-2535-1.

21. Sharma, A., Jha, N., Kishor, K. Predict COVID-19 with chest X-ray. In: Gupta D., Polkowski Z., Khanna A., Bhattacharyya S., Castillo O. (eds) *Proceedings of Data Analytics and Management. Lecture Notes on Data Engineering and Communications Technologies*, vol. 90, Springer, Singapore, 2022. DOI: 10.1007/978-981-16-6289-8_16.

22. Jain, A., Sharma, Y., Kishor, K. Financial supervision and management system using Ml algorithm. *Solid State Technology*, 63(6), 18974–18982, 2020. http://solidstatetechnology.us/index.php/JSST/article/view/8080.

23. Wan, D., Greenway, A., Harris, J. G., Alter, A. E. 2010.

24. HarishGoud, B., Shankar, T.N., Sahoo, P.K., Cheng, W.H. A novel method for routing packet between patient and doctor using sensor and cloud. In: *2021 6th International Conference for Convergence in Technology (I2CT)*. IEEE, 1–5, 2021.

25. Potluri, S., Rao, K.S. Quality of service based task scheduling algorithms in cloud computing. *International Journal of Electrical and Computer Engineering*, 7(2), 1088, 2017.

26. Thirupathi Rao, N., Bhattacharyya, D. Energy diminution methods in green cloud computing. *International Journal of Cloud-Computing and Super-Computing*, 6(1), 1–8, 2019.

27. Kuo, A. M. Opportunities and challenges of cloud computing to improve health care services. *Journal of Medical Internet Research*, 13(3), e67, 2011.

28. Korea IT Times. *Telstra Plans Launch of E-Health Cloud Services*, Tip of the Iceberg for Opportunity, 2010. URL: http://www.koreaittimes.com/story/9826/telstra-plans-launch-e-healthcloud-services-tip-iceberg-opportunity.

29. Rui, Z., Ling, L. Security models and requirements for healthcare application clouds. In: *Cloud Computing (CLOUD), 2010 IEEE 3rd International Conference*, 2010.

30. Kuo, A. M. Opportunities and challenges of cloud computing to improve health care services. *Journal of Medical Internet Research*, 13(3), e67, 2011. DOI: 10.2196/jmir.1867. PMID: 21937354; PMCID: PMC3222190.

31. Violino, B. *Accenture, AT&T Offer Cloud-Based Medical Imaging*, Accenture (NYSE: ACN) and AT&T, Chicago, 2011.

32. Kupferman, J., Silverman, J., Jara, P., Browne, J. *Scaling Into the Cloud*, CS270-advanced operating system, 2009.

33. Logic Monitor. *Logic Monitor: Architecture White Paper*, Computing Research Paper, Sponsored by LogicMonitor, 2012.

34. Barry, J., Napatech. *Testing the Cloud: Assuring Availability*, 2011.

35. Kharat, A.T., Safvi, A., Thind, S., Singh, A. Cloud computing for radiologists. *Indian Journal of Radiology and Imaging*, 22(3), 150–4, 2012 Jul. doi: 10.4103/0971-3026.107166. PMID: 23599560; PMCID: PMC3624735.

36. Wang, X., Tan, Y. *Application of Cloud Computing in the Health Information System. Computer Application and System Modeling (ICCASM)*, 2010 International Conference on Computer Application and System Modeling (ICCASM 2010), 1, V1-179–V1-182, 2010.

37. Kalra, D. S. et al., Differentiating algorithms of cloud task scheduling based on various parameters, *IOSR Journal of Computer Engineering (IOSR-JCE)*, 17(6), 35–38, 2015.

38. Selvarani, S. et al., Improved cost-based algorithm for task scheduling in cloud computing, *2010 IEEE International Conference on Computational Intelligence and Computing Research*, 2010.

39. Gunasekhar, T., Rao, K.T., Basu, M.T. Understanding insider attack problem and scope in cloud. In: *2015 International Conference on Circuits, Power and Computing Technologies [ICCPCT-2015]*. IEEE, 1–6, 2015.

40. Vulapula, S.R., Srinivas, M. Review on privacy preserving of medical data in cloud computing system. *Indian Journal of Public Health Research & Development*, 9(12), 2018.

41. Srinivas, P., Pillala, P., Rao, N.T., Bhattacharyya, D. Performance investigation of cloud computing applications using steady-state queuing models. In: Bhattacharyya, D., Thirupathi Rao, N. (eds). *Machine Intelligence and Soft Computing*. Advances in Intelligent Systems and Computing, vol. 1280, Springer, Singapore, 213–225, 2021. DOI: 10.1007/978-981-15-9516-5_19.

42. Tirapathi, R. B., Bhuvanesh Chava, C. H., Susanth Kumar, T., Gopi Kalyan, V. Security key given for group data sharing in cloud computing, *International Journal of Advanced Science and Technology*, 28(16), 596–603, 2019.

43. Kabachinski, J. What's the forecast for cloud computing in healthcare? *Biomedical Instrumentation &Technology*, 45(2), 146–150, 2011.

44. Webb, G. Making the cloud work for healthcare: Cloud computing offers incredible opportunities to improve healthcare, reduce costs and accelerate ability to adopt new IT services, *Health Management Technology*, 33(2), 8–9, 2012.

45. AbuKhousa, E., Mohamed, N., Al-Jaroodi, J. e-Health cloud: Opportunities and challenges. *Future Internet*, 4, 621–645, 2012. DOI: 10.3390/fi4030621.

46. Marks, E.A., Lozano, B. *Executive's Guide to Cloud Computing*. Wiley, Hoboken, NJ, 2010.

47. Stanoevska-Slabeva, K., Wozniak, T., Hoyer, V. Practical guidelines for evolving IT infrastructure towards grids and clouds. In: Stanoevska-Slabeva K., Wozniak T., Ristol S., (eds) *Grid and Cloud Computing: A Business Perspective on Technology and Applications*. Springer, Berlin, 225–243, 2010.

48. US Department of Health & Human Services, Office of the National Coordinator for Health Information Technology. *The ONC-Coordinated Federal Health IT Strategic Plan: 2008–2012*. ONC-HIT, Washington, DC, 2008.

49. Kuo, A. M., Borycki, E., Kushniruk, A., Lee, T. S. A healthcare lean six sigma system for postanesthesia care unit workflow improvement. *Quality Management in Healthcare*, 20(1), 4–14, 2011.

50. Lee, T. S., Kuo, M. H. Toyota A3 report: A tool for process improvement in healthcare. *Studies in Health Technology and Informatics*, 143, 235–240, 2009.

51. European Network and Information Security Agency. ENISA. *Cloud Computing: Benefits, Risks and Recommendations for Information Security*. 2009. URL: http://www.enisa.europa.eu/act/rm/files/deliverables/cloud-computing-risk-assessment.

52. Cloud Security Alliance. *Security Guidance for Critical Areas of Focus in Cloud Computing V2.1*. 2009. URL: http://www.cloudsecurityalliance.org/csaguide.pdf.

53. Jansen, W., Grance, T. National Institute of Standards and Technology, US Department of Commerce. *Guidelines on Security and Privacy in Public Cloud Computing*. 2011. URL: http://csrc.nist.gov/publications/drafts/800-144/Draft-SP-800-144_cloud-computing.pdf.

54. Marston, S., Li, Z., Bandyopadhyay, S., Zhang, J., Ghalsasi, A. Cloud computing: The business perspective. *Decision Support Systems*, 51(1), 176–189, 2011.

55. Buyya, R., Ranjan, R. Special section: Federated resource management in grid and cloud computing systems. *Future Generation Computer Systems*, 26(8), 1189–1191, 2010.

56. Kuo, M. H., Kushniruk, A. W., Borycki, E. M. Design and implementation of a health data interoperability mediator. *Studies in Health Technology and Informatics*, 155, 101–107, 2010.

57. Armbrust, M., Fox, A., Griffth, R., et al. Above the Clouds: A Berkeley View of Cloud Computing. Technical Report No. UCB/EECS-2009-28, University of California Berkeley, Berkeley, USA, 2009. URL: https://www2.eecs.berkeley.edu/Pubs/TechRpts/2009/EECS-2009-28.pdf.

58. Zhang, R., Liu, L. Security models and requirements for healthcare application clouds. In: *Proceedings of the 2010 IEEE 3rd International Conference on Cloud Computing (CLOUD)*. IEEE, New York, NY. 2010.

59. Williams, R., Will, C., Weiner, K., Henwood, F. Navigating standards, encouraging interconnections: infrastructuring digital health platforms. *Information, Communication & Society*, 23(8), 1170–1186. DOI: 10.1080/1369118X.2019.1702709.

60. Gagliardi, F., Muscella, S. Cloud computing: Data confidentiality and interoperability challenges. In: Antonopoulos N., Gillam L., (eds). *Cloud Computing: Principles, Systems and Applications (Computer Communications and Networks)*. Springer, London, 257–270, 2010.

61. Lee, T. S., Kuo, M. H. Toyota A3 report: A tool for process improvement in healthcare. *Studies in Health Technology and Informatics*, 143, 235–240, 2009.

62. Murali, M. V. *Optimal Design of Multi Objective Quality of Service Aware Resource Scheduling Strategies for Cloud Computing*, 2020. URL: http://localhost:8080/xmlui/handle/123456789/555

63. Manekar, A., Gera, P. Studying cloud as IaaS for big data analytics: Opportunity, challenges. *International Journal of Engineering & Technology*, 7(2), 909–912, 2018.

4

Cloud Computing in Artificial Neural Network

Shivani Agarwal and Akanksha Shukla

Ajay Kumar Garg Engineering College

CONTENTS

4.1 Introduction

Cloud computing is a high-demand platform in this current scenario. By using the various applications of cloud computing, we can easily enhance the performance of utilizing resources, managing data, and easily enhancing the network facilities. It is a promising archetype that provides a platform for fast admittance of data in a well-defined structure with complete information while minimizing human or machine efforts. It provided a totally eco-friendly system. This is a very elegant skill that will change the world with minimum effort and minimum time. All of the conventional approaches have issues with how they can handle the data if they train the network with massive amounts of data, which creates a highly problematic condition in an artificial neural network (ANN). So those are minimized by using cloud computing in ANN. Another much-trained utilities of cloud computing are in education, telecommunication, crime branches, water and gas supply, railways, and many more. Actually, the work level is reduced after implementation

DOI: 10.1201/9781003213895-4

of this new technology in this era. In education system, it provides the technologies in the market that is unexpected education services through the network within affordable price and high quality. Students are very much happy to achieve the good skills and knowledge in very less price and quality [1,2]. In telecommunications, implementing the computing environment improves every record, such as calling system, network, and data bandwidth; in fact, it will help to find out the criminals in a very short time because we have a huge space to record the data and find out the similar crime types to fetch the required information, so it provides the boom in the market. So, this is the major advantage, and it occurs only when cloud computing is in market.

Cloud computing makes an easy environment for all the users who want to use huge amount of data and resources, so everything users have to use is in handy environment via the Internet. Cloud Computing solves many problems like weather forecasting, medical drug discovery, and bank transaction system. In study, we observed that ANN provides a better platform for data security. ANN in cloud environment plays a vital role for storing the data, ensuring the good quality of data, data reliability, and providing secure services for the users. It allows users to fetch the information or required data from computer-generated environment that will reduce the cost of processing and data storage that will be executed by the enhancement of ANN techniques in cloud computing. In this environment of research, we have to focus on the association between cloud computing and ANN, which is focused on online services, network sharing, and managing well-established communication network with high speed of access to data, whereas in the cloud computing environment, the security of data and the use of data are haphazard. So, using neural network architectures, we have to enhance that data in a defined and easy way. Also, focus on the security of data so that third party does not mutate that data. In the cloud computing space, the main focus is resource scheduling, so we defined some functions and tasks that are used to classify the data and solve the problems computationally (Figure 4.1).

4.2 Characteristics of Cloud Computing

Cloud computing has many characteristics, some important characteristics are as follows:

1. **Resource assembling:** Resource assembling means all the resources are assembled in one physical space. If multiple clients want a resource so shared resources are used in the network.

2. **Quick resistance:** It means all the resources are scalable as per demand by the clients. The services are very quick, and it's on demand as per the customer requirement. Cloud computing services are not required any human intervention for sharing the resources or managing the resources [3].

3. **Location independent:** Cloud computing interfaces are independent, and it can be accessed from any place, any location of the user. User should access the services of cloud computing universally.

4. **Quality of conformance:** Cloud computing provides the assurance about the quality to the user so that customers are fully satisfied [4].

5. **Limited cost:** The expense of services used by clients is very low, which means no extra cost is involved in cloud architecture.

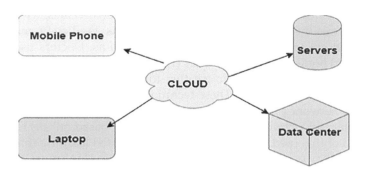

FIGURE 4.1
Cloud computing structure.

6. **Low maintenance:** This is the best service of cloud computing. By using this service, cloud servers and data are easily maintained without the high effort of users and it updates in a very easy and effective manner.

   Security: It is a very useful characteristic of cloud computing, everyone wants that their data is secured in the cloud and that no unwanted parties have accessed that data, so that data is prevented and secured [5,6].

   Wireless network: A distributed system consists of autonomous computers linked by a network and middleware to coordinate their operations and share system resources so users view it as a single, integrated computing facility [5,6]. Wi-Fi access points, base stations, or satellites link mobile nodes to the Internet. Mobile cloud computing is limited to infrastructure-based communication methods and not mobile ad hoc. Mobile ad hoc cloud computing leverages mobile devices to create a virtual supercomputer. A mobile ad hoc network offers network discovery, monitoring, and routing. Cloud middleware handles tasks, failures, mobility, and communications. It conceals complexity and gives users and apps a uniform system view [7–9].

7. **Automation:** This is a very critical and demanding characteristic of cloud computing. Users demand that every service in cloud computing be installed, updated, and configured automatically.

4.3 Scope of Cloud Computing in Artificial Neural Network

Cloud computing plays a vital role in the learning network of ANN. It is the model that simulates the activities of Brain in computational model. In this model, information is distributed across number of neuron nodes in different layered architecture, with neurons from each layer connected to those from other layers as interconnected layered architecture as an input layer, hidden layers, and an output layer [10,11]. So when there are variable numbers of hidden layers, data gathering is very high and rate of data processing is also very high so that it is very difficult without the involvement of cloud computing. Prediction and analysis are the very important application of ANN in the computer science field. That is used to find the rules for predicting known and unknown values, which enhances the results and improves the performance for better analysis. Prediction analysis is used to predict drugs that are totally dependent on the symptoms. Doctors used the decision-making analysis to predict the drug analysis [12].

Predictive analysis is also helpful in weather forecasting. It is used the learning techniques of ANN for data prediction. These techniques are supervised, unsupervised, and recurrent neural network [13,14]. If we use the supervised learning technique, we have the resultant data, and technical analyst takes a decision based on this learning method. Another method of this predictive analysis is unsupervised learning that is used to predict the information by using k-means clustering. Each piece of information is stored in the database as a cloud. So the predictive results also save in the cloud databases. So everyone can fetch these results, and it can be transferred from one network to another [15,16].

4.3.1 Basics of BNN

Biological neural network (BNN) is the essential method of neural network. BNN is made up of neurons. In human minds, there are billions of neurons. Each neuron is tied to another neuron, and information transfers from one neuron to another. Each neuron collects information from other neurons, and collectively, information is processed. This processed information is checked with a level of threshold. If this threshold value is matched with the desired value, then this is the excitation state; otherwise, it is known as the inhibitory state. The fundamental working structure of artificial neurons is the same as that of biological neurons, i.e., the transmission of information processed from one neuron to another neuron after collecting information from synaptic weights from other neurons. This same information processing is done by artificial neurons, like in brain construction.

Biological neural network has a large database of collective information but this data is very huge.so this database is not secured. This huge database handled by using cloud computing. One of the most important characteristic of biological field that is data monopolization that is very helpful in medical field for saving data, time, and cost. We can access data and retrieve information in a very simple and efficient manner by using this technology [17] (Figure 4.2).

This diagram represents the synapses; these are divided into two parts: presynapse and postsynapse; presynapse means taking the information from the connecting neuron and transferring it from one to another by using the postsynapse; these are like buttons;

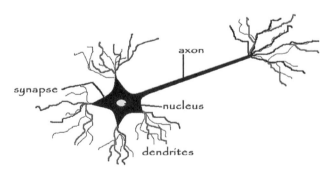

FIGURE 4.2
Biological neuron Structure.

dendrites receive the information from postsynapse, and this collective information is processed to the soma or cell; dendrites are leaf-like structure that collect the information from other neurons; if this collective information reached the defined threshold, then it is delivered to another neuron by using an axon; otherwise, it is not. So, this is the basic working of BNN.

4.4 Basics of ANN

ANN is a greatly gigantic network of computers or nodes, each node united with another one like as distributed network. ANN working is completely dependent on BNN which, in the form of input and weights, is processed in the form of x and w; this processed information summarizes and uses activation function to receive the final output in the form of y (Figure 4.3).

The basic architecture of ANN is made up of basic three-layered architecture. First is input layer, second is hidden layer, and third is output layer. There is always single input layer and output layer but variable hidden layers are used in different applications. Variation of hidden layers is completely dependent on different applications, and that is dependent on the level of complexity.

The raw information is fed into input layer as the variable input values in the form of x, and each input value is attached to the variable weight value in the form of w. This cumulative information is processed from input to hidden layer [18–21]. Then, information processed from one to other hidden layers in the form of matrix. Then transfer the information from hidden input to output neuron. One of the most important things to always consider is that the input value is fixed, and weight values are variable according to the desired outcome. These architectures are divided into two basic categories that are single-layer and multilayer architecture. In single layer, there is only an input layer and an output layer, so there is a straight link from the input layer to the output layer. But in multilayer, there is an input layer, a hidden layer, and an output layer, so there is no straight link between the input layer and the output layer. Various applications like medical diagnosis and weather forecasting used the concept of neural network, but the problem is that

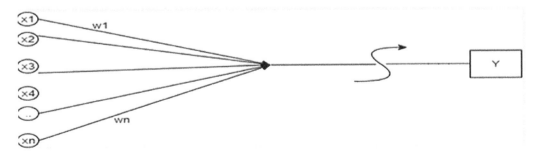

FIGURE 4.3
Artificial neural networks.

learning is difficult due to huge amount of data, so that problem can be minimized by the implementation of cloud computing.

4.4.1 Services of Cloud Computing Inherited in Artificial Neural Network

A very interesting technology named as cloud computing comes in the field that solved many problems like data integrity, security, privacy, load balancing, and data transmission. Cloud computing is one of the top most important research area for the researchers nowadays. It offers many services to the clients as data storage, accessing the data from data store from anywhere to anyone [22]. By using cloud computing, we can easily learn our network with minimum time and cost, so the efficiency of learning our network is fast and very easy. Many companies charge for their cloud services, and these are so flexible and scalable in nature [23]. It provides platform for such diversified services like as software, infrastructure, platform, and expert [24].

4.4.2 Cloud Service as Software in ANN

Everything is everywhere via Internet using cloud computing, so when any user wants any application to install or download, then it is easily accessible, which creates a dynamic environment in a very easy way. Because of its ability to handle large databases via Internet and all data in a secure manner, all companies are completely dependent on this technology. The use of ANN techniques is useful for taking the decisions after learning the network. So, it provides an optimum solution of any business application by using the techniques of neural network. Various business applications easily implement and handle by using cloud computing and learning of that network by using ANN like as job scheduling, load balancing, and many more applications are easily implemented by these concepts. So, solution of these business applications provides a high prediction of resource utilization.

4.4.3 ANN in Job Scheduling

Job scheduling is the biggest problem, which means if many requests come for a resource, then this problem can be minimized by using ANN and maintaining all the data by using cloud computing [25]. The implementation of these technologies necessitates that the cloud service provider fulfills every service request. Every user request for a resource in a cloud environment so which user requests fulfill at which time with proper resource utilization and reduce cost and time. This time it becomes a very hot area of research. This process easily handles by using the concept of network learning. Scheduling of any job for allocate the resource by learn from environment on the basis of the time, cost, and utility. These parameters are used to find the best resource for a best time to allocate for a user scheduling of each user request means find the best way of allocating the resources for the required request [26]. The core mission of job scheduling is to discover the best solution of the resource from cloud by using cloud computing technique (Figure 4.4).

This diagram depicts the procedure to find the way of job scheduling with minimum time and cost, and the steps are as follows:

1. Collect all the requested jobs in a cloud environment by the user.
2. Defined all the parameters for selecting a job or for completion of job by using three main functions as cost, time, and utility.

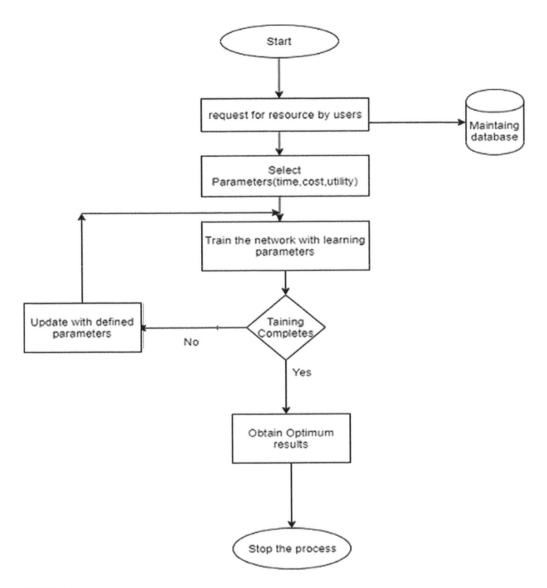

FIGURE 4.4
Job scheduling by using ANN.

3. Input parameters and weight parameters are defined in the network for training. So that network is trained and finds the best way to determine which request to fulfill first.
4. When training completes, find out the best resultant of job scheduling. If the training is uncompleted, then network is again trained and finds the best solution till it's completed.
5. After that stop the process.

4.4.4 ANN in Textiles

In textile industry, many forecast problems are occurred and these problems are solved by using ANN. There are some very small issues focused like fiber prediction and cotton prediction, so that we have to identify properly after trained the network by implementing the concept of neural network.

ANN provides a platform for predicting the symphony of copolymers in a very easy way. It can be supervised or unsupervised learning environment. Start processing with collecting the images from data base and then dig out the automatically identified parameters from that image and then arrange these parameters with their complex levels and accuracy of that model [27]. Accuracy of that model is completely dependent on the number of samples; if samples increases, then the network complexity increases accordingly, and it creates a large database, so that the problem is resolved by cloud computing. Cloud computing maintains the large databases with a secured environment and provides the facility to process the data in an efficient manner.

ANN is focused on textiles by defining some important factors:

1. ANN can help predict the high quality of fiber.
2. ANN focused on production control parameters.
3. It is used to provide the optimum results.
4. ANN is used to classify the grades after extracting the defects in packaging or material.
5. It is useful for maintaining the relationship between variables and structure.

4.4.5 Cloud Service as Infrastructure in ANN

The involvement of cloud computing and ANN to enhance the functionalities of infrastructure, emphasize the functional concepts, and improve the quality standards. But this is the very weak part that quality standards are not met due to only basic standards are followed. So that provides the judgment how to move on to provide best service as infrastructure.

This is a very beautiful concept that without interruption of any one (either special member or team management) data and resources are accesses from any platform by the Internet using Cloud concept. There are two types of computing named as edge computing and mobile computing those are used for handling all the resources and also work on the key points of data like time management, response time, load balancing, and data transmission scheme. When data transmission between client to client or online transaction takes place, some challenges are faced like data security. This problem can be minimized by using the learning techniques of ANN as supervised learning and unsupervised learning [28].

4.4.6 Supervised Learning

Supervised learning means learning from experiences in the real world. Supervised learning is the learning mechanism that based on past history, and based on that history, we find the results of the present work [14]. In supervised learning, the results are known and have a predefined approach that is useful for comparing the required information and target information so that error of finding the correct information is minimized and easily captured [29,30].

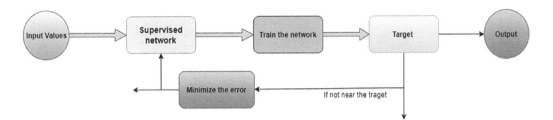

FIGURE 4.5
Supervised learning.

It allows collecting the data bases according to the problem and having the results also; for achieving these results, we train the network and optimize the results with the help of the supervisor (Figure 4.5).

The problems are solved by using this learning categorized by two models:
(1) Classification Model and (2) Regression Model

1. **Classification model:** This is the very important model to solve the problems by using categorical categories. This is very helpful for realistic problems, these types of problems are used to predict sentiment analysis, voting type problems, and other various real type problems, and each one is classified either true or false concept means two-class classification or multiclass classification.

2. **Regression model:** This model is a prediction model based on statistics data that is totally dependent on dependent or independent data. This is totally dependent on cause-and-effect relationship model. This is used to solve the real problems of banking sectors and share marketing issue [31].

4.4.7 Unsupervised Learning

Unsupervised learning is the different method from the supervised learning. This is the method that uses to train the data without the use of classification technique. It means there is no trainer is present for supervising. It learns itself without having the past history and experiences. This is the idea to help the large database of unknown patterns and find the known one.

In unsupervised learning, results are unknown so that it uses cluster analysis to deduct the required results. To reduce the error in results, train the network and analyze each result with the required information so it uses k-means clustering (Figure 4.6).

There are two methods that are used for unsupervised learning:

1. **Clustering method:** This is the one very good technique of unsupervised method. This is completely deals with unlabeled data rather than labeled data. Data is scattered and find out the similarities in data and make clusters with the same features data. This data we have to fetch out with the number of parameters by use the concept of k-means clustering. This is used for divided the databases as per the same scale of parameters like when we distinguish the student data base with the parameters are the result, attendance. So defined database is clustered on this and k-means clustering is used for undefined databases.

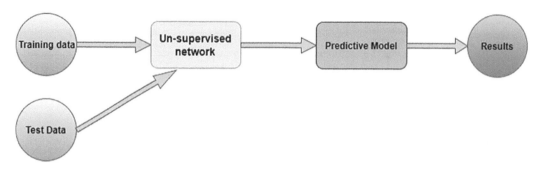

FIGURE 4.6
Unsupervised learning.

2. **Anomaly detection:** This is the very interesting method nowadays. There are many anomalies present in the persons mind in many fields. This is the best method to find the criminal background, detect the medical issues, and detect the bank frauds also.

4.4.8 Cloud Service as Platform in ANN

Cloud computing plays a vital role for communicating things from anywhere by any one at any time. The most important thing is that how securely data transmission is done, which technique used for transfer the data. The data is secured and authentic or not. Which type of measures and techniques used for monitoring the data? These all are very crucial concepts [3,32,33].

So, the proposed solutions are defined supervised model of ANN with different layers for providing data integrity, data encryption, enhanced security, and detection of threats by using back-propagation model.

Cloud computing is designed for balancing the demand of services by using the Internet for expanding the aspect of resource utilization. This is the symbol for defining the network of networks. This is very useful for developing the market of online business, social media platforms. This is used for the expansion of this business and expands the platforms. It shows that how we utilize the resources in a better way and in an easy way. When resources stored in the cloud network, we have to enhance the storage in cloud for better utilization and improve scalability in the market.

4.4.9 How the Security Applies in Cloud Data by Using ANN

Data security is one of the main issues in computer science field. The major issue in this field is that everyone knows that storage of data is stored globally as how much space is required to save that data. But no one knows how this data is stored globally and provides the security of that data . Data security is a major concept in transmission of data from one end to another end. Cloud computing is usually utilized in technical departments in industry and storage of research papers, journals, books, and some academics data but in protected environment, so this is the major fields for providing protection and security [34,35].

Data security enhanced so, use the concept of neural network as a layered architecture, in first layer use the concept of data encryption, in second layer use the method of

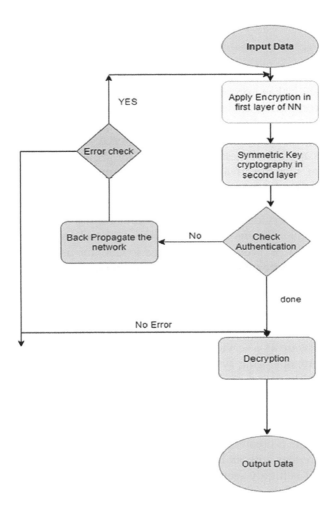

FIGURE 4.7
Security by using ANN.

symmetric key cryptography for providing maximum security when data store in cloud (Figure 4.7).

In this diagram, use the data security scheme for transferring the data from one place to another place in secured manner. Take the input data and apply the encryption scheme on that data, it is applicable in the first layer of neural network, this encrypted data passes on from first layer of neural network to second layer of neural network, in this second layer apply the symmetric key cryptography scheme for enhancement in data security, then check the authentication if it is valid then they decrypt the data by using same key [36–40], if it is invalid then back-propagate it for correct the error. This error checking schemes takes number of epochs for providing high security, it stops when met the authorize user and finally decrypt the data by authentic user. This transmission process provides high security in transmission of data in the cloud network by enhancing the cryptography scheme with neural network methodology.

4.5 Reviews

Cloud computing is the main bough of computational technology. In this, we focus on security-related, data leakage problems that are exploding in the business. In this paper, we use two cloud computing models like deployment model and service delivery model. A business organization fetches data from cloud computing, but they face many issues like leakage of data, corruption in data, and unauthorized data access. So that the use of cloud computing is applied in these organizations for providing higher security by using security mechanism. One big advantage of cloud computing is that data can be accessed from anywhere, anytime, so accessing data is fast [41,42].

In this chapter [43], we define five actors in cloud computing model: CSC (Cloud service consumer), CSP (cloud Service Provider), CA (cloud auditor), and CB (Cloud broker), and CC (Cloud Carrier). CSC obtains the service from CSP and pays for the amount of data required at that price. CSP provides the service to CSC for use the data.CA affords the assessment of cloud services independent's grant interaction between CSC and CSP.CC grants the connectivity between CSP and CSC to smooth the accessing.

In this paper [445], we investigate many challenges like security, leakage, authorization, and work on to solve these problems by defining various methods. In this, we define three service delivery models, namely infrastructure as a service (IaaS), platform as a service (PaaS), and software as a service (SaaS), and nine services, namely application, data, runtime, middleware, operating system, virtualization, server, storage, and networking. These all are applied to data security issues and finding solutions to security problems. These solutions apply not only to organizations' internal customers but also to their external customers.

In this, we classify six stages in life cycle of data, namely create, store, use, share, archive, and destroy. When data is created, one of the most crucial points is that data moves freely from one place to another without hindering. This data is in encrypted form by AES and RSA algorithms so it is highly secure and authorized. That enhances the precision, uniformity, and fidelity of data. Hash and auditing methods are used to enhance the quality of data.

In cloud computing, one of the important aspects is data. Security of data and privacy of data are the key areas in research and methodology. So, the main concern area of this paper is how we provide security from data leakage and provide data protection.

In this paper [45], we use classification technique and some privacy parameters to provide security from various unwanted users or unauthorized users in cloud. If the data is secure, then it helps to various organizations that they fetch any type of data from cloud in restricted or private mode. One essential assess of security of data is how the data is more consistent and more accurate in cloud. In this paper, we spotlight on the properties of data classification like access control mechanism, content, and storage. It means how we recurrently access the data and how we repeatedly modernize the data and focus on legality of the data, specific the data and provided backup of data store. In this, we use some encryption technique that defines the size of the key used to encrypt the data. We use some quality standard to increase the level of security. In this paper [45], data classification technique used to analyze the elements of personal data, categorize these data, and apply security mechanism like encryption. This is important to sustain data quality with defined benchmarks and provide accessibility. Therefore, it is very much unlighted to provide security or access data from cloud in very efficiently and securely.

In this paper [46], it proposes a model that is used for detect the intrusion in the system by using principal component analysis, feature reduction or dimensionality reduction algorithm for minimize the traffic in cloud. Basically, it uses a hybrid approach to solve the problem of high data space in cloud network so the traffic jam increases. This is the approach that minimizes the meaningless data by minimizing the features so that if data is attacked, then we can easily find out that detection is done with a minimum number of resources and use the trained network for obtaining the new attacks.

In this work, we emphasize the following characteristics:

1. Increase the speed of detection
2. Enhancement in security of data and accuracy by rapid detection
3. Reduce the dimensionality of data so reduces the complexity.
4. Focus on feature selection and feature extraction.

   This paper [47] describes the basic architecture of cloud computing, issues, and characteristics of cloud computing. The basic aim of cloud computing is that it utilizes the maximum resources to provide the high throughput and solve the problems of computations. It helps to provide the highly scalability, maintainability, and trustable environment. Some of those characteristics are defined in this paper:

   1. By using the Internet service, client admitted the data and applications by third party.
   2. Resource sharing with less cost for high users demand and high utilization of resources.
   3. High maintenance and high security used for transmission of data or maximum use of data for high performance.

For providing the cloud computing solution in this paper, we define four types of cloud deployment, namely public cloud, private cloud, hybrid cloud, and community cloud. Public cloud defines that how the users use data of cloud, with a define cost according to time and usage. The main disadvantage of public cloud is less secured environment. The only solution of this problem is the usage of security checks or validation. Private cloud is used within organization so the main advantage of this is highly secured network with highly managed environment. Hybrid cloud means it is combination of public and private cloud, and it is highly secured. Community cloud means when two or more organizations joint together and accessed by using third party. Various advantages are easy management, fast computing, high management, and high resource utilization.

In this paper [48], it proposes a model that is used to detect the attack in cloud network that observes the traffic flow in the network either in or out form in the network. They divide their algorithm in following three modes: training database module, preprocessor module, and classifier module.

In training database module, it used supervised classifier for training purpose that provides helps for find the attackers. In this, it uses the database of both types like normal and malicious data; then, it extracts the features and converts each one with numeric value and normalizes it. This is a very crucial and important process to find out the contributed values. Second, the preprocessor module processes the traffic data and captures this data with the defined time interval; it is a continuous process, and all the data samples are captured by the tool. All the captured data now classifies in different classes with same feature value and make it in different files of that data. In the third phase, the classifier module uses ELM, which is extreme large machine classifier used that is a kind of ANN model with a single hidden layer, an input layer, and an output layer. The construction of this model is like as input layer connected to hidden layer with defined weights and hidden layer to output layer. Train the network to improve the performance and accuracy.

4.6 Proposed Model

In this proposed model, we use the basic technique of machine learning that is ANN. There are many algorithms present for learning the network for enhancing the system. Various algorithms are PERCEPTRON, HEBBIAN, ADALINE, and MADALINE. These learning algorithms have different–different layers with variable number of neurons in different layers as per the desired resultants according to their work. Various numbers of neurons are tried in the input and hidden layers but the optimal results produced are used in this proposed model. Similarly, multiple hidden layers are increased for achieving the good results but the complexity of the system is very high so to reduce this complexity, the optimal solution is that two hidden layers are proposed in this model. So, in this proposed model, initially we can take 25 neurons in first input layer and 30 neurons in second hidden layer and third hidden layer. In output layer, we can use three neurons. By using cloud computing system, we can improve the performance of the system. For improving the performance of the system, we can increase the number of neurons and enhance the number of layers, but when there is a spontaneous increase in the number of layers and neurons, performance degrades (Figure 4.8).

Some Important Points of This Model

1. Variation in number of layers
2. Variation in number of neurons
3. Enhance the quality of data by using cloud system
4. Data is secured and manageable
5. Improve performance and quality
6. Reduce cost and time of delivery

These points are very important for this proposed model when we want to improve the performance and quality of this model with a less complex architecture, so we have to focus on enhancing the number of nodes in each layer with respect to increasing the number of layers, but always keep in mind that if we increase the number of layers, then the complexity of this architecture increases automatically; sometimes, resultant comes in the negative direction. So, we use the optimal number of hidden layers with optimal number of neurons of each layer. Number of neurons of each layer is not pre-decided that is completely dependent on problem to problem but always kept in our mind that variation in layers or variation in neurons is used for find the optimal solution. The main goal is to minimize the error with high data security and improve the quality of the system by using this methodology. All these points are very crucial at the time of implementation of this algorithm and are always used to enhance the quality of the system. The major role is finding the best solution with minimum error and high-quality software.

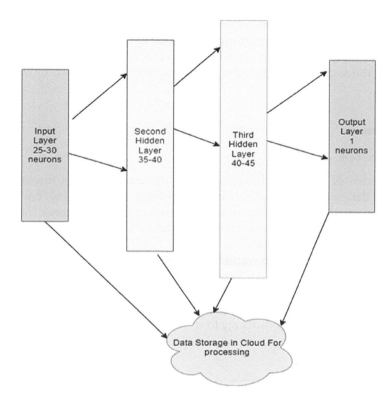

FIGURE 4.8
Proposed model.

4.7 Conclusion

Cloud computing provides a platform for managing the data, data security, and integrity of that data. It comes as demanding technology day by day. But some issues like network traffic, flooding, and unauthorized and unwanted user access increase. So ANN is used for improving the performance of any application, like job scheduling, work load distribution, and many more. By using the multilayer hidden layers and increasing the number of neurons, the matrix size is increased and data management at learning time and data processing is a critical task so that is reduced by using the concept of cloud computing in ANN. In this model, first we use the symmetric key cryptography for authenticating the data and multilayered model for improving the performance. Finally, we say that the neural network classified many fields and provided the effective results and ad-equable solutions from the best approaches in the cloud computing environment. It provides a set of categories on the basis of predefined task so that can be useful for predicting the best analysis for these types of problems.

In this work, a machine learning approach is used to boost the performance of the system and enhance the results of cloud computing environment. For achieving the good results, we have to focus on various layers with various neurons with number of hidden layers for improve the performance of the system with less complex module, so that we find the optimal solution. To calculate the performance of this proposed algorithm, back-propagate the weights from output to hidden layer, hidden to hidden layer, and hidden to input layer for improving the results, thus improving the software quality and minimizing the error.

4.8 Future Scope

Future perspective of this algorithm is highly recommended for e-business, emphasizing the issues like data security and enhancing the schemes of networking. For better utilization, we can discover this concept in different models of ANN and check the performance with different architectures, so the cost of that is reduced and we can speed up delivery of a quality product within a short time.

Cloud computing is one of the future's most important areas in the computer science research field for providing the best solutions in the era of shared resources, network sharing, high productivity, improved business services, and providers that provide help for achieving success. Incorporating neural networks into cloud computing provides a gentle platform to explore the best resources and technology to solve the problem in an optimized way.

References

1. M. Maqableh, H. Karajeh, Job scheduling for cloud computing using neural networks, *Communications and Network*, 6, 191–200, 2014. Published Online August 2014 in SciRes, http://www.scirp.org/journal/cn & http://dx.doi.org/10.4236/cn.2014.63021.
2. MIT Technology Review, *Neural Net Now Available in Cloud*, https://www.technologyreview.com/2014/01/21/82476/neural-nets-now-available-in-the-cloud/.
3. B.A. Milani, N.J. Navimipour, A comprehensive review of the data replication techniques in the cloud environments: Major trends and future directions, *Journal of Network and Computer Applications*, 64, 229–238, 2016.
4. Y.G. Sucahyo, et al., Software as a service quality factors evaluation using analytic hierarchy process, *International Journal of Business Information Systems (IJBIS)*, 24(1), 51–68, 2017.
5. K. Kishor, P. Nand, P. Agarwal, Subnet based ad hoc network algorithm reducing energy consumption in MANET. *International Journal of Applied Engineering Research*, 12(22), 11796–11802, 2017.
6. K. Kishor, P. Nand, P. Agarwal, Secure and efficient subnet routing protocol for MANET, *Indian Journal of Public Health*, 9(12), 200, 2018. http://dx.doi.org/10.5958/0976-5506.2018.01830.2.
7. K. Kishor, P. Nand, P. Agarwal, Notice of retraction design adaptive subnetting hybrid gateway MANET protocol on the basis of dynamic TTL value adjustment. *Aptikom Journal on Computer Science and Information Technologies*, 3(2), 59–65, 2018. https://doi.org/10.11591/APTIKOM.J.CSIT.115.
8. K. Kishor, P. Nand, Review performance analysis and challenges wireless MANET routing protocols. *International Journal of Science, Engineering and Technology Research (IJSETR)*, 2(10), 1854–185, 2013, ISSN 2278-7798.
9. K. Kishor, P. Nand, Performance evaluation of AODV, DSR, TORA and OLSR in with respect to end-to-end delay in MANET. *International Journal of Science and Research (IJSR)*, 3(6), 633–636, 2014, ISSN 2319-7064.

10. K. Kishor, R. Sharma, M. Chhabra, Student performance prediction using technology of machine learning. In: Sharma D.K., Peng SL., Sharma R., Zaitsev D.A. (eds) *Micro-Electronics and Telecommunication Engineering. Lecture Notes in Networks and Systems*, vol. 373. Springer, Singapore, 2022. https://doi.org/10.1007/978-981-16-8721-1_53.

11. K. Kishor, Communication-efficient federated learning. In: Yadav S.P., Bhati B.S., Mahato D.P., Kumar S. (eds) *Federated Learning for IoT Applications. EAI/Springer Innovations in Communication and Computing.* Springer, Cham, 2022. https://doi.org/10.1007/978-3-030-85559-8_9.

12. C. Tao, J. Gao, Building a cloud-based mobile testing infrastructure service system, *Journal of Systems and Software*, 124, 39–55, 2017.

13. J. Kang, Z. Xiong, D. Niyato, S. Xie, J. Zhang, Incentive mechanism for reliable federated learning: A joint optimization approach to combining reputation and contract theory, *IEEE Internet of Things Journal*, 6(6), 10700–10714, 2019.

14. A. Jain, K. Kishor, Financial supervision and management system using ML algorithm, *Solid State Technology*, 63(6), 18974–18982, 2020.

15. K. Kishor, Personalized federated learning. In: Yadav S.P., Bhati B.S., Mahato D.P., Kumar S. (eds) *Federated Learning for IoT Applications. EAI/Springer Innovations in Communication and Computing.* Springer, Cham, 2022. https://doi.org/10.1007/978-3-030-85559-8_3.

16. S. Gupta, S. Tyagi, K. Kishor, Study and development of self sanitizing smart elevator. In: Gupta D., Polkowski Z., Khanna A., Bhattacharyya S., Castillo O. (eds) *Proceedings of Data Analytics and Management. Lecture Notes on Data Engineering and Communications Technologies*, vol. 90. Springer, Singapore, 2022. https://doi.org/10.1007/978-981-16-6289-8_15.

17. K. Priyam, V. Rastogi, Predicting the secondary structure of protein using back propagation with Madaline. *International Journal of Engineering Technology Science and Research*, 5(3), 204–209, 2018, ISSN 2394-3386.

18. B. McMahan et al., Communication-efficient learning of deep networks from decentralized data, *Proceedings of International Conference on Artificial Intelligence and Statistics (AISTATS)*, 54, 1273–1282, 2017.

19. S.P. Yadav, D.P. Mahato, N.T.D. Linh, *Distributed Artificial Intelligence: A Modern Approach* (1st ed.). CRC Press, 2020. https://doi.org/10.1201/9781003038467.

20. Y. Liu, J. J. Q. Yu, J. Kang, D. Niyato, S. Zhang, Privacy-preserving traffic flow prediction: A federated learning approach, *IEEE Internet of Things Journal*, 1–1, 2020.

21. A. F. Atiya, A. G. Parlos, New results on recurrent network training: Unifying the algorithms and accelerating convergence, *IEEE Transactions on Neural Networks*, 11(3), 697–709, 2000.

22. D. Svantesson, R. Clarke, Privacy and consumer risks in cloud computing. *Computer Law & Security Review*, 26, 391–397, 2010. http://dx.doi.org/10.1016/j.clsr.2010.05.005.

23. K. Kishor, D. Pandey, Study and development of efficient air quality prediction system embedded with machine learning and IoT. In: Gupta D. et al. (eds), *Proceeding International Conference on Innovative Computing and Communications. Lecture Notes in Networks and Systems*, vol. 471, Springer, Singapore, 2022. https://doi.org/10.1007/978-981-19-2535-1.

24. B. K. Rai, S. Sharma, G. Kumar, K. Kishor, Recognition of different bird category using image processing. *International Journal of Online and Biomedical Engineering (iJOE)*, 18(07), 101–114, 2022. https://doi.org/10.3991/ijoe.v18i07.29639.

25. M. Maqableh, Job Scheduling for cloud computing using neural network, *Communications and Network*, 6, 191–200, 2014. Published Online August 2014 in SciRes.

26. M. Ashouraie, N.J. Navimipour, Priority-based task scheduling on heterogeneous resources in the Expert Cloud, *Kybernetes*, 44(10), 1455–1471, 2015.

27. C. S. Sentthil Kumar, Scope for artificial neural network in textiles, *IOSR Journal of Polymer and Textile Engineering (IOSR-JPTE)*, 2(1), 34–39, 2015.

28. U. Ahmed Butt, A review of machine learning algorithms for cloud computing security, *Electronics*, 9(9), 1379, 2020, http://dx.doi.org/10.3390/electronics9091379, https://www.mdpi.com/20799292/9/9/1379/htm.

29. A. Sharma, N. Jha, K. Kishor, Predict COVID-19 with chest X-ray. In: Gupta D., Polkowski Z., Khanna A., Bhattacharyya S., Castillo O. (eds) *Proceedings of Data Analytics and Management. Lecture Notes on Data Engineering and Communications Technologies*, vol. 90, Springer, Singapore, 2022. https://doi.org/10.1007/978-981-16-6289-8_16.

30. A. Jain, Y. Sharma, K. Kishor, Financial supervision and management system using ML algorithm. *Solid State Technology*, 63(6), 18974–18982, 2020. http://solidstatetechnology.us/index.php/JSST/article/view/8080.

31. Y. Huang, Y. Su, S. Ravi, Z. Song, S. Arora, K. Li, Privacy-preserving learning via deep net pruning, *arXiv preprint arXiv: 2003.01876*, 2020. https://doi.org/10.48550/arXiv.2003.01876.

32. N.J. Navimipour, F.S. Milani, Task scheduling in the cloud computing based on the cuckoo search algorithm, *International Journal of Modeling and Optimization*, 5(1), 44, 2015.

33. M. Malathi, Cloud computing concepts. In: *3rd International Conference on Electronics Computer Technology (ICECT). arXiv preprint arXiv:1610.05492*, 2016. 2011.

34. N.J. Navimipour, et al., Expert cloud: A Cloud-based framework to share the knowledge and skills of human resources, *Computers in Human Behavior*, 46, 57–74, 2015.

35. V. Jyothsna, V.V. Rama Prasad, FCAAIS: Anomaly based network intrusion detection through feature correlation analysis and association impact scale, *ICT Express*, 2(3), 103–116, 2016.

36. S. Jo, H. Sung, B. Ahn, A comparative study on the performance of intrusion detection using decision tree and artificial neural network models, *Journal of Korea Society of Digital Industry and Information Management*, 11(4), 33–45, 2015.

37. P.L. Lin, et al., A size-insensitive integrity-based fuzzy c-means method for data clustering, *Pattern Recognition*, 47(5), 2042–2056, 2014.

38. S. Ghosh, S.K. Dubey, Comparative analysis of k-means and fuzzy c-means algorithms, *International Journal of Advanced Computer Science and Applications*, 4(4), 35–39, 2013.

39. J. Li, et al., Brief introduction of back propagation (BP) neural network algorithm and its improvement, *Advances in Computer Science and Information Engineering*, 169, 553–558, 2012. ISBN: 978-3-642-30222-0, https://doi.org/10.1007/978-3-642-30223-7_87.

40. B. Hajimirzae, et al., Intrusion detection for cloud computing using neural networks and artificial bee colony optimization algorithm, *ICT Express*, 5(1), 56–59, 2019.

41. Z. Jiang, A. Balu, C. Hegde, S. Sarkar, Collaborative deep learning in fixed topology networks, Advances in Neural Information Processing Systems, 5904–5914, 2017.

42. N. Bassiliades, et al., A semantic recommendation algorithm for the PaaSport platform-as-a-service marketplace, *Expert Systems with Applications*, 67, 203–227, 2017.

43. X. Xu, From cloud computing to cloud manufacturing. *Robotics and Computer Integrated Manufacturing*, 28, 75–86, 2012. http://dx.doi.org/10.1016/j.rcim.2011.07.002.

44. P. Ravi Kumar, P. Herbert Raj, P. Jelciana, Exploring security issues and solutions in cloud computing services – A survey. *Cybernetics and Information Technologies*, 17(4), 3–31, 2017. https://doi.org/10.1515/cait-2017-0039.

45. R. Shaikha, M. Sasikumar, Data classification for achieving security in cloud computing, *Procedia Computer Science*, 45, 493–498, 2015.

46. S. G. Kene, D. P. Theng, "A review on intrusion detection techniques for cloud computing and security challenges," 2015 2nd International Conference on Electronics and Communication Systems (ICECS), 2015, pp. 227-232, doi: 10.1109/ECS.2015.7124898.

47. Y. Jadeja, K. Modi, Cloud computing – Concepts, architecture and challenges. *2012 International Conference on Computing, Electronics and Electrical Technologies (ICCEET)*,), Kumaracoil, 21–22 March 2012, 877–880, 2012. http://dx.doi.org/10.1109/ICCEET.2012.6203873.

48. Rashmi, Securing software as a service model of cloud computing: Issues and solutions, *International Journal on Cloud Computing: Services and Architecture (IJCCSA)*, 3(4), 1–11, 2013.

5

Cloud Computing in Blockchain

Kaushal Kishor

ABES Institute of Technology

CONTENTS

DOI: 10.1201/9781003213895-5

5.1 Introduction

Recent advances in information processing technologies have attracted consumers seeking greater data storage. Cloud computing is a benefit for cloud users. Cloud users may access, share, and trade data based on their premises. It suggests that cloud customers don't have direct control over uploaded resources. The cloud provider delivers as-is and as-available services [1]. As we enter the "information era," the amount, pace, and diversity of online data increase dramatically. Mobile devices, sensors, archives, and social networks may generate data. Data explosions raise major research challenges like "how to effectively and optimally administrate vast volumes of data and detect new preservation techniques of accessing knowledge." Millions of sensitive heterogeneous and homogeneous transactions are created [2]. Information processing units enable several financial markets for next-generation financial technologies for safe network and user communication. Blockchain technology addresses financial security. It's a public ledger network that improves internet security. Blockchain customers execute virtual transactions using blockchain authentication. This block is updated frequently to reflect the newest electronic money transaction facts.

Blockchain technology uses cryptographically signed transactions [3]. Block-wise. Every block is encrypted. At each point of failure, transactions should be authenticated. It uses P2P functionalities. This strategy doesn't charge broker fees for the transactions. Since blockchain technology guarantees strong and scalable end-system security, its rise is expected. Hackers have trouble exploiting transaction system flaws. Transactions are simpler and more transparent.

Hashes: It's a key part of the blockchain model's many usage cases. It encrypts block data. Data of any size is computed. Input changes may affect output. Real-time apps employ SHA-256.

Ledgers: These include transactions. Each node has a transaction ledger. Traditional ledgers are kept using pen and paper. New computer technologies use the same approach. So, a centralised ledger is employed with certain drawbacks, such as sudden data loss and centralised transaction verification via a third-party agent.

End-users provide each block node with a transaction id. With this transaction index, the procedure continues. Transactional mid-operations won't save. All committed transactions are stored in a queue. Every mining node updates the transaction process. A block contains all transactions. Blockchain rejects invalid transactions. This approach demonstrates data rigidity since the produced hash changes drastically with a single-bit change. Every block's hash is shared across nodes to boost security. Every node may verify the hash to avoid changes.

5.1.1 Blockchain Model Blocks Include

- Block number (or height)
- Hash values of current and previous blocks; Merkle tree root hash; timestamp; block size; transaction list in block

5.1.1.1 Blockchain

Organisations own most blockchain nodes. Node communication depends on ledger content. Node agreement reduces system performance. The blockchain accepts user-submitted transaction requests to accomplish its function. One or more ledgers keep a permanent record of the transaction after its completion. This ensures the blockchain's immutability.

5.1.1.2 Blockchain Security

Transaction data and parameters are near to business logic. Blockchain transactions employ asymmetric key cryptography. Entire transactions employ public and private keys. The private key verifies transaction signatures. The public key verifies the private key-generated signature (Figure 5.1).

5.1.2 Ad Hoc Mobile Cloud Infrastructure

A distributed system comprises autonomous computers linked by a network and distribution middleware, which allows them to coordinate their actions and share system resources so users see it as a single, integrated computing facility [4,5]. Distributed systems are cluster, grid, and cloud. In the cluster, dispersed computing equipment is linked by a local area network, while the grid uses a wide area network. Cloud computing originates from the cluster and grid computing and integrates hardware virtualisation, utility computing, autonomic computing, ubiquitous computing, and service-oriented architecture. Cloud computing delivers computer power, communication infrastructure, and applications through a network. Cloud computing has solved complicated challenges. These systems have strong computers and fast networks. Due to developments in mobile computing and networking, robots, aerial vehicles, sensors, and smartphones may be integrated with cloud computing systems. Mobile cloud computing and mobile ad hoc cloud computing are two ways to integrate mobile devices with cloud systems. Mobile devices are connected to a cloud computing system over a cellular network in mobile cloud computing. Mobile devices with cloud computing access massive processing power and storage space. This lets mobile devices run data- and CPU-intensive apps like image and video processing. Cloud storage and application execution increase mobile device dependability and battery life. Figure 5.2 shows the mobile cloud system architecture. Mobile nodes like a robot or smartphone are linked to the internet through a Wi-Fi access point, base station, or satellite. Mobile cloud computing is limited to infrastructure-based communication technologies and cannot be employed in mobile ad hoc contexts. Mobile ad hoc cloud computing combines many mobile devices to build a virtual supercomputing node. Figure 5.3 shows the mobile ad hoc cloud system design. Mobile nodes interact over a mobile ad hoc network that enables network discovery, monitoring, and routing. Cloud middleware manages resources, failures, mobility, communications, and tasks. It conceals complexity and gives a single-system picture to users and applications [6–8].

Machine learning (ML), a subset of AI, tries to construct systems/machines that can automatically learn from data patterns and experiences and improve their predictions without being explicitly programmed. ML covers the study of algorithms and the creation of self-training computer systems [9–11]. Applying ML methods (decision tree, logistic regression, linear regression, support vector machine, K-nearest neighbor, etc.) to vast volumes of data

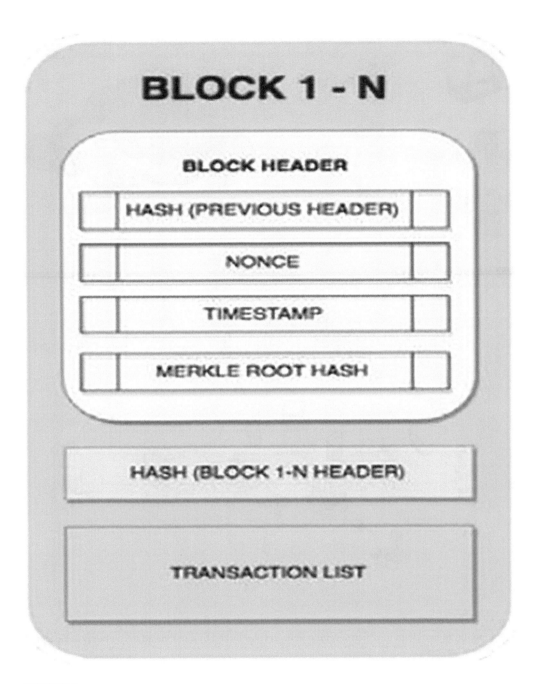

FIGURE 5.1
Generic blockchain model.

may be difficult. Traditional ML libraries don't handle huge datasets; hence, new techniques were needed [12–14]. ML was out of reach for small- and medium-sized businesses since it was expensive to apply ML technology and solutions. Cloud computing improves and expands ML applications. "Intelligent cloud" is ML in the cloud. Cloud ML increases the capabilities of both the cloud and ML algorithms [15,16].

FIGURE 5.2
Model cloud computing system architecture.

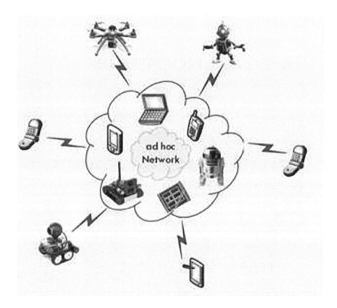

FIGURE 5.3
Depicts a mobile ad hoc cloud in which several mobile devices linked by a mobile ad hoc network act as a unified computing resource.

5.1.3 Bitcoin

Bitcoin is an electronic monetary system based on digital signatures. Each owner digitally signs messages and transfers coins depending on current and past hash transactions. Payees may check signatures based on ownership [17]. Bitcoin works as follows:

a. All nodes get new transactions.
b. Each block node collects new transactions.

c. Every block needs proof of work (PoW).

d. When a node finds PoW, a broadcast message is sent to all nodes in the block.

e. Transactions are processed, not spent.

f. Nodes accept block hash facilities.

5.1.4 Cloud Computing Authentication

Cloud computing's resource sharing and virtualisation provide appealing computing services. Cloud computing introduces security as a service. A company may provide end-users with several application services. E-mail and web servers are active server pages. All approved customers must embrace the company's services. Before consuming any service, the client must have a security context for each application server [18]. A user may access resources in several security domains. Multiple security credentials are not a secure, coordinated, or manageable solution. Similar concerns arise with cloud migration. Variable entities obtain these services, requiring a robust security system. Access control management becomes complicated and costly as services develop. Most apps emphasise system and organisational value. Single security policy administration provides flexible, scalable authorisation systems. A single place for policy administration makes policy changes easier. Protection and auditing of authorisation systems are maintained independently, making compromise difficult.

5.1.5 Blockchain Specifications

5.1.5.1 E-Cash and Its Security

E-cash revolutionises e-commerce. It replaces old paper and coin. Credit card is an e-cash option. This approach demands merchants' and agents' confidence. Consumers must request E-cash from a bank or issuer while making a payment [19]. Offline e-cash is stored on a smart card or token. Each implementation is traceable or anonymous (untraceable). By identified implementation, each transaction requires third-party verification, such as a bank. This approach improves security by encrypting and digitally signing E-cash messages. Figure 5.4 shows the e-cash workflow, in which the bank, customer, and merchant should be mutually trusted.

5.1.5.2 Access Control

Systems secure data. Data, services, and computational systems are valuable. Entities with varying access privileges establish a trustworthy environment. Some cases demand transferable access privileges. A user might sell their access right [20]. An employee who wants to conduct a calculation on a virtual machine (VM) deputises another employee who needs to access the same machine.

5.1.5.3 Blockchain and Cloud Computing Security

Cloud computing includes huge networks of virtualised hardware and software. Any service belongs to data centres, often called data farms [21].

Blockchain may be integrated into cloud systems in two ways:

a. Integrating blockchain with the cloud for enterprise storage, replication, and database access.

b. Integrating task and cloud data security.

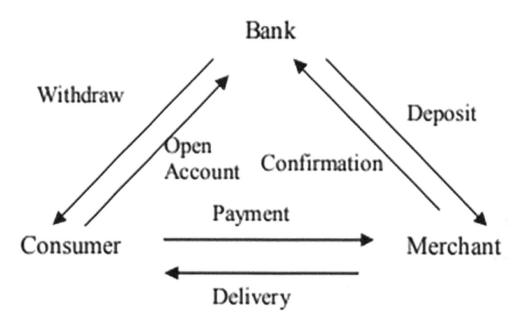

FIGURE 5.4
Workflow of e-cash.

Cloud-based blockchain transactions have limitations and needs [22]. Blockchain transactions are massive. Dynamic cloud systems are elastic and scalable.

a. For security, user data is concealed in data centres. Transactional tasks should be tuned. It implies that consumers may decide where their data is kept and handled.

b. System resilience and fault tolerance: If a node fails, the system should identify a replacement; thus, data centre node replication and numerous software apps.

Software should be centrally assigned in dispersed cloud environments and various software applications.

5.2 Cloud Computing

Today, the web hosts millions of websites. The hosted site requires expensive servers. These servers must have consistent traffic and be constantly monitored and maintained. To arrange and maintain these servers, additional workers will be needed. Data centres hold everything. So, maintaining the server and workers may derail corporate objectives. We're embracing "cloud computing" to prevent stressful maintenance. Cloud computing stores, manages, and processes data from anywhere in the globe utilising a network of distant computers. It replaces a local server or PC. Cloud computing services are given to an organisation's devices through the internet [23]. Cloud computing combines data centres, resources, and servers over the internet. Pay-per-use governs these services. The worldwide, low-cost offerings improve staff cooperation. The cloud's software is automatically updated, making it manageable. The service consumer will control cloud documents. It's limited [24]. As cloud data is flexible, it poses security, privacy, and assault risks. With many users, the cloud may have downtimes.

Cloud services are mostly delivered in three ways. First is Software as a Service (SaaS), an internet-hosted application for clients. The cloud service provider offers numerous services for many customers on a single platform of cloud-based applications or projects. Customers don't control cloud infrastructure. SaaS includes Amazon Web Services, SalesForce.com, and Google Mail. The second is Platform as a Service (PaaS). The cloud service provider lets us install our app and programming languages. SaaS hosts the application on the cloud, whereas PaaS offers the platform. PaaS is best shown by Google. Infrastructure as a Service (IaaS) gives users direct network access to storage, computation, and other resources. IaaS uses virtualisation to suit cloud clients' resource needs. Setting up autonomous VMs apart from hardware and other VMs is the best virtualisation strategy. Servers have a unique IP address for security. Amazon EC2, GoGrid is IaaS [25].

5.2.1 Cloud Deployment Models

Public Cloud: Customers that need to share servers may utilise providers' public cloud. Cloud infrastructure is public and may be dynamically bought by several businesses. Providers host and manage clouds. Cloud providers may host customers to reduce risk and expense for short-term extensions. App Engine and Azure are examples [24]. Private Cloud: This is created for single customers, enabling data ownership, security, and client delicateness. It deploys client infrastructure and apps. Compared to a public cloud, it's secure and pricey. Private clouds have security and bandwidth regulations. Clients may limit user access and private cloud networks. A private cloud's example is Eucalyptus system. Hybrid cloud merges cloud deployment models. Hybrid cloud delivers on-demand scaling. These rely on public cloud resources to compute from private data centres. A well-built hybrid cloud can deliver security services, but developing and regulating one is difficult. A hybrid cloud is Amazon Web Services.

5.2.2 Community Cloud

This is designed for a group of organisations with similar needs. One or more local firms may own, manage, and run it. This cloud is beneficial in banking and education. Community clouds include Facebook. Five criteria define cloud computing. Users may spontaneously supply network storage using on-demand self-service. Broad network access delivers network wide service with common techniques to promote different client platforms. Resource pooling uses a multi-tenant architecture to service numerous users. Metered service is when metering capabilities own, manage, and optimise resources. Elastic scalability adapts IT resources to shifting demands. A programme may automatically construct new servers as needed [26]. The cloud has numerous pros and cons. Some are [27]:

5.2.3 Data Security

Most cloud services protect data using security measures. Sometimes data leaks. Most of the celebrities' info leaked from iCloud previously. Keeping data on the cloud allows access without the user's knowledge. Security is the main reason companies avoid cloud services. Cloud services are typically always accessible; however, some have planned time-outs. They pause service for maintenance. Some services are time-limited.

5.2.4 Restrictions

Cloud users will have minimal data control. Most control is in IaaS, where they configure virtual computers to their requirements.

5.2.5 Reputation

Cloud service availability is internet-dependent. Some nations lack a functional network, even if internet access is widespread. Cloud services make providers ignore non-internet areas. People don't utilise mobile data for an intensive app running anymore. Wi-Fi is not everywhere, however.

5.2.6 No-Vendor Legal Liability

Even cloud providers hold data securely, a breach isn't liable. Legal complications aren't involved when using cloud data from another nation. Which country's laws will govern data provision and privacy?

5.2.7 Cloud-Based Research

5.2.7.1 Reliability

Cloud users have access 24/7. The server stops due to maintenance or limited time. Cloud consumers anticipate additional services, standards, and best practices. Cloud servers are like local ones. They suffer server downtimes and rely heavily on a cloud provider. When a user selects a server, they may be locked in, posing a business risk [29].

5.2.7.2 Requirement

There are several rules on data access, usage, reporting, and audit trails. Customers may have compliance requirements for cloud providers' data centres.

5.2.7.3 SLAs

Cloud services will be delivered based on Service Level Agreements (SLAs) that enable numerous copies of one application on many servers based on priority. The cloud may shut down or reduce a low-priority app. Cloud customers must evaluate SLAs with cloud suppliers. Most suppliers design SLAs that suit them while offering little data protection, downtime, and pricing. Before signing a contract, cloud customers should carefully consider these issues.

5.2.7.4 Cloud Data Management

Managing unstructured or semi-structured cloud data is a research priority. Since they don't have access to the data centre's physical security system, service providers depend on the infrastructure provider for total data protection. Even on virtual computers, the supplier may remotely set security conditions without knowing whether it's safe. In these scenarios, the infrastructure provider must provide application auditability, data confidentiality, and secure data access and transfer. Cryptographic protocols provide confidentiality, while remote attestation ensures audibility. VMs move dynamically; therefore, it's not always feasible. So, remote attestation won't work.

5.2.7.5 Data Encryption

Encryption protects data. Low-, intermediate-, and high-level securities are provided. Consider web services APIs used to reach the cloud via an application or client. SSL encryption is standard. The data is encrypted and saved in the cloud when the item arrives. Decrypting and storing data without encryption before cloud storage compromises data security.

5.2.7.6 Interoperability

Internal system communication is crucial for exchanging and using data. Closed public cloud networks aren't meant to connect. The industry can't merge cloud IT systems due to a lack of internal communication. Enterprises require a single toolkit to connect different apps across current systems and cloud providers.

5.3 Blockchain Technology

5.3.1 Emergence of Blockchain-Bitcoin

Bitcoin brought blockchain technology. Bitcoin was created in 2008 by a fake person named Satoshi Nakamoto. He wrote "Bitcoin: A Peer to Peer Electronic Cash System," which allows direct internet payments without a third party [30]. This electronic cash solution overcomes the problem of double-spending money since digital currency may be easily duplicated and spent twice. Each transaction is tamper-resistantly linked to the next. The public ledger links tamper-resistant transactions. With this ledger, a network may check a user's transaction history and confirm that the money hasn't been spent [31].

Blockchain is a technology that cryptocurrencies like Bitcoin use for secure and anonymous transactions [32]. Bitcoin thrives on anonymity, but the blockchain is transparent. Blockchain transmits data, rights, etc., unlike Bitcoin. Blockchain's uses are broader than Bitcoin's [33]. Blockchains are transparent-distributed ledgers holding digitally signed transactions in blocks. Each block contains a cryptographic hash value, timestamp, and transaction data. The design prevents blockchain data manipulation [34]. It is a distributed, open ledger that records transactions forever.

Blockchain is an indestructible digital record of economic transactions that can be configured to support anything of value. Blockchain technology eliminates government interference and fraudulence due to consensus confirmation. By eliminating third parties, rapid transactions may be made without transaction expenses. This boosts financial efficiency [28]. Despite its merits, blockchain remains volatile. Anonymous, untraceable transactions might increase society's crimes.

5.3.2 Differentials

5.3.2.1 Decentralisation

Traditional centralised networks validate nodes by a central server. This causes communication delays and raises calculation expenses. Blockchain uses peer-to-peer blocks without a third party. Blockchain doesn't require a centralised server to store and update numerous systems. All nodes in this distributed network actively transact with a decentralised server [35].

5.3.2.2 Persistence

Honest miners store transaction data on the blockchain. Rolling back or deleting transactions is tough if they're on the list [36]. Other miners verify these blocks, so they can't be changed.

5.3.2.3 Auditability

All blockchain transactions will be digitally signed by the sender, storing the block with a timestamp for easy tracking and verification.

5.3.2.4 Anonymity

Asymmetric encryption secures blockchain data. Digitally signed payments verify the receiver. The sender uses the blockchain to construct a self-generated email and generates a separate set of addresses to hide their identity. A centralised owner will keep users' genuine identities, minimising sender identity leakage [37].

5.3.2.5 Autonomous

As no organisation controls the blockchain network, we may publish signed nodes and see whether other nodes accept them. Accepting a node by every other node in the network ensures data flow in the blockchain.

5.3.2.6 Immunity

Before entering the block, transaction data is checked [38]. Blockchain records transactions forever. Block data is unchangeable. If someone attempts to modify the data, it would be quickly noticed since it's connected via the hash key and would invalidate the following blocks.

5.3.2.7 Transparency

All parties may publish records on the blockchain and query node data. Blockchain technology stores transaction data in an open distributed ledger [39]. All network nodes may access this open and accurate data.

5.3.2.8 Traceability

Hashing encrypts blockchain data blocks. Each hash block. Each network block includes its predecessor's hash key [40]. In the blockchain network, tracking a block's hash key is easy.

5.3.3 Blockchain Types

Blockchain is characterised by user availability and accessibility [41].

5.3.3.1 Public Blockchain

A public blockchain is a decentralised, open ledger where any node may process, store, and validate transaction data using a consensus method.

5.3.3.2 Private Blockchain

No one can join the private blockchain rapidly. It's a centrally controlled blockchain for access. The public may selectively examine private blockchain data. Private blockchain is for small businesses. Private blockchain applications include vote counting, digital identity, asset ownership, and supply chain management.

5.3.3.3 Consortium Blockchain

A consortium blockchain is somewhat decentralised. The pre-selected node may pick the service type. The remaining nodes may access blockchain transactions, but not consensus. Consortium blockchains are Hyperledger and R3CEV.

5.3.4 Blockchain Phases

Blockchain has three generations. Blockchain 1.0 is digital cash, 2.0 is the digital economy, and 3.0 is a digital society [42].

5.3.4.1 First-Generation Blockchain

Bitcoin introduces blockchain technology to the globe. Satoshi Nakamoto created Bitcoin, a digital currency. Digital currencies benefit from blockchain technology. Transaction data is encrypted in chunks and connected using complicated cryptographic mechanisms. Immutable data in blocks prevents updates. Blockchain's open distributed ledger prevents double-spending. Blockchain PoW has spawned several digital currencies. Digital currencies lower transaction fees. Credit cards are also anonymous.

5.3.4.2 Second-Generation Blockchain

Blockchain technology's rise demonstrated that it could be utilised for bank-related loans, mortgages, and equities. Second-generation smart contracts extended digital currencies and created a digital economy. A smart contract is a self-executing line of code triggered when a buyer and seller meet agreed requirements. Each has a unique address. Smart contracts run in every network node depending on code conditions. These build trust between strangers. As contract code is run openly on the network and is verifiable, it enables parties to examine and forecast the result. Smart contract data is kept in tamper-proof, anti-counterfeit blockchain blocks. Insurance, commercial agreements, financial data recording, mortgages, food supply networks, etc. use smart contracts. Smart contracts include Ethereum.

5.3.4.3 Third-Generation Blockchain

In its progress, blockchain overcame its scaling difficulty. Blockchain 3.0 increases non-financial uses. Smart cities, smart governance, smart resource use by smart population, smart economics. Integrating blockchain with the Internet of Things will enable smart property transactions and data payment without third-party intervention. This may create a machine-to-machine power market and manage electronic medical records. Blockchain 3.0 helps unbanked clients preserve digital identities so banks can complete Know Your Customer and access bank accounts. Many online transactions are between strangers. Using blockchain to store data and conduct transactions will bring more trustworthy consumers, reducing fraud [40].

5.3.4.4 Mining

Mining involves adding blocks to the blockchain, a publicly distributed record. More Bitcoin mining is rewarded. Each node's miners mine blocks and are occasionally rewarded.

5.3.4.5 Blockchain Nodes

A blockchain node is a network device. Nodes are classified by their function. Nodes vary. It's: Mining nodes create blockchain blocks. These nodes check whether a block may be added during mining. Mining nodes only build and add blocks to the chain. Full nodes verify new blocks and add them to the blockchain.

Full nodes retain and deliver block copies to all network nodes. During publishing, they verify transactions till the genesis block. After validation, data is delivered to all network nodes to confirm the blockchain's integrity. A decentralised network with more nodes is harder to hack. A complete node's transaction count determines if it's a super node. Super nodes are constantly active and link the remaining complete nodes.

Light nodes behave similarly to full nodes but contain less of the block. They include the previous transaction blocker, verify the blockchain, and alert the remaining nodes. Light nodes are linked to full nodes and are weaker. When a full node is hacked and holds damaged data, a light node may capture and disregard that blockchain as fake and transfer the whole node information to a sustaining blockchain. As they take up less data space than complete nodes, they help decentralise the network and go further for less.

5.3.4.6 Blockchain Layers

Blockchain lacks hierarchy. Data, network, consensus, contract, service, and application (Figure 5.5) describe it. Data and network layers verify data. Consensus methods verify the consensus layer [43]. Contract layer smart contracts establish trust. Services and app layers integrate blockchain. Data block, timestamp, Merkle root tree, and hashing are in the data layer. Peer-to-peer, verification, and wide protocols are network layer components. PoW, proof of stake (PoS), Byzantine fault, etc. are in the consensus layer. Smart contracts, incentive systems, and scripting are in the contract layer. Ethereum, Hyperledger Fabric, IBM Azure, etc. are service layer technologies.

5.3.4.7 Hashing

Hashing is identifying a distinct item among similar ones. Hash functions transform data into a hash key. A hash table stores the hash function's output. Hash function maps a hash table's dataset: hash value or hash code [44].

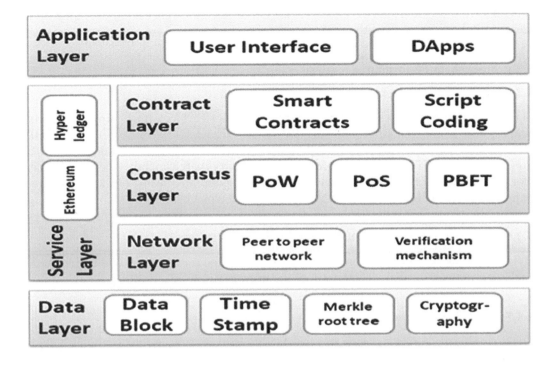

FIGURE 5.5
Layers of blockchain.

5.3.4.8 Smart Contracts

Nick Szabo created smart contracts as a transaction mechanism in 1994. Smart contracts predate blockchain. Smart contracts are digital agreements [45]. The parties' relationship is predicated on trust-building standards. Smart contracts are programmable programmes that operate in a blockchain environment. The blockchain executes the block's contents, providing trustworthiness and uniqueness. Smart contract data on the blockchain is tamper-proof and anti-counterfeiting. The smart contract self-executes when a certain network condition is satisfied [46]. It helps parties forecast outcomes since contract execution relies on public network code and is verifiable [40]. Smart contracts can manage claims and transactions. Loans, mortgages, and commercial agreements also employ them. Smart contracts can assess efficacy, availability, and scalability, according to studies. Test-driven development and behavior-driven development analyse smart contract correctness. Ethereum builds smart contracts best [47].

5.3.5 Digital Signatures

Digitally signed data delivered one-to-one or one-to-many ensures no data loss. Clients have private and public keys. A client must produce a hash value from transaction data and encrypt it with their private key to transfer data. The digital signature is a process, and signing is the stage. The network's nodes receive digitally signed transactions. The recipient's public key decrypts payment information [48]. The decrypted hash value is compared to the sender's hash value. Verification. Blockchain verification uses an elliptic curve digital signature algorithm [49].

5.3.6 Blockchain Performance Analysis

5.3.6.1 Bitcoin and Ethereum Performance Comparison

Bitcoin and Ethereum blockchains are compared. Block size, block time, number of transactions, and block creation complexity [50] were examined. Bitcoin blocks are 1 MB, whereas Ethereum blocks are 2000–2800 bytes. Bitcoin's block creation time is 600 to 10 minutes, whereas Ethereum's is 15 seconds. Transactions: As Bitcoin takes longer to build a block and transact, Ethereum has grown increasingly popular. Bitcoin's block construction requires 25 million Terhash per second, but Ethereum won't be tough.

5.3.6.2 Hyperledger and Ethereum Comparison

Hyperledger fabric and Ethereum are compared. Average throughput, CPU usage, memory usage, network usage, execution time, and average delay [50].

5.3.7 Blockchain Applications

The use of blockchain technology in everyday life is increasing. A few examples include the food supply chain; asset management; insurance claims; smart automobile; smartphones; e-passports; smart appliances; healthcare management; and keeping track of one's own health and medical information.

5.3.7.1 Financial Blockchain

Banks facilitate conventional methods and system transactions. Many intermediaries keep track of such payments, causing inaccuracies. This involves time and money [45]. Blockchain technology employs a distributed public ledger where miners validate transactions using "PoW." Blockchain offers financial services. They include:

Many cryptocurrencies employ blockchain technology like Bitcoin. Traditional systems don't require a third party like a bank. Check and adjust all payments.

Global payments take longer because several middlemen validate them. Blockchain is helpful here. Decentralised public ledger simplifies verification. Global payments are quicker, verifiable, immutable, and safer using peer-to-peer networks.

Many fake insurance claims are filed. Blockchain-distributed ledger technology may prevent fraudulent claims.

5.3.7.2 Healthcare Blockchain

Blockchain benefits health databases and information sharing centres. It provides medical assistance and analysis. The EHR contains test results, treatment records, medications, and diagnostic data (EHR). Continuous data processing on cloud servers enhances safety and accuracy. Clinicians check a patient's health using data and records. The database speeds up diagnoses. Hospitals and research institutes analyse and mine the medical database. Smart contracts may help create medical contracts and vouchers [40].

5.3.7.3 Blockchain in Data Provenance

Data provenance involves processing, state, and source. Managing scientific data, data storage, and data assets involves provenance. Blockchain technology and smart contracts can verify asset integrity and data provenance. It promotes traceability and may have a multi-stakeholder chain. Forensics and accountability also utilise it.

5.3.7.4 5G Blockchain

5G networks must coordinate heterogeneous devices and applications to increase energy efficiency, network capacity, and resource availability. We may use blockchain and smart contracts to streamline industrial automation and manufacturing equipment. Traditional resource allocation requires a network slice broker [51]. Using blockchain, cloud radio over an optical fibre network might adopt an anonymous access identification technique to cut operating and connecting costs and reach a cooperative agreement.

5.3.7.5 Aviation Blockchain

Blockchain will create digital operator and product supplier partnerships for decentralised travel services and goods. Smart contracts may function across corporations and divisions.

5.3.7.6 Supply Chain Blockchain

Traditional supply chain systems employ smart sensors to gather information as the chain moves. Soon, there will be more sensors. Blockchain technology would assist retain the vast volume of gathered and processed data. Distributed network information is reliable.

5.3.7.7 Blockchain in Smart Homes

Integrating blockchain with IoT will make smart home appliances secure and efficient.

5.3.7.8 Blockchain in Smart Property

Distributed ledger technology may represent homes, automobiles, and smart gadgets. Blockchain tracks device actions. We may distribute the records to legitimate people anytime we wish [48].

Hard money lending is prevalent. The borrower requires collateral to borrow money. Borrowers may commit fraud by utilising illegal assets as collateral or by adopting dishonest practices. Blockchain technology and smart contracts can examine the property before taking it as collateral. It increases trust, transparency, and security among strangers. Personal electronics and autos are safeguarded by authentication keys and smart keys. Cryptography can secure this. Authentication fails if the key is stolen, duplicated, or transferred. A blockchain ledger may replace and recreate lost credentials.

5.3.7.9 Blockchain Elsewhere

An Internet of Battlefield Things (IoBT)-based cyber-physical system includes a vehicle-based cyber-physical system, as well as a vehicle-based cyber-physical system. The internet's growth will be fuelled by blockchain's decentralised, trustworthy, open, and scalable network.

5.3.8 Blockchain Architecture

Blockchain is a series of blocks that contain a network's data in a public ledger. Blocks have a header and body. Figure 5.2 shows the block header's six basic components [52]. They are:

1. **Block version:** Follows block validation requirements.
2. **Merkle root hash:** When a transaction happens, data is encrypted and sent to each node. The blockchain employed the Merkle tree algorithm to obtain a final hash value and Merkle tree root since each node block may include thousands of transaction data.
3. **Timestamp:** Gives each block the current time in seconds.
4. **Target difficulty:** Valid hash block threshold.
5. **Nonce:** A 4-byte field that increments with each hash computation. 256-bit hash points to the preceding block.
6. **Previous block hash**: Hash pointer holds the hash of the preceding block's contents and the block's address. This little adjustment makes blockchains reliable and innovative.

5.3.8.1 Blockchain's Workings

Blockchain technology uses connected data chunks. Each block header links them. If any data in the prior block is altered, the hash key will change, causing a mismatch. It safeguards data. A user's transaction data is delivered as a block. Blockchain blocks must be disseminated to all network nodes. The transaction needs miners' approval. When a block is generated, miners gain approval by solving computationally difficult issues. Authenticating the block completes the transaction. Following, choose the next block's author. Validated blocks are linked to build a blockchain network [38].

5.3.8.2 Consensus Algorithms

All network nodes must verify a block before adding it to the blockchain. Consensus algorithms are a technology that helps the blockchain nodes decide a transaction order and filter erroneous transactions. Multiple transactions compete to be published and get the reward. Consensus algorithms handle decision problems. Distributed blockchain network makes it hard for the miners to obtain consensus [38].

5.3.8.3 Proof of Work

In this PoW consensus paradigm, user power equals system computing power. Consensus models aim to eliminate fraudulent and honest nodes. In a decentralised network, one node must record all transactions. One way is a random node selection that may be attacked. If a user or node records transactions, they must prove their network's security.

To obtain the reward when a node is added to the blockchain, the user must solve a computationally tough issue. This network node will measure SHA-256 using a block header and nonce. Change the nonce to obtain various hash values. Miners compute a value equal to or less than a consensus. When a miner reaches the desired value, the miner block is sent to all network nodes, who must confirm the hash value. Upon approval, other miners will add the new block to the network. When several miners find the desired value concurrently, legitimate blocks may be created in parallel. In these circumstances, blocks create competing forks. Longer chains are regarded as legitimate in this PoW technique. In PoW, miners conduct several computer computations [52]. This wastes resources. Some PoW side apps, like Prime Coin, hunt for mathematical prime number chains.

5.3.8.4 Proof of Stake

PoW's greatest resource-efficient alternative is PoS. More block miners are less likely to assault the PoS network. The miner may make the next coin with more. This selection is unfair since the richest miner would dominate. Most systems compare a miner's blocks to the network's. Peer coin encourages age-based selection. The peer coin's next block is likely to be bigger or older. Blackcoin randomises the next block generator. It chooses the equation and stake size with the lowest hash value. Many blockchains want to switch to PoS [53].

5.3.8.5 Practical Byzantine Fault Tolerance (PBFT)

PBFT is like Byzantine-proof principles. Hyperledger fabric employs PBFT as its consensus algorithm since it handles one-third of Byzantine copies. Each round decides on a new block and chooses the main node to organise transactions. PBFT has three phases: prepared, committed, and committed. When two-thirds of the nodes vote, the node advances. PBFT needs familiarity at every network node. Antshares must implement delegated PBFT based on the PBFT protocol, in which professional nodes vote to record transactions.

5.3.8.6 Delegated Stake Proof

PoS is democratic, but delegated proof of stake (DPoS) is a democratic representative. Network stakeholders choose the block publisher and validator. Fewer nodes to verify transactions can simply check the block, leading to early transaction confirmation. Delegates may change block size and interval. Bitshares uses DPoS.

5.3.8.7 Ripple

Ripple uses trustworthy sub-networks throughout its large network. This network has two kinds of nodes: consensus process participating server and client to transfer funds only. Each server's unique node list (UNL) is necessary. The database will ask UNL nodes whether to publish a transaction in the ledger, and if more than 80% is approved, the transaction will be included. The ledger will authenticate nodes as long as UNL nodes are less than 20%.

5.3.8.8 Tendermint

Tendermint resembles PBFT consensus. If an unconfirmed block is introduced to a round, a proposer is chosen. This approach includes pre-vote, pre-commit, and commit. Validators vote on whether to broadcast the proposed frame's prediction. Pre-commit is sent to the block if more than two-thirds of pre-votes are cast. The node gets two-thirds of pre-commitments; it commits. In the commit phase, the node verifies the block and sends the commit done. If more than two-thirds of nodes commit, the block is approved.

5.3.8.9 Node Identity Management

PBFT requires each user's identification to pick a principal user for each round, whereas Tendermint knows all valuators to select a proposer. In the remaining algorithms, nodes connect freely.

5.3.8.10 Energy Saving

PoW uses more energy since miners are constantly calculating. PoS and DPoS require less energy since their search space is small. The rest of the algorithms conserve energy since there's no mining.

5.3.8.11 Tolerated Adversary Power

The node needs 51% of the network's hash power to seize control. By possessing 25% of the hashing power in PoW, miners may make more money. PBFT and Tendermint can handle up to one-third of defective nodes in ripple if the faulty nodes in a UNL are less than 20%. This comparison shows that various strategies promote decentralisation or efficiency. PoW is very scalable compared to other algorithms [28]. PoS reduces power consumption compared to PoW. Stake reduces power usage, processes transactions quicker, and requires less hardware than PoW. The lack of hashing energy to access the next block reduces energy use in PBFT. DPoS distributes rewards with real-time voting security and reduces blockchain network expenses. Ripple is decentralised, consumes less energy, and verifies transactions instantly.

5.3.9 Blockchain Challenges

Blockchain is a promising technology, but it has obstacles. These issues restrict blockchain's use. Consensus procedures, data management, storage, chain systems, regulation, governance, etc. [48]. Challenges include:

5.3.9.1 Scalability

Daily blockchain transactions mean more data to store. All nodes must validate all transactions. Blockchain can only handle seven transactions per second due to block size and creation time. Small transactions may be delayed because miners prioritise those with a greater fee. Scalability is difficult [53].

5.3.9.2 Privacy Leak

Blockchain transactions are secure because users use generated addresses instead of actual identities. Users may generate several addresses if data leaks. The blockchain cannot ensure transactional privacy because any public key may see transaction values. Blockchain must improve payment anonymity [54].

5.3.9.3 Laws

Blockchain has changed society, especially legal and law systems. Early legal oversight of blockchain led to legal difficulties. After understanding blockchain's features, rules and regulations may be reinforced. Most nations implemented blockchain by increasing regulations [38].

5.3.9.4 Governing

Blockchain provides tremendous government and infrastructure deployment potential and might transform government activities and responsibilities. It simplifies government organisational structures, data security, and governance and service procedures. Since blockchain is a distributed network without a third party, it enables larger policy development possibilities [42].

5.4 Support Blockchain for Cloud Computing

A. Blockchain support for cloud computing Blockchain and cloud computing deliver new data security and service availability. Blockchain's features transcend cloud research problems.

5.4.1 Interoperability

Public clouds don't enable internal communication, hence many industries avoid them. Consider cloud nodes when integrating with blockchain. Blockchain enables inter-node communication. All nodes in a network share data, so each has a copy of transactions. It's network transparency. They update the ledger, which is published to all nodes. Companies may add any number of networks and keep data accessible, bringing validity to the network.

5.4.2 Data Encryption

Decrypting data before saving it in the cloud concerns its integrity. Using cryptographic techniques, the blockchain network turns block data into a hash code and creates a hash key for each block. Consider using blockchain to maintain cloud task scheduling. The control system that gathers job scheduling data develops hash code and registers it in the blockchain network instantly to guarantee timeliness and data integrity. Blockchain's block discovery consensus algorithms ensure block data integrity. Each node in the network stores a copy of each transaction, providing availability and persistence to survive faults and assaults. Blockchain nodes increase data availability and authenticity by providing an on-demand service with minimal downtime.

5.4.3 SLAs

Without equal justice, cloud agreements benefit the service provider or consumer. Blockchain smart contracts can fix this problem. A blockchain smart contract enables unknown parties to create confidence. Smart contracts are programmable programmes that operate in a blockchain environment. When a condition is satisfied on all blockchain nodes, the smart contract executes itself. It helps parties forecast outcomes since contract execution relies on a public network's code, and signed contracts are verifiable.

5.4.4 Cloud Data Management

Unstructured cloud data, blockchain data is organised. Every block's hash key traces the contents. Each block includes the preceding block's hash key to trace the network. Network nodes may access verified block data. Cloud can accommodate fluctuating computational demands. Using a distributed ledger, this may be readily addressed by controlling several events that trigger smart contracts, maintaining service quality. Blockchain guarantees the user's privacy and may securely erase the user's record to prevent third-party access. Cloud and blockchain integration will boost corporate confidence and provide an on-demand service.

5.4.5 Blockchain–Cloud Analysis

Different papers promote blockchain's cloud computing. To our knowledge, this is the first blockchain–cloud literature review. Below these tables is a bar graph showing a year-by-year examination of digital library articles. All these investigations show that blockchain and cloud computing are well-researched. Figure 5.6 shows a year-by-year examination of digital library articles. Blockchain enables data transparency, authorisation, and cost-effective cloud solutions. Figure 5.7 shows some of the blockchain's cloud advantages. As blockchain may be implemented in public, private, and community modes and provides decentralisation, we compared blockchain and cloud services based on security. Cloud services lack data security. Based on our study, implementing blockchain will make cloud data more secure.

Figure 5.6 shows blockchain's cloud services. As blockchain may be implemented in public, private, and community modes and provides decentralisation, we compared

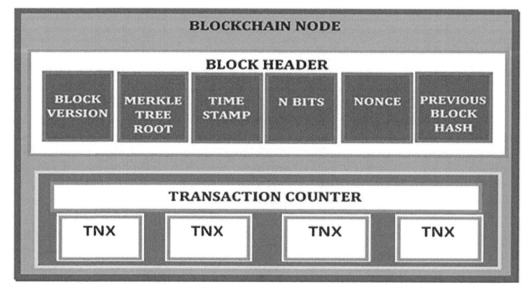

FIGURE 5.6
The general architecture of a blockchain.

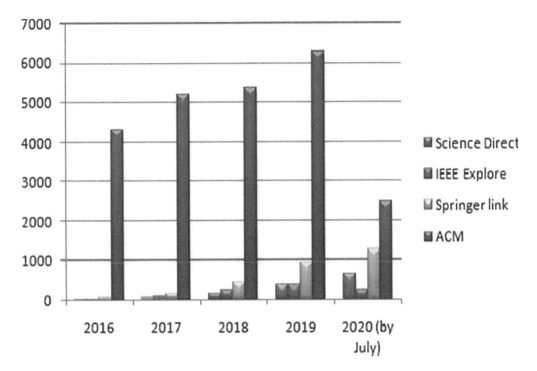

FIGURE 5.7
Year-wise analysis of articles being published in digital libraries.

blockchain and cloud services based on security. Cloud services lack data security. Based on our study, implementing blockchain will make cloud data more secure. Many blockchain–cloud apps may be used in everyday life to safeguard data. Blockchain–cloud serves several sectors. This connection may give additional storage flexibility and verified data. Monitoring network authorisation promotes network resiliency. Figure 5.7 shows several blockchain-cloud apps. Figure 5.6 shows blockchain data flow with cloud data. Blockchain services may increase cloud data security. The blockchain data is separated into tiny bits and encrypted using hashing algorithms. A consensus method validates data before adding it to the chain. Depending on the need, the provider may employ a permissioned, permissionless, public, or private blockchain (Figure 5.8).

5.5 Conclusion

Computing on the cloud is an outdated technology. The use of cloud computing still faces challenges in terms of data security, data management, interoperability, and other areas. The reliability and veracity of blockchain technology are gaining widespread support across the world. When blockchain technology is combined with cloud computing, usability, trust, security, scalability, and data management will all see significant improvements. The concepts of cloud computing and blockchain were presented in this chapter.

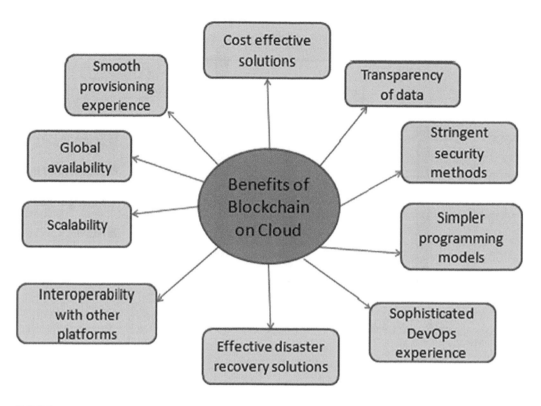

FIGURE 5.8
Benefits that blockchain provide to cloud.

The blockchain network should be integrated with a scalable cloud environment so that trust, server service, data security, and user data management can all be improved.

References

1. l-Kwon, L., Young-Hyuk, K., Jae-Gwang, L., Jae-Pil, L. The analysis and countermeasures on security breach of bitcoin. In: *Proceedings of the International Conference on Computational Science and Its Applications, Guimarães, Portugal, 30 June–3 July 2014.* Springer International Publishing: Cham, 2014.
2. Beikverdi, A., JooSeok, S. Trend of centralization in Bitcoin's distributed network. In: *Proceedings of the 2015 16th IEEE/ACIS International Conference on Software Engineering, Artificial Intelligence, Networking and Parallel/Distributed Computing (SNPD), Takamatsu, Japan, 1–3 June 2015.*
3. Christidis, K., Michael, D. Blockchains and smart contracts for the internet of things. *IEEE Access*, 2016, 4, 2292–2303.
4. Kishor, K., Nand, P., Agarwal, P. Subnet based ad hoc network algorithm reducing energy consumption in MANET. *International Journal of Applied Engineering Research*, 2017, 12(22), 11796–11802.

5. Kishor, K., Nand, P., Agarwal, P. Secure and efficient subnet routing protocol for MANET. *Indian Journal of Public Health*, 2018, 9(12), 200. DOI: 10.5958/0976-5506.2018.01830.2.

6. Kishor, K., Nand, P., Agarwal, P. Notice of retraction design adaptive subnetting hybrid gateway MANET protocol on the basis of dynamic TTL value adjustment. *Aptikom Journal on Computer Science and Information Technologies*, 2018, 3(2), 59–65. DOI: 10.11591/APTIKOM.J.CSIT.115.

7. Kaushal, K., Nand, P. Review performance analysis and challenges wireless MANET routing protocols. *International Journal of Science, Engineering and Technology Research (IJSETR)*, 2013, 2(10), 1854–185, ISSN 2278-7798.

8. Kaushal, K., Nand, P. Performance Evaluation of AODV, DSR, TORA and OLSR in with respect to end-to-end delay in MANET. *International Journal of Science and Research (IJSR)*, 2014, 3(6), 633–636.

9. Kishor, K., Sharma, R., Chhabra, M. Student performance prediction using technology of machine learning. In: Sharma D.K., Peng SL., Sharma R., Zaitsev D.A. (eds) *Micro-Electronics and Telecommunication Engineering. Lecture Notes in Networks and Systems*, vol 373. Springer, Singapore, 2022. DOI: 10.1007/978-981-16-8721-1_53.

10. Kishor, K. Communication-efficient federated learning. In: Yadav S.P., Bhati B.S., Mahato D.P., Kumar S. (eds) *Federated Learning for IoT Applications. EAI/Springer Innovations in Communication and Computing*. Springer, Cham, 2022. DOI: 10.1007/978-3-030-85559-8_9.

11. Kishor, K. Personalized federated learning. In: Yadav S.P., Bhati B.S., Mahato D.P., Kumar S. (eds) *Federated Learning for IoT Applications. EAI/Springer Innovations in Communication and Computing*. Springer, Cham, 2022. DOI: 10.1007/978-3-030-85559-8_3.

12. Gupta, S., Tyagi, S., Kishor, K. Study and development of self sanitizing smart elevator. In: Gupta D., Polkowski Z., Khanna A., Bhattacharyya S., Castillo O. (eds) *Proceedings of Data Analytics and Management. Lecture Notes on Data Engineering and Communications Technologies*, vol 90. Springer, Singapore, 2022. DOI: 10.1007/978-981-16-6289-8_15.

13. Kishor, K., Pandey, D. Study and development of efficient air quality prediction system embedded with machine learning and IoT. In: Gupta D. et al. (eds) *Proceeding International Conference on Innovative Computing and Communications. Lecture Notes in Networks and Systems*, vol. 471, Springer, Singapore, 2022, DOI: 10.1007/978-981-19-2535-1.

14. Rai, B. K., Sharma, S., Kumar, G., Kishor, K. Recognition of different bird category using image processing. *International Journal of Online and Biomedical Engineering (IJOE)*, 2022, 18(07), 101–114. DOI: 10.3991/ijoe.v18i07.29639.

15. Sharma, A., Jha, N., Kishor, K. Predict COVID-19 with chest X-ray. In: Gupta D., Polkowski Z., Khanna A., Bhattacharyya S., Castillo O. (eds) *Proceedings of Data Analytics and Management. Lecture Notes on Data Engineering and Communications Technologies*, vol 90. Springer, Singapore, 2022. DOI: 10.1007/978-981-16-6289-8_16.

16. Jain, A., Sharma, Y., Kishor, K. Financial supervision and management system using ML algorithm. *Solid State Technology*, 2020, 63(6), 18974–18982. http://solidstatetechnology.us/index.php/JSST/article/view/8080.

17. Huang, H., Chen, X., Wu, Q., Huang, X., Shen, J. Bitcoin-based fair payments for outsourcing computation of fog devices. *Future Generation Computer Systems*, 2016, 78, 850–858.

18. Huh, S., Sangrae, C., Soohyung, K. Managing IoT devices using blockchain platform. In: *Proceedings of the 2017 19th International Conference on Advanced Communication Technology (ICACT), Bongpyeong, Korea*, 19–22 February 2017.

19. Armknecht, F., Karame, G., Mandal, A., Youssef, F., Zenner, E. Ripple: Overview and outlook. In: Conti M., Schunter M., Askoxylakis I. (eds) *Trust and Trustworthy Computing*. Springer International Publishing, Cham, pp. 163–180, 2015.

20. Vasek, M., Moore, T. There's no free lunch, even using bitcoin: Tracking the popularity and profits of virtual currency scams. In: *Proceedings of the International Conference on Financial Cryptography and Data Security, San Juan, Puerto Rico, 26–30 January 2015*. Springer, Berlin/Heidelberg, 2015.

21. Zhang, J., Nian, X., Xin, H. A secure system for pervasive social network-based healthcare. *IEEE Access*, 2016, 4, 9239–9250.

22. Singh, S., Jeong, Y.-S., Park, J.H. A survey on cloud computing security: Issues, threats, and solutions. *Journal of Network and Computer Applications*, 2016, 75, 200–222.

23. W. Venters, E. A. Whitley, A critical review of cloud computing: Researching desires and realities. *Journal of Information Technology*, 27(3), pp. 179–197, 2012.

24. S. Sharma, G. Gupta, P. R. Laxmi, A survey on cloud security issues and techniques, *arXiv:1403.5627*. 2014. Available: http://arxiv.org/abs/1403.5627.

25. S. Kirkman, A data movement policy framework for improving trust in the cloud using smart contracts and blockchains, In: *Proceedings of the IEEE International Conference on Cloud Engineering (IC2E)*, 2018, pp. 270–273.

26. D. Agrawal, A. A. El Abbadi, S. Das, A. J. Elmore, Database scalability, elasticity, and autonomy in the cloud, In: *Proceedings of International Conference on Database Systems for Advanced Applications (DASFAA)*. Springer, Berlin, 2011, pp. 2–15.

27. D. A. Fernandes, L. F. Soares, J. V. Gomes, M. M. Freire, P. R. Inácio, Security issues in cloud environments: A survey, *International Journal of Information Security*, 13(2), 113–170, 2014.

28. A. Harshavardhan, T. Vijayakumar, S. R. Mugunthan, Blockchain technology in cloud computing to overcome security vulnerabilities, In: *Proceedings of 2018 2nd International Conference on I-SMAC (IoT in Social, Mobile, Analytics and Cloud)*, 2018, pp. 408–414.

29. M. Risius, K. Spohrer, A blockchain research framework, *Business & Information Systems Engineering*, 59(6), 385–409, 2017.

30. S. Nakamoto, *Bitcoin: A Peer-To-Peer Electronic Cash System*, Saint Kitts and Nevis, Technical Report, 2008.

31. J. Kołodziej, A. Wilczynski, D. Fernandez-Cerero, A. Fernandez-Montes, Blockchain secure cloud: A new generation integrated cloud and blockchain platforms–general concepts and challenges, *European Cybersecurity*, 4(2), 28–35, 2018.

32. I. Eyal, A. E. Gencer, E. G. Sirer, R. Van Renesse, Bitcoin-NG: A scalable blockchain protocol, In: *Proceedings of 13th USENIX Symposium on Networked Systems Design and Implementation*. 2016, pp. 45–59.

33. H. Halaburda, G. Haeringer, *Bitcoin and Blockchain: What We Know and What Questions Are Still Open*, NYU Stern School Business, New York, NY, Tech. Rep., 2019.

34. L. Popovski, G. Soussou, P. B. Webb, *A Brief History of Blockchain*, Patterson Belknap Webb & Tyler, New York, NY, Tech. Rep., 2014.

35. A. Vatankhah Barenji, H. Guo, Z. Tian, Z. Li, W. M. Wang, G. Q. Huang, Blockchain-based cloud manufacturing: Decentralization, *arXiv:1901.10403*, 2019. Available: http://arxiv.org/abs/1901.10403.

36. D. C. Nguyen, P. N. Pathirana, M. Ding, A. Seneviratne, Integration of blockchain and cloud of things: Architecture, applications and challenges, *arXiv:1908.09058*, 2019. Available: http://arxiv.org/abs/1908.09058.

37. Bansal, Aniket, Satyam Kumar, Ashutosh Pandey, and Kaushal Kishor. "Attendance Management System through Fingerprint." *International Journal for Research in Applied Science & Engineering Technology (IJRASET)* 6, no. 9 (2018). DOI : 10.22214/ijraset.2018.4368, http://ijraset.com/fileserve.php?FID=15925

38. M. R. Islam, M. M. Rahman, M. Mahmud, M. A. Rahman, M. H. S. Mohamad and A. H. Embong, "A Review on Blockchain Security Issues and Challenges," 2021 IEEE 12th Control and System Graduate Research Colloquium (ICSGRC), Shah Alam, Malaysia, 2021, pp. 227–232, doi: 10.1109/ICSGRC53186.2021.9515276.

39. G. Zhao, S. Liu, C. Lopez, H. Lu, S. Elgueta, H. Chen, B. M. Boshkoska, Blockchain technology in agri-food value chain management: A synthesis of applications, challenges and future research directions, *Computers in Industry*, 109, 83–99, 2019.

40. Y. Lu, The blockchain: State-of-the-art and research challenges, *Journal of Industrial Information Integration*, 15, 80–90, 2019.

41. M. Niranjanamurthy, B. N. Nithya, S. Jagannatha, Analysis of blockchain technology: Pros, cons and SWOT, *Cluster Computing*, 22(6), 14743–14757, 2019.

42. D. Efanov, P. Roschin, The all-pervasiveness of the blockchain technology, *Procedia Computer Science*, 123, 116–121, 2018, DOI: 10.1016/j.procs.2018.01.019.
43. H. A. Reddy, K. R. Bhat, M. Pavithra, N. Mandara, S. Ramya, Blockchain for financial applications using IoT, *International Research Journal of Computer Science*, 6(6), 369–377, 2019.
44. S. Nayak, N. C. Narendra, A. Shukla, J. Kempf, Saranyu: Using smart contracts and blockchain for cloud tenant management, In: *Proceedings of IEEE 11th International Conference on Cloud Computing (CLOUD)*, 2018, pp. 857–861.
45. L. Zhu, K. Gai, M. Li, Blockchain and the Internet of Things, In: *Blockchain Technology in Internet of Things*. Springer, Cham, 2019, pp. 9–28.
46. S. Wang, X. Wang, Y. Zhang, A secure cloud storage framework with access control based on blockchain, *IEEE Access*, 7, 112713–112725, 2019.
47. S. Nanayakkara, S. Perera, S. Senaratne, Stakeholders' perspective on blockchain and smart contracts solutions for construction supply chains, In: *Proceedings of CIB World Building Congress*, 2019, pp. 1–11.
48. Z. Zheng, S. Xie, H. N. Dai, X. Chen, H. Wang, Blockchain challenges and opportunities: A survey, *International Journal of Web and Grid Services*, 14(4), 352–375, 2018.
49. D. Johnson, A. Menezes, S. Vanstone, The elliptic curve digital signature algorithm (ECDSA), *International Journal of Information Security*, 1, 36–63, 2001.
50. P. S. Maharjan, *Performance Analysis of Blockchain Platforms*, Howard R. Hughes College Engineering, University of Nevada, Las Vegas, Las Vegas, NV, Tech. Rep., 2018.
51. D. B. Rawat, V. Chaudhary, R. Doku, Blockchain: Emerging applications and use cases, *arXiv:1904.12247*, 2019. Available: https://arxiv.org/abs/1904.12247.
52. K. Bendiab, N. Kolokotronis, S. Shiaeles, S. Boucherkha, WiP: A novel blockchain-based trust model for cloud identity management, In: *Proceedings of 2018 IEEE 16th International Conference on Dependable, Autonomic and Secure Computing, 16th International Conference on Pervasive Intelligence and Computing, 4th International Conference on Big Data Intelligence and Computing and Cyber Science and Technology Congress (DASC/PiCom/DataCom/CyberSciTech)*, 2018, pp. 724–729.
53. D. K. Tosh, S. Shetty, X. Liang, C. Kamhoua, L. Njilla, Consensus protocols for blockchain-based data provenance: Challenges and opportunities, In: *Proceedings of IEEE 8th Annual Ubiquitous Computing, Electronics & Mobile Communication Conference (UEMCON)*, 2017, pp. 469–474.
54. C. V. N. U. B. Murthy, M. L. Shri, A survey on integrating cloud computing with blockchain, In: *Proceedings of International Conference on Emerging Trends in Engineering and Technology (IC-ETITE)*, 2020, pp. 1–6.

6

Cloud Computing for Machine Learning and Cognitive Application

Atul Kumar Singh

Galgotia University

Aditya Sam Koshy and Megha Gupta

IMS Engineering College

CONTENTS

DOI: 10.1201/9781003213895-6

6.1 Introduction

Edge computing is another approach for attaining the cloud computing services for applications that require better higher accessibility speed [1]. This is most useful for time-sensitive applications. It readily deploys. The services and information are processed and maintained at the edges before it is moved to the cloud.

The cloud computing is designed to cater the needs at locations that are too remote to reach or provide hands-on services via the help of hardware resources. To achieve such feats, there are multiple ways the cloud computing does just that. The three major deployment techniques for cloud computing are infrastructure as a service (IaaS), platform as a service (PaaS), and software as a service (SaaS) [2].

The aim of cloud computing is to remove the human mediation from in-between the service deployment procedure/service. The machine learning is now becoming more and more inevitable in many a turns of society. The machine learning tends to create machines that are trained via different methodologies based on the applications, need, and other biases. This is a perfect partner for cloud computing in maintaining the needlessness of human interface and mediation between cloud and end users. Not only does the machine learning help in that regard, it also helps in figuring out the flaws that arise in the cloud computing, which is a major concern with anything that is used to cater the needs of masses. The machine learning concerns with the advancement of the computer technology to such an extent that it is able to perform and carry out the tasks in lieu of a human supervision [3]. The merger of cloud computing and machine learning gives us a whole new field of opportunities for applications that once seemed out of touch from reality.

6.1.1 Cloud Computing

Cloud computing has, as already established, opened many facets for business and development. This in turn also requires a push from researchers and scholars, to continuously put in the work to enhance the current state of the technology. This is because the sheer amount of competition for the lions' share in market has increased as well. So, to one-up each other, the companies need innovation and sustainable development. The cloud computing provides services in three different deployment manners, which are discussed below:

6.1.2 Software as a Service

The method of making an application available as a service on the Internet is known as software as a service. Instead of installing the software on their computer, users simply access the software over the Internet [4]. This eliminates the need for users to manage complex software and hardware. SaaS users do not need to purchase, maintain, or upgrade software or hardware. Users simply connect to the Internet and access the application is very easy (e.g., Microsoft Office 365, Google Apps).

SaaS reduces customers in advance prices with the aid of using putting off the want to completely buy software program or spend money on a sturdy on-premise IT infrastructure—as is the case with conventional software program. SaaS clients must spend money on speedy community hardware; however, on account that provider overall performance is decided with the aid of using net connection speeds. Examples of SaaS encompass software provider vendors (ASPs) like Google Docs and Microsoft Office 365, in addition to business enterprise offerings that supply human aid software program, e-trade systems, patron courting control tools, and included improvement environments (IDEs). Software providers usually select one—or both—of two not unusual place deployment models: In their personal statistics center, or Through a public cloud provider issuer like AWS, Azure, or IBM Cloud, that manages the cloud surroundings on which the SaaS answer is hosted. SaaS packages take benefit of multitenant structure to isolate patron statistics. Software upgrades, trojan horse fixes, and different standard app preservation are looked after with the aid of using the SaaS issuer, at the same time as customers have interaction with the software program thru an Internet browser. SaaS answers are commonly absolutely functional; however, every so often comprise custom integration through software programming interfaces (APIs)—like REST or SOAP—to hook up with different functions. The nature of SaaS makes it simpler for vendors to roll out new functions to their clients. Most SaaS packages are preconfigured plug-and-play merchandize wherein the SaaS issuer manages the whole thing at the back of the app, including hardware components, such as networking, storage, and data center servers; platforms such as virtualization, the running system, and middleware; and software requirements such as runtimes, statistics, and the app itself.

6.1.3 Platform as a Service

PaaS is typically accessed over the Internet, but can also be deployed in on-premises or hybrid mode. Anyway, the underlying infrastructure on which the application runs is managed by the service provider. Customers often have the choice of where to physically host the application and the strength or security of their environment, but at many additional costs.

Typical PaaS components are as follows:

Managed infrastructure: The provider manages the server, storage, data center, and network resources needed to run the application.

Design, testing, and development tools: The integrated development environment brings together the tools you need to actually build your software, including source code editors, compilers, and debuggers. Some vendors also offer collaboration tools that allow developers to share and contribute to each other's work.

Middleware: PaaS often contains the tools needed to integrate user applications with different operating systems.

Operating system and database: PaaS provides an operating system on which you can run your applications and a variety of managed database options.

6.1.4 Infrastructure as a Service

Infrastructure as a service (IaaS) is a model that defines how providers provide cloud-based virtualization resources over the Internet.

IaaS is usually in contrast to the other two cloud computing patterns. The platform as a service (PaaS) model adds a layer of managed services to IaaS resources. The software as a service (SaaS) model provides fully managed software that is delivered directly to end users. See the IaaS and PaaS and SaaS section below.

Typical IaaS use cases are as follows:

Testing and Development—Teams can quickly create development and test environments to bring new applications to market faster. IaaS allows teams to automatically create test and development environments as part of their development pipeline.

Web App—IaaS provides all the infrastructures needed to run large web applications such as storage, web servers, and networks. Enterprises can use IaaS to quickly deploy web applications and easily scale their infrastructure as application demands increase or decrease.

Storage, Backup, and Recovery—Organizations can avoid the high initial cost of storage and the complexity of storage management. Cloud storage services eliminate the need for trained personnel to manage data and comply with regulatory requirements, enabling organizations to meet their storage needs as needed. It also simplifies the planning and management of backup and recovery systems.

High-Performance Computing—High-performance computing (HPC) helps solve complex and complex problems involving millions of variables and computations by running on supercomputers or large computing clusters. Leading IaaS providers offer services that bring HPC within the normal business reach and enable you to use HPC on demand instead of making a significant investment in your HPC infrastructure. For example, read the HPC guide on Azure.

Big Data Analysis—Big data processing and analysis are important in today's economy and require complex infrastructure such as large storage systems, distributed processing engines, and high-speed databases. IaaS providers offer all of the infrastructures as managed services, most of which also offer PaaS that can perform real-world analysis such as machine learning and AI.

6.2 Machine Learning

6.2.1 Supervised Learning

Supervised gadget mastering builds a version that makes predictions primarily based totally on proof with inside the presence of uncertainty [5,6]. A supervised mastering set of rules takes a acknowledged set of enter records and acknowledged responses to the records (output) and trains a version to generate affordable predictions for the reaction to new records. When you have acknowledged records for the output you are aiming to achieve, use supervised mastering [7,8].

Supervised mastering makes use of type and regression strategies to broaden gadget mastering fashions.

Classification strategies are expecting discrete responses—for example, whether or not an email is actual or spam, or whether or not a tumor is cancerous or benign. Classification fashions classify enter records into categories. Typical programs consist of scientific imaging, speech popularity, and credit scoring.

Use type in case your records may be tagged, categorized, or separated into particular businesses or classes. For example, programs for handwriting popularity use type to understand letters and numbers. In photo-processing and pc vision, unsupervised sample popularity strategies are used for item detection and photo segmentation.

Common algorithms for appearing type consist of help vector gadget (SVM), boosted and bagged choice trees, k-nearest neighbor, Naïve Bayes, discriminant evaluation, logistic regression, and neural networks [9,10].

Regression strategies are expecting non-stop responses—for example, modifications in temperature or fluctuations in electricity demand. Typical programs consist of strength load forecasting and algorithmic trading.

Use regression strategies in case you are running with a records variety or if the character of your reaction is an actual number, which includes temperature or the time till failure for a bit of equipment.

Common regression algorithms consist of linear version, nonlinear version, regularization, stepwise regression, boosted and bagged choice trees, neural networks, and adaptive neuro-fuzzy mastering.

6.2.2 Unsupervised Learning

Unsupervised mastering unearths hidden styles or intrinsic systems in records. It is used to attract inferences from datasets which include enter records without categorized responses.

Clustering is the maximum not unusual place unsupervised mastering technique. It is used for exploratory record evaluation to discover hidden styles or groupings in records. Applications for cluster evaluation consist of gene collection evaluation, marketplace research, and item popularity [11,12].

Common algorithms for appearing clustering consist of k-method, hierarchical clustering, Gaussian aggregate fashions, hidden Markov fashions, self-organizing maps, fuzzy c-method clustering, and subtractive clustering.

6.3 Literature Review

As we have already mentioned the popularity of cloud computing and machine learning among the academicians and enterprises, the plethora of work previously done helps us understand these technologies better. A major application of cloud computing lies in Healthcare Services as it is able to improve it drastically. In [13], authors propose a model for the health care system based on cloud computing by the help parallel particle swarm optimization which assists in optimizing the selection of VMs. The authors have made use of a new chronic kidney disease detection system to check the performance of their new VM. The system currently lacks provision for other diseases. An interesting study has been carried out by authors in [14], where they have made use of different machine learning algorithms to analyze user behaviors in a working environment and real conditions in a hospital.

In [15], authors have discussed major challenges that are faced when deploying the cloud using IaaS approach. It focuses on different technicalities that we come across when talking about scheduling and resource allocation. In [16], authors propose a model for content-based image retrieval (CBIR), via the help of Microsoft Azure hybrid cloud. The architecture is implemented for software as a service (SaaS), allowing a huge collection of images to be accessed and processed making it optimum for hybrid applications. In [17], the authors make use of trust-based approach to ensure genuineness and legitimacy of cloud resources and its end users. They figure this out by assigning a trust value to the user which is computed based on the past behavior and the accesses of the said user. For their application, various machine learning techniques are employed such as Naïve Bays, decision tree, logistic regression, etc., which helps them tackle unwanted requests.

In [18], the authors have presented a trust model which is built on quality of service and the speed of implementation of the resources of the cloud. The proposed model was able to provide reliable service in terms of quality and speed as compared to other similar models.

In [19], the authors discuss their approach to help masses working on machine learning, by providing a distributed architecture that covers all of the machine learning development cycle. This architecture provides access to its users in a transparent manner and all the while providing resources in distributed manner which is even more efficient in grand scheme of things.

The machine learning is also used majorly in boosting security aspects of cloud computing. In [20], the authors have investigated the problems arising due to resource provisioning in edge-cloud environments along with other parameters and also provided different methods for the betterment in the reliability of the distributed applications in various environments.

In [21], the authors have worked on public as well as private cloud and their security problems and provided a three-tier security architecture. The authors have also discussed the open issues that arise. In [22], the authors provide an account on how the machine learning models can help in boosting the strength of data security which is of utmost importance. While in [23], the researchers have taken assistance of a model to face the threats to security and the problems that arise in concern of the distributed computing. The researchers in the [24] have drawn out a comparison between different machine learning algorithms, for the defense system. Algorithm strategies are compared and chosen based on their high accuracy in malware detection.

6.3.1 Cloud Computing

First, we must understand how this computing model has evolved to understand cloud computing. In the beginning, Internet service provider (ISP 1.0) provides Internet services to individuals and organizations over dial-up telephone services. As the uses of Internet increase and work as commodity, ISP started to search for value-added services like access to emails and servers for query-solving which is considered as ISP 2.0. These services lead to some specialized facilities like hosting organizations servers with supporting infrastructure and application running on them [25,26]. These facilities are defined as collocation facilities (ISP 3.0). Those specialized services are worked as data centers where individuals or organization locate networks, server, and data storage to interconnect with several intercommunication and other network service provider with less cost and complexity [27]. The emergence of application service providers (ASPs) is the next evolutionary stage as collecting facilities spread and became commodities. ASPs concentrated on delivering more value-added applications for end users rather than simply the computer infrastructure (ISP 4.0). ASPs offer applications to end users they own for execution as well as the necessary infrastructure. A new computing model called cloud computing (ISP 5.0) is created with the inclusion of ASPs, and it defines that the SPI model refers to SaaS, PaaS, and IaaS. With growing interest, cloud computing is a young and constantly developing concept with continuous announcements of new and improved features. Some have argued that as cloud computing has received more attention, businesses are making more and more claims to be "cloudy," leading some to believe it is just hype. Many companies are said to operate on the cloud. Several computing organizations have stated their plans to spread the word about various aspects of cloud computing. Some of these organizations, such as the Cloud Computing Security Alliance and the National Institute of Standards and Technology (NIST), are already well-established [28,29].

Cloud computing, as defined by NIST, is a model for providing ubiquitous, practical, on-demand network access to a shared pool of reconfigurable computing resources (such as networks, servers, storage, applications, and services) that can be swiftly provisioned and released with little management work or service provider interaction. Five characteristics are essential to cloud computing: multitenancy (shared resources), huge scalability, elasticity, pay-as-you-go, and resource self-provisioning [30].

6.3.2 Multitenancy

While cloud computing offers business models where resources are shared, earlier computer paradigms allocate all resources to a single user. At several levels of cloud computing, including network, host, and application levels, resources are shared.

6.3.3 Huge Scalability

Some organizations have the capacity to host hundreds or thousands of systems, but cloud computing may expand this number to tens of thousands of systems. In addition, it has a huge amount of storage capacity and massive bandwidth.

6.3.4 Elasticity

End users have the option of changing how much resources they consume based on their needs. As they no longer need resources, they may also release them for other uses.

6.3.5 Pay-as-You-Go

Only the resources that the end user uses must be paid for. In other words, the user just needs to pay while the resources are being used.

6.3.6 Self-Provision of Resources

End users have the option of self-provisioning resources including extra processing power, software, storage, and network resources.

Because it may provide consumers solutions for a fraction of the expense of purchasing such a solution with supercomputer-like capacity, cloud computing is gaining popularity. As a mix of already existing technologies, cloud computing is not a technology in and of itself. These technologies are applied at various speeds and in various situations; they are intended to work together to provide a technological ecosystem for cloud computing. New developments in processor power, virtualization technology, storage, broadband network connectivity, and quick, affordable servers have come together to provide a more comprehensive cloud computing solution.

6.4 The SPI Framework for Cloud Computing

The abbreviation "SPI" stands for a standard framework for cloud computing that has been designed for specifying cloud services. SaaS, PaaS, and IaaS are the three main cloud services represented by this acronym (SPI). Figure 6.1 shows the relationship between services delivery model, uses, and deployment model of clouds [31,32].

6.4.1 The Cloud Services Delivery Model

The SPI framework for cloud computing includes three approved approaches for delivering cloud services.

6.4.1.1 The Software as a Service Model

In this delivery model, a cloud service provider provides end customers with a variety of applications or software to use on a subscription- or pay-per-use basis. End users need not to purchase software for their uses. Cloud technology occasionally offers free services for certain purposes. Hardware, software, and support for these bought or subscribed services are all complete. Client can use these services through any authorized device. To create organization-specific data for various services and to interact with other applications that are not SaaS platforms, preparation work is occasionally necessary. With the help

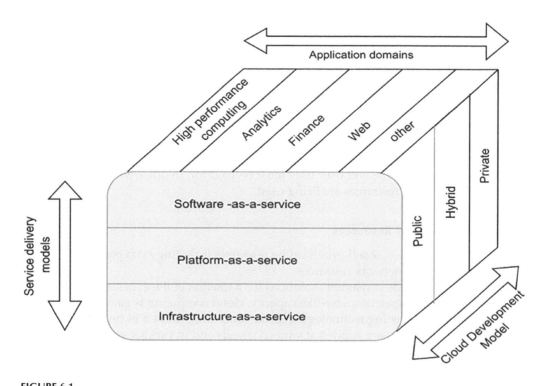

FIGURE 6.1
Figure shows the relationship between services delivery model.

of SaaS, businesses may delegate the hosting and operation of their applications to a third party, saving money on the cost of licenses, servers, and other infrastructure.

6.4.1.2 The Platform as a Service Model

In the PaaS model, the provider gives application developers an integrated development environment (IDE) for developing applications, and the resulting services are made available through the provider's platform. The developers build a framework and best practices for creating applications, as well as a distribution and payment channel. This allows for the quick creation of software, minimal entry costs, and the use of established channels for client acquisition [33].

Development environment is made available as a service under the PaaS, which is a variation of SaaS. To create their own apps, developers leverage the cloud service provider's building blocks. The cloud is where developed tools or applications are stored and accessible. With the aid of PaaS, users may create web applications without having to download any software or acquire specialist system management knowledge. Multitenant development tools, deployment frameworks, integrated administration, and integrated pricing are all provided by PaaS. Throughout the whole software life cycle, it must facilitate both informal and formal collaboration while ensuring the confidentiality of the source code and any associated intellectual property [34].

6.4.1.3 The Infrastructure as a Service Model

To execute client-developed applications in a conventional hosted application environment, the vendor offers the whole infrastructure. This specifically designated hosted application makes use of hardware that was either acquired or leased specifically for this function. The hardware infrastructure required to execute applications is similarly provided by the IaaS model in cloud computing, but it also enables end users to use this hardware infrastructure on a pay-per-use basis and scale the service in response to demand. From the standpoint of the resource supplier, construct an infrastructure that can cope with fluctuating resource demand over time. This IaaS concept, which provides computing services like utility computing did, is comparable to utility computing. This implies that you only pay for the resources, like as processing power, disc storage, and so forth that you really use. IaaS offers online services that shield the customer from specifics relating to computer resources, location, data partitioning, scalability, security, backup, and other issues. In cloud computing, the infrastructure is completely under the provider's control [35].

6.4.1.4 Cloud Deployment Model

The term "cloud computing" refers to a condensed depiction of the intricately interconnected gadgets and Internet connections. The physical setting for cloud platforms, infrastructure, and applications is defined by the deployment model. While small businesses use public clouds, major businesses create private ones to meet their demands. Based on how a cloud is related to a company, private and public clouds can be viewed as internal and external clouds, respectively. With the help of public and private computing, a business or vendor may charge clients a fee in exchange for providing dynamic, scalable, virtualized resources through an Internet connection. Clients may not necessarily need to be knowledgeable about, skilled in, or in charge of the IT infrastructure [36].

Reliable services are delivered through various data centers and are created on servers using various virtualization technologies in a variety of cloud computing infrastructures. If networking infrastructure is present, the services can be accessed from anywhere. All consumer computer demands appear to be met by cloud computing as a single point of access.

6.4.2 Public Clouds

Public clouds, also known as external clouds, are what is meant by "cloud computing" in the conventional sense. In this definition, resources are dynamically provided as needed by users over the Internet via web applications or web services from an off-site, third-party provider who shares resources and bills on a fine-grained, utility-computing basis [37].

Public cloud was operated, hosted, and maintained by a third-party provider from one or more data centers. The provision of security measures and regular operation is the duty of the third-party provider who owns the public cloud. Customers of public cloud services have little control and supervision over the system's physical components [38].

6.4.3 Private Clouds

The term "private cloud" refers to an organization's own cloud. On private networks, it provides cloud computing. It offers cloud computing advantages without the drawbacks, corporate governance issues, or dependability worries. Less intensive management and cheaper initial capital expenses are not advantages for businesses that created and run their own private clouds. The management of private cloud is the customer's responsibility.

Because private cloud is devoted to a single entity and is not shared with other resources, it differs from public cloud in terms of the network, computing, and storage infrastructures connected with it. Daily services or security mechanisms are often provided or controlled by internal IT or a third party who creates the private cloud for an organization under the private cloud computing paradigm. In it, the client has more control over the system's physical components, including the hypervisor and the hosted virtualized operating system. It is very simple for a consumer to cope with established corporate security standards, policies, and regulatory compliance when there is transparency and a high degree of control [39].

6.4.4 Hybrid Clouds

Both public and private clouds are included in a hybrid cloud system. A business can utilize a hybrid cloud to store and run non-essential applications in a public cloud environment while keeping sensitive data and key applications on-site in a private cloud. The integration of cloud components is increasing, barriers are being removed, and capabilities are being created to deliver services in a hybrid cloud. Trusting that a company's or a person's information is secure and confidential is a major problem. An important step toward widespread acceptance of cloud computing is the development of hybrid computing.

6.4.5 The Impact of Cloud Computing on Users

The following section provides the impact of cloud computing on several types of users:

- Individual business
- Individual customers

- Start-ups
- Small- and medium-sized business
- Enterprise businesses

6.4.6 Individual Business

Many people are now utilizing cloud computing technologies to launch their businesses. They are motivated by cloud computing cheap barrier to entry. Some development tools are also free to use, or users simply need to pay for more resources or stores. Customers can host their websites to attract customers, use various cloud portals to sell and market their goods, use virtual marketing tools to reach customers around the world, place product ads with search engines, manage their funds using online banking features, manage their finances using online accountancy services, and schedule appointments using office calendars. The cloud may offer all of these benefits.

6.4.7 Individual Customers

Cloud computing is already widely used by many technologically competent people in today's world. Despite the fact that home computers have their own storage, they nonetheless depend on cloud computing services to meet their growing storage and computational needs. Individual consumers can purchase music from cloud service providers, save personal information to facilitate cooperation on social networking sites, create their own personal website in the cloud, and preserve their personal emails and photographs there. Customers may monitor their participation in exercise programmers, make purchases, conduct searches, and use the Internet to research the most recent news. These days, tax returns are also created and kept on the cloud. Many of the cloud's terms and conditions might provide privacy hazards that people could find concerning. There may be an unintentional loss or unauthorized fraudulent access by a Content Security Policy (CSP).

6.4.8 Start-Ups

When a company wants to launch a new venture, they want to set up operations in a flexible, scalable way. When compared to promoting a product and funding R&D, creating an IT department is a low priority. By putting in place and hosting an effective enterprise resource planning (ERP) solution on-site, a business might show that it is scalable. The majority of IT infrastructure is currently outsourced via the cloud, and a lean IT shop is maintained. The difficulties presently are in becoming bound by provider contracts and service levels that the CSP offers. Startups pioneer some of the cloud computing technologies for integrated business, but they have less data, fewer processes, and fewer applications than established organizations.

6.4.9 Small- and Medium-Sized Business

Numerous small businesses are created as spin-offs or acquired by major businesses. Awareness the maturity and entrenchment of legacy processes and data requires an understanding of the age of small- and medium-sized organizations. In contrast to large enterprises, requirements for data security and privacy are no longer a concern for small- and medium-sized businesses. Since there are fewer IT departments, fewer knowledge and skill sets are needed. The ability to justify significant IT projects may become more challenging. Small businesses need to upgrade their IT structures as soon as possible without spending excessive amounts of money. These firms have a smaller number of people making most of the decisions. Small and medium company environments have several necessary elements that might improve the adoption of cloud computing depending on the particular case.

6.4.10 Enterprise Businesses

Because cloud computing enables customers to access services outside of the company firewall, mature firms are using it more often every day. Utilizing cloud computing enables businesses to provide productivity-enhancing services like travel and research. Companies do not utilize individually identifying information while conducting various surveys among their personnel to populate broad attributes. Instead, they use corporate applications. Applications for salesforce.com document management, buying, and logistics are examples of business-critical departments and operations that may employ cloud computing. Data redundancy between the CSP and the conventional corporation is a crucial factor that businesses take into account while utilizing the cloud. Time to market, where a noisy application is the only workable option given cost and time restrictions, is the accumulating case for a cloud solution.

6.5 Conclusions

It is impossible to resist the buzz being generated by cloud computing. By influencing the distribution and usage of technology, this new computing paradigm has the potential to be a disruptive force. The next evolutionary step in the field of mainframes, PCs, servers, smartphones, and other technologies might be cloud computing, which will fundamentally alter how businesses handle their IT. Consumers, businesses, and financial analysts are all paying attention to it. It has been noted that millions of articles are found online when you search "cloud computing," defining, praising, mocking, and marketing it.

Although predictions differ, many financial analysts believe that over the next few years, cloud computing will significantly increase both IT investment and income streams. It is an extensive and varied phenomenon. The migration of conventional IT services to the new cloud model accounts for the majority of the growth, but cloud computing also offers room for the development of significant new companies and income streams.

With the help of cloud computing, IT services may now be provided that are free at the time of use and funded by advertising rather than through direct purchase and payment. The majorities of cloud services are presently and will continue to be financed by advertising.

There are a number of indications suggesting people and corporate entities regarded cloud computing as a substitute for the way they already utilize information technology. These arguments imply that in the near future, the organizational structure and traditional IT service model will need to alter in order to handle the processing capacity that can be quickly provided through cloud computing. Cloud computing is increasingly being used because it offers low-cost solutions, is responsive and flexible, gives enterprises full control over technological decisions, and bridges the gap between consumer and corporate applications.

6.6 Future Scope

The internal IT paradigm, in which you purchase servers, PC servers, software, and licensed applications to expand your organization, is beginning to fade from the computer world. We may now utilize new IT services for people, small companies, and start-ups to leverage computer power, apps, and storage thanks to a new era of computing known as cloud computing. Numerous applications may be used on the cloud at any time, from any location, on a range of devices. A company may provide its new hires access to these services through the cloud without buying new gear or software licenses. Organizations may expand their infrastructure, thanks to the elastic nature of cloud computing.

As cloud computing has an enormous impact in the field of computing, the future of cloud computing has become a crucial problem and has to be recognized. Several organizations depend on this computing. It overgrows over time. The growth of cloud computing is expected to speed up in the upcoming years, and several academics and IT support its uses. The trend of cloud computing is set to take off like wildfire due to how frequently it is used in the modern digital environment.

Cloud storage is used by many people and businesses to store their data, including sensitive data; hence, it is vital to offer security and privacy procedures to protect the data. Since it enables pooled resources and processing power based on a pay-as-you-go model and will draw numerous businesses and individuals, cloud service providers must incorporate a greater security mechanism. Because the loss of a client system does not jeopardize data or software in a cloud-based software environment, physical security is greater.

The utilization of cloud computing in state-full applications like n-tier web services can be improved by expanding the hybrid cloud computing model. Cloud computing still has to address a number of difficulties, such as session management, service time estimate, and data consistency.

References

1. C. Fauzi, A. Azila, A. Noraziah, H. Tutut, Z. Noriyani, On cloud computing security issues. *Intelligent Information and Database Systems: Lecture Notes in Computer Science*, 7197, 560–569, 2012.
2. C. Gong, J. Liu, Q. Zhang, H. Chen, Z. Gong, The characteristics of cloud computing. In *2010 39th International Conference on Parallel Processing Workshops (ICPPW)*. IEEE, pp. 275–279, 2010.
3. M. Callara, P. Wira, User behavior analysis with machine learning techniques in cloud computing architectures. In *Proceedings of the 2018 International Conference on Applied Smart Systems, Médéa, Algeria*, pp. 1–6, 24–25 November 2018.
4. H. Yang, M. Tate, A descriptive literature review and classification of cloud computing research. *Communications of the Association for Information Systems*, 31, 35–60, 2012.
5. K. Kishor, R. Sharma, M. Chhabra, Student performance prediction using technology of machine learning. In: Sharma D.K., Peng SL., Sharma R., Zaitsev D.A. (eds) *Micro-Electronics and Telecommunication Engineering. Lecture Notes in Networks and Systems*, vol. 373. Springer, Singapore, 2022. https://doi.org/10.1007/978-981-16-8721-1_53
6. K. Kishor, Communication-efficient federated learning. In Yadav S.P., Bhati B.S., Mahato D.P., Kumar S. (eds) *Federated Learning for IoT Applications. EAI/Springer Innovations in Communication and Computing*. Springer, Cham, 2022. https://doi.org/10.1007/978-3-030-85559-8_9.

7. K. Kishor, Personalized federated learning. In Yadav S.P., Bhati B.S., Mahato D.P., Kumar S. (eds) *Federated Learning for IoT Applications. EAI/Springer Innovations in Communication and Computing.* Springer, Cham, 2022. https://doi.org/10.1007/978-3-030-85559-8_3.

8. S. Gupta, S. Tyagi, K. Kishor, Study and development of self sanitizing smart elevator. In Gupta D., Polkowski Z., Khanna A., Bhattacharyya S., Castillo O. (eds) *Proceedings of Data Analytics and Management. Lecture Notes on Data Engineering and Communications Technologies,* vol. 90. Springer, Singapore, 2022. https://doi.org/10.1007/978-981-16-6289-8_15.

9. K. Kishor, D. Pandey, Study and development of efficient air quality prediction system embedded with machine learning and IoT. In Gupta D. et al. (eds), *Proceeding International Conference on Innovative Computing and Communications. Lecture Notes in Networks and Systems,* vol. 471, Springer, Singapore, 2022. DOI: 10.1007/978-981-19-2535-1.

10. B. K. Rai, S. Sharma, G. Kumar, K. Kishor, Recognition of different bird category using image processing. *International Journal of Online and Biomedical Engineering (iJOE),* 18(07), 101–114, 2022. DOI: 10.3991/ijoe.v18i07.29639.

11. A. Sharma, N. Jha, K. Kishor, Predict COVID-19 with chest X-ray. In Gupta D., Polkowski Z., Khanna A., Bhattacharyya S., Castillo O. (eds) *Proceedings of Data Analytics and Management. Lecture Notes on Data Engineering and Communications Technologies,* vol. 90. Springer, Singapore, 2022. DOI: 10.1007/978-981-16-6289-8_16.

12. A. Jain, Y. Sharma, K. Kishor, Financial supervision and management system using ML algorithm. *Solid State Technology,* 63(6), 18974–18982, 2020. http://solidstatetechnology.us/index.php/JSST/article/view/8080

13. A. Abdelaziz, M. Elhoseny, A.S. Salama, A.M. Riad. A machine learning model for improving healthcare services on cloud computing environment. *Measurement,* 117–128, 2018.

14. M. Callara, P. Wira, User behavior analysis with machine learning techniques in cloud computing architectures, *2018 International Conference on Applied Smart Systems (ICASS),* 2018, pp. 1–6, DOI: 10.1109/ICASS.2018.8651961.

15. Á. López García, E. Fernández-del Castillo, P. Orviz Fernández, I. Campos Plasencia, J. Marco de Lucas. Resource provisioning in Science Clouds: Requirements and challenges. *Software: Practice and Experience,* 48(3), 486–498, 2018.

16. M. Meena, A. R. Singh, V. A. Bharadi, Architecture for software as a service (SaaS) model of CBIR on hybrid cloud of Microsoft Azure. *Procedia Computer Science,* 79, 569–578, ISSN: 1877-0509, 2016. DOI: 10.1016/j.procs.2016.03.072.

17. P.M. Khilar, V, Chaudhari, R.R., Swain, Trust-based access control in cloud computing using machine learning. In Das, H., Barik, R., Dubey, H., Roy, D. (eds) *Cloud Computing for Geospatial Big Data Analytics. Studies in Big Data,* vol. 49. Springer, Cham, 2018. DOI: 10.1007/978-3-030-03359-0_3.

18. A. Gholami, M.G. Arani, A trust model based on quality of service in cloud computing environment. *International Journal of Database Theory and Application,* 8(5), 161–170, 2015.

19. L. G. Alvaro, T. Viet, A. S. Alic, C. Miguel, C. P. Isabel, C. Alessandro, D. Stefan et al. A cloud-based framework for machine learning workloads and applications. *IEEE Access,* 1, 2020. DOI: 10.1109/ACCESS.2020.2964386.

20. Le, T., Garcia, R., Casari, P., Östberg, P-O. Machine learning methods for reliable resource provisioning in edge-cloud computing: A survey. *ACM Computing Surveys,* 52, 1–39, 2019. DOI: 10.1145/3341145.

21. S. Singh, Y.-S. Jeong, J. Park, A survey on cloud computing security: Issues, threats, and solutions. *Journal of Network and Computer Applications,* 75, 200–222, 2016.

22. D. Bhamare, T. Salman, M. Samaka, A. Erbad, R. Jain, Feasibility of supervised machine earning for cloud security. In *Proceedings of the International Conference on Information Science and Security, Jaipur, India,* 16–20 December 2016, pp. 1–5.

23. P. Purniemaa, R. Kannan, N. Jaisankar, Security threat and attack in cloud infrastructure: A survey. *International Journal of Computers and Applications,* 2, 1–12, 2013.

24. N. Selamat, F. Ali, Comparison of malware detection techniques using machine learning algorithm. *Indonesian Journal of Electrical Engineering and Computer Science,* 16, 435, 2019.

25. S. M. Thompson, M. D. Dean, Advancing information Technology in health care, *Communications of the ACM*, 52(6), 2009.

26. P. Kumar Paul, M. K. Ghose, Cloud Computing: possibilities, challenges and opportunities with special reference to its emerging need in the academic and working area of Information Science, *International Conference on Modelling optimization and Computing, Procedia Engineering*, 38, 2222–2227, 2012.

27. L. Peiyua, L. Dong, The new risk assessment model for information system in cloud computing environment, *Procedia Engineering*, 15, 3200–3204, 2011.

28. Z. Jian Xun, G. Zhi Min. Survey of research progress on cloud computing. *Application Research of Computers*, 27(2), 429–433, 2010.

29. F. DengGuo, Z. Min, Z. Yan, X. Zhen, Study on cloud computing security. *Journal of Software*, 22(1), 71–83, 2011.

30. S. Qiang, H. Youtao, D. Yuxin, Research on a quantitative information security risk assessment model. *Journal of Computer Research and Development*, 43, 594–598, 2006.

31. F. Deng-guo, Z. Yang, Z. Yu-qing, Survey of information security risk assessment. *Journal of China Institute of Communications*, 7(25), 10–18, 2004.

32. K. Mukherjee, Cloud computing: Future framework for e-governance, *International Journal of Computer Applications (0975-8887)*, 7(7), 1–8, ISSN: 2278–3075, 2010.

33. M. Kayali, N. Safie, M. Mukhtar, The effect of individual factors mediated by trust and moderated by IT knowledge on students' adoption of cloud based e-learning, *International Journal of Innovative Technology and Exploring Engineering (IJITEE)*, 9(2), 987–993, 2019.

34. N. Zhao, M. Xia, Z. Xu, W. Mi, Y. Shen, A cloud computing-based college-enterprise classroom training method, *World Transactions on Engineering and Technology Education 2015*, WIETE, Vol. 13, No. 1, 2015.

35. T. D. Nguyen, T. M. Nguyen, Q. T. Pham, S. Misra, Acceptance and use of e-learning based on cloud computing: The role of consumer innovativeness, In Murgante B. et al. (eds) *Computational Science and Its Applications – ICCSA*, pp. 159–174, 2014.

36. L. Wang, G. V. Laszewski, A. Younge, X. He, M. Kunze, J. Tao, C. Fu, Cloud computing: a perspective study, *New Generation Computing*, 28(2), 137–146, 2010.

37. M. Rodriguez-Martinez, H. Valdivia, J. Rivera, J. Seguel, M. Greer, MedBook: A cloud-based healthcare billing and record management system, *2012 IEEE Fifth International Conference on Cloud Computing*, pp. 899–905, 24–29 June 2012, DOI: 10.1109/CLOUD.2012.133.

38. P. Mell, T. Grance, *Draft NIST Working Definition of Cloud Computing – v15*, National Institutes of Standard and Technology, Information Technology Laboratory, 19th, August 2009.

39. T. Dillon, C. Wu, E. hang, Cloud computing: Issues and challenges, In *24th IEEE International Conference, Perth, WA, AINA*, pp. 27–33, 20–23, April 2010.

7

Edge Cloud Computing-Based Model for IoT

Arvind Kumar
Raj Kumar Goel Institute of Technology

Raj Kishor Verma and Rupa Rani
ABES Institute of Technology

CONTENTS

DOI: 10.1201/9781003213895-7

7.1 Introduction

Computing at the edge processes information close to its origin. As more and more appliances become Internet of Things (IoT) enabled, there will be an explosion of information. Assuming 5G mobile phones are successful, considerably more information might be generated. According to Cisco [1], there will be 500 ZB of data generated by IoT devices in 2019. Increased from 3.4 ZB in 2014 to 10.4 ZB in 2020 [2]. The number of connected devices using streaming services is expected to reach 50 million by 2020 [3] and maybe even more by 2025. "Edge computing" refers to the practice of doing data processing directly on the end device. It is possible that this volume of information is too much for cloud storage to handle. With edge computing, data are processed in part or in whole at the edge of the network, often close to the data source. It enhances response speed, data analysis, and latency [4].

Smart cities, smart healthcare, and smart homes are all impacted by IoT development and implementation [5]. There are now tens of billions of connected objects [6], and another 50 billion IoT devices are predicted to be in use by 2020 [7]. The performance, security, reliability, and privacy of IoT devices are impacted by their limited storage and processing capacity [8,9]. Many applications have been enhanced by the IoT and cloud computing. Smart cities [10], smart homes [11], smart metering [9], and video surveillance [9], including smart urban surveillance [12], are all examples.

With the help of IoT, a wide variety of high-tech devices may be linked to the web [13]. Improvised protocols [14–17] are used for data perception, data collection, and data sharing between nodes. Providing services to end users requires processing the massive amounts of data generated by these devices. Classical computing, in which nodes send data to a cloud server, runs it through its paces and then sends back its results and a response is inefficient and wasteful of bandwidth and other resources. Smart transportation [18], smart cities [19–21], smart grid [22,23], and smart healthcare [24] are all time-sensitive applications that would be compromised by increased transmission times as more data are sent. Due to the short battery life of IoT devices, it is recommended that data be sent to a nearby edge device that can better analyse and store the information. Processing data locally minimizes the need for long-distance transmission as well as associated expenses in terms of both time and energy [25].

The standard of living in urban areas will rise as a consequence of more interactions between people and IoT devices and services [26].

The IoT is implemented in IoT-based pest management, power grid optimization, bee population preservation, enhancing the effectiveness of garbage collection, preventing illegal fishing, ending high-risk police pursuits, using UAVs to aid in rainforest conservation; redefining field-based intelligence for the oil and gas industry, using sensors to improve road safety and enhanced traffic management.

7.1.1 Cloud Computing

"Cloud computing" provides software and network infrastructure (including servers, databases, and storage) through the Internet on demand [27]. Reference [28] describes four cloud deployment methods: "public cloud" refers to cloud computing accessible over the Internet. Cloud service providers own, maintain, and manage this infrastructure [29]. Private clouds are owned and maintained by a single firm yet serve many consumers [30]. This infrastructure is owned, operated, and managed [28]. Community cloud: This infrastructure gives services to a specific consumer from various organisations that share shared interests, such as when several schools utilise the same platform given by certain corporations [31]. "Hybrid cloud" combines two or more cloud computing infrastructures. Each prototype is unique. Combining Google's public and Amazon's private clouds is one example (AWS). Data and application portability regulations [28] are their glue. "Cloud computing" provides several services online. Based on benefits, these services split into three categories.

7.1.2 Software-as-a-Service (SaaS)

In this strategy, manufacturers supply end users with software or a browser-based application to perform and save work online [32,33].

7.1.3 Platform-as-a-Service (PaaS)

End users may install and operate new apps without building or maintaining the infrastructure [33].

7.1.4 Infrastructure-as-a-Service (IaaS)

Vendors offer hardware, data centres, network components, and storage as hardware-as-a-service [34]. Cloud computing handles IoT storage and networking difficulties [35].

7.1.5 Cloud Computing at the Edge Offers Many Benefits for LSD-IoT

To store this information, cloud computing provides safe, low-cost storage, and computation services for the IoT [36]. The data are always accessible from any device, and the customer just pays for the space they use.

7.1.5.1 Scalable

With cloud computing, you can monitor and maintain a growing population of IoT gadgets. IoT applications may benefit from enhanced bandwidth and storage [37–39].

7.1.5.2 Performance

Cloud computing has the potential to enhance IoT performance by offloading data processing from IoT devices to remote servers [39].

While cloud architectures are essential to the IoT, they aren't without flaws. Cloud services aren't always able to determine the most efficient approach to handle data processing and storage. Keeping records of every sensor reading would be inefficient. To address these issues, a new design is required:

Many IoT applications, such as e-health apps, interface with the physical environment via sensing and actuation. This issue, which arises from the physical separation of IoT devices and cloud computing resources, may be solved by integrating the two [40,41].

7.1.5.3 Data Size

More IoT devices means more bandwidth required to transport IoT data to the cloud, especially when smart phones can send streaming videos and images to the cloud, leading to placing cloud-like services near the end user to conserve bandwidth [42].

Sensors are examples of IoT devices that use a loT of power. In order to keep the quality of the IoT network intact, devices with limited resources need to be placed in close proximity to cloud services [43].

7.1.5.4 Availability

In time-sensitive applications, IoT devices must be connected to the cloud. They need to be online all the time, which might be taxing for low-powered gadgets [44]. IoT edge computing is defined here, along with its implementation and some analysis of the phenomenon. Through the usage of edge computing, data and computer applications are moved away from centralized nodes and closer to the point of use. There are an estimated 500 zettabytes of data created by IoT devices per year [44]. There are implications for bandwidth, storage, and computation. The use of edge computing helps lower response times for real-time programmes [44]. Computing power is brought all the way out to the edge of a network via edge computing. While cloud computing handles the backend of the network, edge computing ensures that services will always be available to users. Devices in the network's periphery (the "edge") are responsible for moving data storage, processing, and transmission closer to the end users. In many ways, edge computing enhances the network.

7.1.5.5 Effectiveness

An edge device divides up the work of storing data, processing it, and exercising control between the individual user and the cloud. Devices in the IoT may make efficient use of centralized edge computing resources.

Users' wants are taken into account by edge devices [45]. The physical health of patients is monitored by IoT devices, and computing resources are distributed according to patients' health risk categories [46]. With data processing and storage so close to the end user, edge devices, and clients provide more agility via reduced cost and time to market [47]. By performing data analysis and processing closer to the end user, edge computing helps time-critical applications deal with latency [48].

7.2 Edge Computing: Why You Need It

Many industries produce data in a digitalizing world. These data must be processed fast for current technology (real-time applications). Small- and medium-sized enterprises and research organizations no longer need a computer to calculate. End users must still send and receive data. Edge computing does computations where the data are in real time. IoT may need rapid response times, private data, and big data, straining the network. Cloud computing can't handle these problems. Figures 7.1a and 7.2 illustrate edge computing.

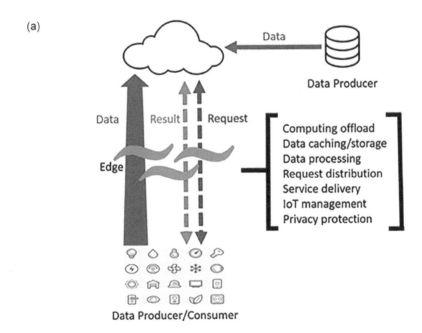

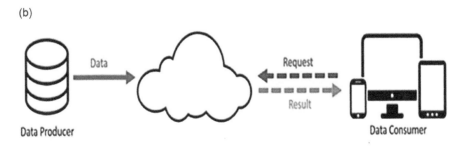

FIGURE 7.1
(a) and (b) Workflow models of cloud and edge computing paradigm. (a) Edge computing paradigm. (b) Cloud computing paradigm.

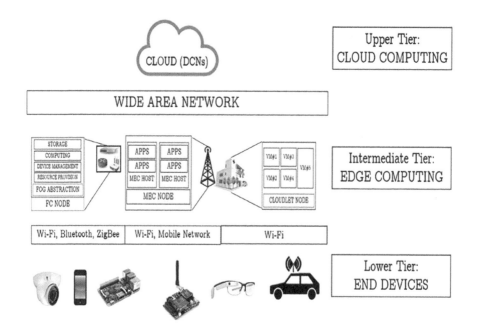

FIGURE 7.2
Edge computing example.

Edge computing doesn't compete with cloud or supercomputers but spreads the burden. More energy-efficient small/embedded devices will improve computations.

7.2.1 Push from the Cloud Services

Cloud computing is highly efficient in terms of computing; however, there must be an alternate approach to minimize data transmission bottlenecks. Edge computing fixes this. A Boeing 787 generates 5 GB of data per minute [49], which is inefficient for data processing on a satellite or the ground. Autonomous cars also need constant information processing to steer correctly. The network's bandwidth makes cloud processing impractical. Edge computing utilizes less energy than cloud owing to embedded devices [50].

7.2.2 Push from the IoT

LEDs, security cameras, and air quality sensors create and consume a lot of data as part of the IoT. Future IoT connections will include additional technological items. Bandwidth and latency make cloud processing impractical. This implies edge devices must process certain data. Edge computing may reduce cloud privacy concerns by limiting edge data. Figure 7.1b demonstrates the classic cloud computing paradigm, where raw data are created and sent to the cloud and users seek access. This structure isn't optimum since a lot of data must be exchanged, and data privacy is an issue.

7.2.2.1 Go from Data Consumer to Data Creator

A device at the edge both consumes and creates cloud data. Edge users pull data from the cloud while browsing YouTube, Facebook, and Instagram. Edge devices create data, such as collecting photos or movies. Depending on the resolution, edge users may upload a lot of data to the cloud. These increases upload bandwidth. Before uploading data to the cloud, the edge device may modify the resolution [51].

7.3 Related Work

7.3.1 Edge Computing Architecture

Edge computing designs often consist of many layers, each of which plays a critical part in the proper functioning of the corresponding paradigm [52]. Edge computing environments may be broken down into many distinct types, as shown in Figure 7.2 is themselves classified by one of several different deployment patterns.

7.3.2 Cloudlet Computing

It refers to a network of computers (small clusters) that may be accessed by users. In a nutshell, it is a little data centre that connects to wireless local area networks (WLANs) and offers computing and storage resources to end users. Three distinct layers form the foundation of cloudlet computing: component, node, and cloudlet. For application latency reduction, this is intended to have more bandwidth.

7.3.3 Fog Computing

It is a decentralised resource between the cloud and end users. It uses FCNs [53]. Switches, routers, and access points are heterogeneous FCNs. FCNs diverse environment allows devices at multiple protocol levels and non-IP-based technologies to interact. End users can't see FCNs, assuring security.

Multi-access edge computing (MEC) reduces latency in the radio access network. Mobile edge computing is an ETSI-defined network architecture near the RNC or macro base station. The edge orchestrator organises the MEC provides load and capacity statistics and gives end users location and network information.

IoT devices and sensors create a lot of data. These monitor and operate the infrastructure and exchange data across a contemporary communication network. Edge users employ IoT devices and sensors [54].

Edge computing is often complicated or diverse. Some edge computing applications can't employ this complicated design. Edge computing works well with various software systems.

7.3.4 Virtualization

When talking about an OS, computer resources, storage device, or network device, the term "virtualization" is used. When used in the context of computers, the word "virtualization" often refers to the process of creating a virtual machine that is controlled by a hypervisor, a piece of middleware that acts as an abstraction or emulation layer between the operating system and the hardware [55]. Each virtual machine operating inside the hypervisor emulator is known as a guest, while the hardware running the hypervisor is called the host. Figure 7.3 depicts the two primary varieties of hypervisors now in use:

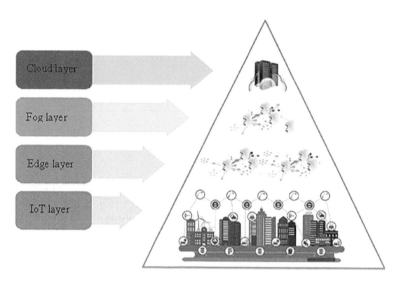

FIGURE 7.3
Overview of edge computing architectures.

Getting closer to the aims of IoT technology will be aided by developments in fields such as sensors, Big Data, embedded systems, ubiquitous computing, cloud computing, communication networks, and nanoelectronics. Figure 7.1 depicts the three distinct IoT communication models.

7.4 Models of IoT Communication

7.4.1 Device to Device Communication (D2D)

When this occurs, no additional hardware is required for the IoT nodes to exchange data with one another [56]. The hybrid protocols used in this machine-to-machine network enable for the provision of services of a certain quality. Due to the tiny size and low data rate of the sent packets, this paradigm is useful in a wide variety of contexts. From a user's standpoint, however, incompatibility between devices from various suppliers, such as that between Z-wave protocol and ZigBee protocol devices [57], is a major drawback of this paradigm. Developing ad hoc wireless networks is a prime use for this model type. Sensor networks are easy to deploy in the environment (Figure 7.4).

7.4.2 Device to Cloud Communication (D2C)

Due to the restricted computational and storage capacities of end devices, this communication paradigm has end devices acquire services like compute and storage from cloud service providers [56]. This model's main benefit is that it makes use of pre-existing components and infrastructure in the communication network. However, as the number of

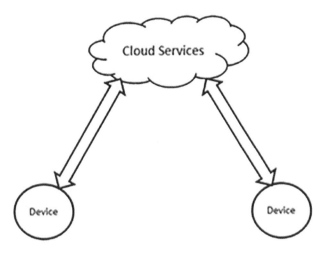

FIGURE 7.4
Device to device communications.

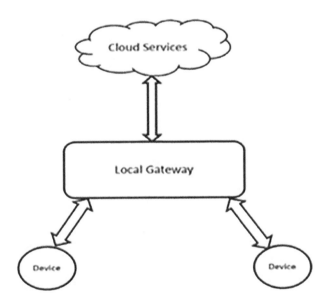

FIGURE 7.5
Devices to cloud communication (D2C).

connected devices grows, the limitations of bandwidth and other network resources become more apparent. To boost the effectiveness of such a model, network optimization is a crucial step (Figure 7.5).

7.4.3 Device to Gateway Communication (D2G)

In this configuration, the gateway is responsible for handling tasks such as data/protocol translation, security scanning, and so on. This separates the IoT nodes from the cloud provider and functions as a firewall. The gateway's role in this architecture is analogous to that of a piece of middleware, relaying information between the device layer and the application layer. The efficiency of low-power devices is much improved by this network type, and IoT security and adaptability are also greatly bolstered. When compared to other communication models, this one's advantages lie in the fact that the gateway handles security, protocol translation, and so on, on behalf of the IoT devices.

7.5 Edge Computing Architecture

The basic architecture of edge computing is shown in Figure 7.6.

7.5.1 Far End

The front end is made up of the IoT nodes that are physically located in the closest proximity to the sensing environment. To improve the quality of service in real-time applications, front-end devices may give a more comprehensive picture of the environment being sensed. Due to their inherent limitations, front-end devices must pass most service requests up the stack.

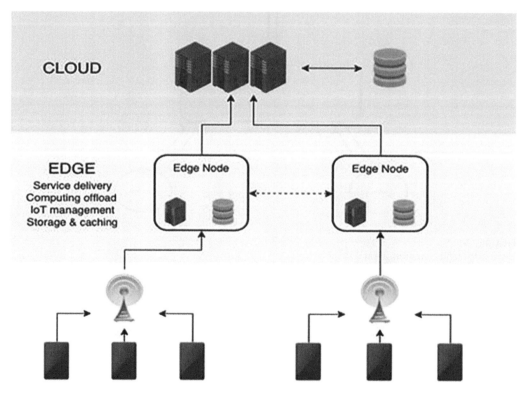

FIGURE 7.6
Traditional architecture of edge computing.

7.5.2 Near End

Close to the front line of devices are the near end servers, which have additional resources, such processor power, storage space, and so on. We refer to them as "edge servers" in the industry. Services like as real-time computing, data storage, and retrieval, and edge offloading may all be provided by edge servers located at the network's periphery (Figure 7.7).

7.6 Cloud Architecture Based on IoT

Multiple components, including sensors, gateways, RFID, and others, are embedded to create a smart network of interconnected objects [11]. In this example, shown in Figure 7.8, we see a basic cloud setup for the IoT. Perception layer data comes from IoT gadgets and human-worn sensors. Internet gateways provide access to data at the network layer. The data are prepared for analysis and storage by being cleaned and processed at the edge computing layer. Machine learning algorithms of varying sophistication were deployed to the cloud for further data analysis and forecasting. IoT proponents say their product will improve and simplify people's lives by allowing them to make more informed decisions or by reducing stress, routine tasks, and interpersonal interaction [11] (Figure 7.9).

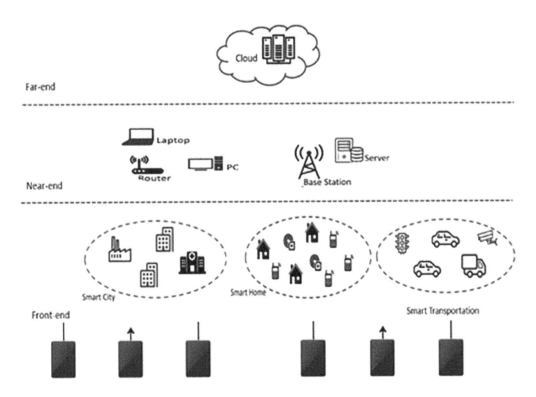

FIGURE 7.7
Basic IoT cloud architecture.

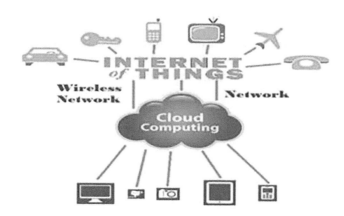

FIGURE 7.8
IoT cloud architecture.

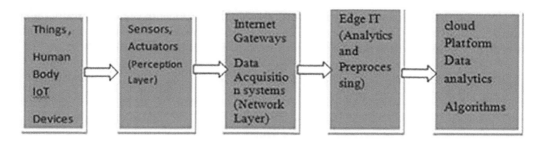

FIGURE 7.9
Basic IoT cloud architecture.

7.6.1 IoT Applications in Detail

There is a huge demand for IoT-enabled systems for easy living in each sector. A couple of the fields are listed below [19].

7.6.1.1 Smart Cities

To harness the information generated by your neighbourhood and city and transform it into a "smart city." Intelligent Highways with climate-specific warning notices, and diversions, and unforeseen events like accidents or jams are all a part of the picture, as is the monitoring of parking space availability, the calculation of the energy radiated by cellular stations and Wi-Fi routers, monitoring at the vehicle and pedestrian level to improve driving and walking paths, and so on.

7.6.1.2 Smart Security

Including the detection of gas leaks and levels in industrial settings, chemical plant settings, and mines, as well as the identification and tracking of persons in restricted and off-limits regions.

7.6.1.3 Smart Medical Field

This entails a wide range of services, from aid for the elderly and handicapped to the tracking and monitoring of antibiotic, vaccine, and organic component storage freezers to the monitoring of patients in healthcare facilities and the old's own homes.

7.6.1.4 Intelligent Agriculture

Monitoring soil moisture and vineyard trunk diameter to manage grape sugar and grapevine health, regulating microclimate conditions to promote fruit and vegetable output and quality, and researching field weather conditions to anticipate ice formation, rainfall, drought, snow, or wind.

7.6.1.5 Smart Industrial Control

Autodiagnosis and system management, oxygen, and dangerous gas monitoring in chemical facilities to safeguard personnel and goods, industrial temperature monitoring [58].

7.6.1.6 Smart Entertainment and Media

IoT delivers high communication between people by exchanging media over the cloud [59].

7.6.1.7 Smart Legal System

IoT introduces improved analytics, superior facts, and quicker processes to judicial systems, boosting strategies, removing immoderate procedures, handling corruption, minimising expenses, and enhancing pride.

7.7 Benefits of the Internet of Things

Due to limited processing power and storage, IoT faces performance, security, privacy, and reliability challenges. Integrating IoT with cloud computing solves most problems.

7.7.1 Communication

Cloud-based IoT emphasizes application and data exchange. IoT can transmit ubiquitous applications and automate data distribution and collection to reduce costs. Using built-in apps and customised portals, the cloud can connect, manage, and track anything.

7.7.2 Storage

IoT includes billions of devices, information sources, and semi-structured or unstructured data. Cloud storage is one of the most cost-effective and acceptable alternatives for IoT data.

7.7.3 Processing Capabilities

IoT devices have limited processing capabilities, preventing on-site data processing. Instead, high-capability nodes aggregate and analyse acquired data. Cloud offers limitless virtual processing and on-demand use.

7.7.4 New Abilities

IoT devices, protocols, and technologies are heterogeneous. Reliability, scalability, interoperability, security, availability, and efficiency might be difficult. It is easy to use and has cheap implementation costs.

7.8 Advantages of IoT and Cloud Computing Integration

The combination of cloud and IoT systems has various advantages. Several advantages are described as follows.

7.8.1 Analysis

Large amounts of unstructured sensor data are gathered on the cloud platform, and aggregated sensor networks are collected using the cloud computing prototype. This integration allows for the investigation of this knowledge.

7.8.2 Scalability

If the firm needs to extend its resources, it utilises any more cloud merchant services at no cost. This is referred to as the scalability of a sensor cloud.

7.8.3 Visualization

The sensor's cloud architecture allows for innovative data collection and retrieval. The collaboration sensor cloud lets retailers share sensor data, linking physical sensor networks. Improving data storage and processing-allocating storage and processing resources, and delivering a large-data application. Dynamic service processing lets sensor clouds access data from anywhere, anytime.

7.8.4 Flexibility

It enables the user to extend the prior calculation procedure. It enables us to store and distribute sensor data in a flexible setting.

7.8.5 Fast Reaction Time

Wireless sensor network (WSN) concatenation and cloud computing give a quick response time to the user. As a result, it is classified as a real-time application.

7.8.6 Automation

Automation is important in cloud computing for sensors. It also lengthens the transmission time for critical revisions.

7.8.7 Multitenancy

This is a feature that distributes services to several users while also sharing cloud resources for sensors. It also makes sensor data accessible from anywhere and at any time.

7.9 Future Work

Without a doubt, this study may serve as a foundation for future work addressing the difficulties that arise when two well-established technologies are combined. Growth in the IoT is meteoric, yet many businesses still struggle with how to ensure their IoT projects and deployments are safe. Making certain that devices and services have trustworthy identities that may communicate inside safe ecosystems is an essential part of IoT security. The complicated nature of these settings needs more sophisticated authentication methods than simple certificates can provide. When businesses embrace a strong managed PKI solution, they can offer their devices to satisfy these criteria more securely and affordably than they could on their own. By using Oracle Cloud Infrastructure's multi-cloud architecture, you can maximise both the efficiency and economy of your cloud-based resources.

7.10 Conclusion

Cloud computing and the IoT are discussed in this article, along with the many ways in which they may be combined, with regard to healthcare specifically. As a result of virtualization and cloud computing, users may now access and use the sensors of several wireless sensor networks. In order for the cloud to provide sensor-as-a-service to its end customers, virtualization makes it much easier to build virtual sensor networks employing a wide range of physical sensors. This study concludes that merging cloud and sensor networks is beneficial for their respective users. Real-time monitoring in the healthcare sector is greatly facilitated by the sensor cloud, paving the door for improved medical services for final customers. Therefore, this kind of integration is a must in the 21st century. Important future standards for this technology include energy efficiency, security, service quality, user usability, real-time updates, data processing, and graphics or warnings, all of which will be greatly aided by the usage of several IoT cloud platforms and medical sensors.

References

1. Cisco. Cisco annual internet report (2018–2023) White Paper. *White Paper*, 2020.
2. Cisco. Global cloud index: Forecast and methodology, 2014–2019. *White Paper*, 2014.
3. *Cisco Edge-to-Enterprise IoT Analytics for Electric Utilities Solution Overview.* URL: https://www.cisco.com/c/en/us/solutions/collateral/data-center-virtualization/big-data/solution-overview-c22–740248.html.
4. Aazam, M., Zeadally, S., Harras, K.A. Fog computing architecture, evaluation, and future research directions. *IEEE Commun. Mag.*, 2018, 56, 46–52.
5. Sarkar, S., Chatterjee, S., Misra, S. Assessment of the suitability of fog computing in the context of internet of things. *IEEE Trans. Cloud Comput.*, 2015, 6, 46–59.
6. Kishor, K. Communication-efficient federated learning. In: Yadav S.P., Bhati B.S., Mahato D.P., Kumar S. (eds) *Federated Learning for IoT Applications. EAI/Springer Innovations in Communication and Computing.* Springer, Cham, 2022. https://doi.org/10.1007/978-3-030-85559-8_9
7. Botta, A., De Donato, W., Persico, V., Pescapé, A. Integration of cloud computing and internet of things: A survey. *Future Gener. Comput. Syst.*, 2016, 56, 684–700.
8. Babu, S.M., Lakshmi, A.J., Rao, B.T. A study on cloud based Internet of Things: CloudIoT. In *Proceedings of the 2015 Global Conference on Communication Technologies (GCCT), Thuckalay, India,* 23–24 April 2015, pp. 60–65.
9. Yang, Z., Zhou, Q., Lei, L., Zheng, K., Xiang, W. An IoT-cloud based wearable ECG monitoring system for smart healthcare. *J. Med. Syst.*, 2016, 40, 286.
10. Petrolo, R., Loscri, V., Mitton, N. Towards a smart city based on cloud of things, a survey on the smart city vision and paradigms. *Trans. Emerg. Telecommun. Technol.*, 2017, 28, e2931.
11. Chen, N., Chen, Y., You, Y., Ling, H., Liang, P., Zimmermann, R. Dynamic urban surveillance video stream processing using fog computing. In *Proceedings of the 2016 IEEE Second International Conference on Multimedia Big Data (BigMM), Taipei, Taiwan,* 20–22 April 2016, pp. 105–112.
12. Kishor, K. Personalized Federated Learning. In: Yadav S.P., Bhati B.S., Mahato D.P., Kumar S. (eds) *Federated Learning for IoT Applications. EAI/Springer Innovations in Communication and Computing.* Springer, Cham, 2022. https://doi.org/10.1007/978-3-030-85559-8_3
13. Hossain, M.S., Muhammad, G. Cloud-assisted industrial internet of things (IIoT) – Enabled framework for health monitoring. *Comput. Netw.*, 2016, 101, 192–202.
14. J. Lin, W. Yu, N. Zhang, X. Yang, H. Zhang, W. Zhao, A survey on Internet of Things: Architecture, enabling technologies, security, and privacy, and applications, *IEEE Internet Things J.*, 2017, 4(5), 1125–1142.
15. J. A. Stankovic, Research directions for the Internet of Things, *IEEE Internet Things J.*, 2014, 1(1), 3–9.
16. J. Wu, W. Zhao, Design and realization of internet: From net of things to Internet of Things, *ACM Trans. Cyber-Phys. Syst.*, 2016, 1(1), 2:1–2:12. [Online]. Available: http://doi.acm.org/10.1145/2872332.
17. J. Lin, W. Yu, X. Yang, Q. Yang, X. Fu, W. Zhao, A real-time enroute route guidance decision scheme for transportation-based cyberphysical systems, *IEEE Trans. Veh. Technol.*, 2017, 66(3), 2551–2566.
18. N. Mohamed, J. Al-Jaroodi, I. Jawhar, S. Lazarova-Molnar, S. Mahmoud, SmartCityWare: A service-oriented middleware for cloud and fog enabled smart city services, *IEEE Access*, 2017, 5, 17576–17588.
19. S. Mallapuram, N. Ngwum, F. Yuan, C. Lu, Yu, Smart city: The state of the art, datasets, and evaluation platforms, *Proc. IEEE/ACIS 16th Int. Conf. Comput. Inf. Sci.*, May 2017, 447–452.
20. M. D. Cia et al., Using smart city data in 5G self-organizing networks, *IEEE Internet Things J.*, April 2018, 5(2), 645–654, DOI: 10.1109/JIOT.2017.2752761.
21. Y. Yan, Y. Qian, H. Sharif, D. Tipper, A survey on cybersecurity for smart grid communications, *IEEE Commun. Surveys Tuts.*, 2012, 14(4), 998–1010.

22. J. Lin, W. Yu, X. Yang, Towards multistep electricity prices in smart grid electricity markets, *IEEE Trans. Parallel Distrib. Syst.*, 2016, 27(1), 286–302.

23. L. Catarinucci et al., An IoT-aware architecture for smart healthcare systems, In *IEEE Internet of Things Journal*, vol. 2, no. 6, pp. 515–526, 2015. DOI: 10.1109/JIOT.2015.2417684.

24. Mell, P., Grance, T. *The NIST Definition of Cloud Computing*, NIST: Gaithersburg, MD, 2011.

25. Chen, S.Y., Lai, C.F., Huang, Y.M., Jeng, Y.L. Intelligent home-appliance recognition over IoT cloud network. In *Proceedings of the 2013 9th International Wireless Communications and Mobile Computing Conference (IWCMC), Sardinia, Italy*, 1–5 July 2013, pp. 639–643.

26. https://www.patecco.com/en/blog/what-are-the-benefits-of-integration-are-between-cloud-computing-and-internet-of-things.

27. Lawton, G. Developing software online with platform-as-a-service technology. *Computer*, 2008, 41, 13–15.

28. Kishor, K., Pandey, D. Study and development of efficient air quality prediction system embedded with machine learning and IoT. In D Gupta et al. (eds), *Proceeding International Conference on Innovative Computing and Communications. Lecture Notes in Networks and Systems*, vol. 471, Springer, Singapore, https://doi.org/10.1007/978-981-19-2535-1.

29. Atlam, H.F., Alenezi, A., Alharthi, A., Walters, R.J., Wills, G.B. Integration of cloud computing with internet of things: Challenges and open issues. In *Proceedings of the 2017 IEEE International Conference on Internet of Things (iThings) and IEEE Green Computing and Communications (GreenCom) and IEEE Cyber, Physical and Social Computing (CPSCom) and IEEE Smart Data (SmartData), Exeter, UK*, 21–23 June 2017, pp. 670–675.

30. Mitton, N., Papavassiliou, S., Puliafito, A., Trivedi, K.S. Combining Cloud and sensors in a smart city environment. *EURASIP J. Wirel. Commun. Netw.*, 2012, 2012, 247.

31. Jula, A., Sundararajan, E., Othman, Z. Cloud computing service composition: A systematic literature review. *Expert Syst. Appl.*, 2014, 41, 3809–3824.

32. Lawton, G. Developing software online with platform-as-a-service technology. *Computer*, 2008, 41, 13–15.

33. Manvi, S.S., Shyam, G.K. Resource management for Infrastructure as a Service (IaaS) in cloud computing: A survey. *J. Netw. Comput. Appl.*, 2014, 41, 424–440.

34. Atlam, H.F., Alenezi, A., Alharthi, A., Walters, R.J., Wills, G.B. Integration of cloud computing with internet of things: Challenges and open issues. In *Proceedings of the 2017 IEEE International Conference on Internet of Things (iThings) and IEEE Green Computing and Communications (GreenCom) and IEEE Cyber, Physical and Social Computing (CPSCom) and IEEE Smart Data (SmartData), Exeter, UK*, 21–23 June 2017, pp. 670–675.

35. Doukas, C., Maglogiannis, I. Bringing IoT and cloud computing towards pervasive healthcare. In *Proceedings of the 2012 Sixth International Conference on Innovative Mobile and Internet Services in Ubiquitous Computing, Palermo, Italy*, 4–6 July 2012, pp. 922–926.

36. Taherkordi, A., Eliassen, F. Scalable modeling of cloud-based IoT services for smart cities. In *Proceedings of the 2016 IEEE International Conference on Pervasive Computing and Communication Workshops (PerCom Workshops), Sydney, Australia*, 14–18 March 2016, pp. 1–6.

37. Belgaum, M.R., Soomro, S., Alansari, Z., Musa, S., Alam, M., Su'ud, M.M. Challenges: Bridge between cloud and IoT. In *Proceedings of the 2017 4th IEEE International Conference on Engineering Technologies and Applied Sciences (ICETAS), Salmabad, Bahrain*, 29 November–1 December 2017, pp. 1–5.

38. Li, F., Vögler, M., Claeßens, M., Dustdar, S. Efficient and scalable IoT service delivery on cloud. In *Proceedings of the 2013 IEEE Sixth International Conference on Cloud Computing, Santa Clara, CA, USA*, 28 June–3 July 2013, pp. 740–747.

39. Aburukba, R.O., AliKarrar, M., Landolsi, T., El-Fakih, K. Scheduling Internet of Things requests to minimize latency in hybrid Fog–Cloud computing. *Future Gener. Comput. Syst.*, 2020, 111, 539–551.

40. Breivold, H.P., Sandström, K. Internet of things for industrial automation–challenges and technical solutions. In *Proceedings of the 2015 IEEE International Conference on Data Science and Data Intensive Systems, Sydney, Australia*, 11–13 December 2015, pp. 532–539.

41. Singh, D., Tripathi, G., Jara, A.J. A survey of Internet-of-Things: Future vision, architecture, challenges and services. In *Proceedings of the 2014 IEEE World Forum on Internet of Things (WF-IoT), Seoul, Korea,* 6–8 March 2014, pp. 287–292.

42. Kishor, K., Nand, P., Agarwal, P. Secure and efficient subnet routing protocol for MANET, *Indian J. Public Health,* 2018, 9(12), 200. DOI: 10.5958/0976-5506.2018.01830.2.

43. Shi, W., Cao, J., Zhang, Q., Li, Y., Xu, L. Edge computing: Vision and challenges. *IEEE Internet Things J.,* 2016, 3, 637–646.

44. Gazis, V., Goertz, M., Huber, M., Leonardi, A., Mathioudakis, K., Wiesmaier, A., Zeiger, F. Short paper: IoT: Challenges, projects, architectures. In *Proceedings of the 2015 18th International Conference on Intelligence in Next Generation Networks, Paris, France,* 17–19 February 2015, pp. 145–147.

45. Chen, M., Li, W., Hao, Y., Qian, Y., Humar, I. Edge cognitive computing based smart healthcare system. *Future Gener. Comput. Syst.,* 2018, 86, 403–411.

46. Yi, S., Qin, Z., Li, Q. Security and privacy issues of fog computing: A survey. In *Proceedings of the International Conference on Wireless Algorithms, Systems, and Applications, Qufu, China,* 10–12 August 2015, pp. 685–695.

47. Kishor, K., Nand, P., Agarwal, P. Notice of retraction design adaptive subnetting hybrid gateway MANET protocol on the basis of dynamic TTL value adjustment. *Aptikom J. Comput. Sci. Inf. Technol.,* 2018, 3(2), 59–65. https://doi.org/10.11591/APTIKOM.J.CSIT.115.

48. Kishor, K., Saxena, S., Yadav, S., Yadav, S., Study and development of air monitoring and purification system, *Vivechan Int. J. Res.,* 2019, 10, 2, ISSN 0976-8211.

49. J. Cao, Q. Zhang, W. Shi. *Edge Computing: A Primer.* Springer, 2018.

50. K. Dolui, S. K. Datta. Comparison of edge computing implementations: Fog computing, cloudlet and mobile edge computing. In *2017 Global Internet of Things Summit (GIoTS),* 1–6. IEEE, 2017.

51. S. Tuli, R. Mahmud, S. Tuli, R. Buyya. Fogbus: A blockchain-based lightweight framework for edge and fog computing. *J. Syst. Softw.,* 2019, 154, 22–36.

52. Mao, Y., You, C., Zhang, J., Huang, K., Letaief, K. Mobile edge computing: Survey and research outlook, *arXiv:1701.01090,* 2017.

53. A. Al-Dulaimy, Y. Sharma, M.G. Khan, J. Taheri. Introduction to edge computing. In *Edge Computing: Models, Technologies and Applications,* 3–25, 2020.

54. F. Wortmann, K. Flüchter, Internet of Things, *Bus. Inf. Syst. Eng.,* 2015, 57(3), 221–224.

55. Sharma, V., Tiwari, R. *Int. J. Sci. Eng. Technol. Res.,* 2016, 5(2), 472–476.

56. A. Al-Fuqaha, M. Guizani, M. Mohammadi, M. Aledhari, M. Ayyash, Internet of Things: A survey on enabling technologies, protocols, and applications, *IEEE Commun. Surveys Tuts.,* 2015, 17(4), 2347–2376.

57. https://www.iotworldtoday.com/ 2016/12/07/11-innovative-iot-use-cases/.

58. Reddy, M.T., Mohan, R.K. Applications of IoT: A Study, Special Issue, *Int. J. Trend Res. Dev.,* 2017, 86–87.

59. Dawood, M.S., Margaret, J., Devika, R. *Int. J. Adv. Res. Comput. Eng. Technol.,* 2018, 7(12), 841–845.

8

Cloud-Based License Plate Recognition for Smart City Using Deep Learning

Abhilasha Singh

SRM Institute of Science and Technology

Shivani Agarwal

Ajay Kumar Garg Engineering College

CONTENTS

DOI: 10.1201/9781003213895-8

8.1 Introduction

In today's world, an increasing number of cars and a lack of space for vehicle movement are global concerns for traffic management [1]. The latest advancements in intelligent transportation systems and graphical processing units have prompted significant consideration being given to automatic vehicle license plate recognition (AVLPR) in some research areas. In this current period of innovations and expansion of smart urban areas, AVLPR is an emerging and vital computer vision elucidation in traffic management and vehicle identification. AVLPR may also utilize wireless sensor networks technologies. Different areas where AVLPR can be useful are vehicle recognition, license number expiration date detection, parking management, ticketless parking fee management, highway toll collection, security management of unmanned parking spaces, car theft prevention, speeding control, and traffic safety administration. Presently, in smart cities, installation of cameras is being done at different places to track the movement of vehicles [2].

AVLPR has turned out to be an incredibly significant tool by providing help in the monitoring and organization of vehicles [3]. The vehicles can be recognized using number plates without utilizing any additional data. With regard to security, automatic vehicle number plate recognition systems can serve as a tracking for the security people on duty at the designated places. With regard to safety and legal enforcement, automatic vehicle number plate recognition frameworks play a crucial part in border surveillance, physical intrusion, and protection [4–6].

Unfortunately, recognition of number plates is dreary task, reason being the different layout of different plates namely plate size, character size, plate texture background, changing illumination depending upon the surroundings, speed of the moving vehicle, and distance between the vehicle and camera while acquiring the image. Development of a perfect AVNPR system is a challenging job, primarily when vehicle is located or moving in an open environment due to changing illumination circumstances while image acquiring [7]. Consequently, numerous techniques can be implemented with some constraints restricted (continuous light, limited speed of vehicle and stationary surroundings) [8].

Generally, an automatic vehicle number plate recognition system consists of five steps: image acquisition, detection of number plate, pre-processing, character segmentation, and character identification (Figure 8.1). More accuracy is imperative in initial phase because accuracy and efficiency of the entire system is dependent on it [31]. The system acquires images through the camera and then employs an OCR to detect and recognize the number plate of vehicles parked in the designated place as well the moving ones. When a vehicle is spotted, AVNPR uses an algorithm to find the number plate area. Acquired image is pre-processed and OCR technique is utilized to extract the numbers and character in the number plate. Images and data acquired through such systems can be huge, and thus, this information can be stored on a cloud which can be further utilized for manifold purposes like by transport department, extraction of details about theft or for legal issues related to documentation [9].

Many researchers proposed different approaches to identify and extract the number plates like window scheme, arithmetic morphology, and edge prediction model and line

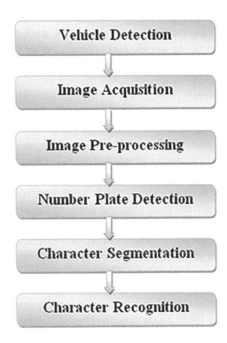

FIGURE 8.1
Basic architecture of automatic vehicle license plate recognition system.

sensitive filters [10]. These approaches are although able to locate and recognize the number plate of the vehicles but with certain restrictions like imposed conditions of illumination in environment, more computation time, and versatility of the system to work in varying conditions [2]. To increase efficiency and accuracy, numerous number plate recognition systems have been put forward using various intelligent computational techniques. Number plate is a standard way of recognizing any vehicle. In recent times, convolutional neural networks (CNN) is being used in the area of image processing and computer vision and are showing tremendous results [11]. This is the reason that CNN has developed into extremely admirable and most frequently used for such applications. In detail, CNN is discussed in further sections [8,12].

This main contribution of the chapter is to propose a model using deep learning technique, which is capable of detecting and recognizing number plates of vehicles in India. Even though number of approaches has been out forward in research till date, deep learning and CNN are drawing remarkable attention of researchers these days in the field of computer vision and pattern recognition. The remainder of the paper is organized as follows: Section 8.2 presents related technologies. Section 8.3 presents literature review, Section 8.4 presents the proposed model/system, and Section 8.5 concludes the work.

8.1.1 Related Technologies

8.1.1.1 Deep Learning

Deep learning is a subset of machine learning (ML), which is explicitly based on artificial neural networks (ANN), more specifically CNN [13,14]. Deep learning models actually mimic human brain. Different types of architectures are utilized in deep learning like recurrent neural networks, deep neural networks, CNN, and deep belief networks. These organizations have been effectively applied in taking care of the issues of medical image analysis, bioinformatics, speech recognition, natural language processing, gaming, and computer vision [15]. Many other areas are also there where deep learning is proactively applied [16,17]. The deep learning demands immense handling power and humongous information, which is by and large effectively accessible nowadays.

Artificial intelligence is doing stupendous advancements in defeating the barriers amid the capabilities of humans and machines. Researchers have worked upon a variety of branches of the field for getting astounding outcomes. One of the most important and massively researched areas is of computer vision [18,19].

The idea behind this work is to empower machines to perceive the world in the similar manner as humans do. Along with this, making them to analyze and utilize the information perceived for number of regular jobs like image and video recognition, image analysis and classification, media recreation, recommendation systems, natural language processing, and so on. The evolution in computer vision with deep learning has been expanded and culminated with time, especially using CNN [20].

A CNN is a deep learning algorithm, which takes input an image, allots importance (learnable loads and inclinations) to different objects/components of the image, and also provides the option to divide them from one another [21]. The preprocessing required on an image in CNN is likely to be lesser as compared to the other classification algorithms. Primitive techniques filters are hand-designed, on the other hand, with sufficient training, CNNs can gain proficiency better than these filters [22]. Fundamental work process of CNN is displayed in Figure 8.2.

ConvNet design closely reflects the human brain's neuron network layout and was driven by the visual cortex. Individual neurons react to enhancements only in the receptive field. Cross-over fields fill the whole visual area [23].

A ConvNet can effectively catch the spatial and temporal conditions in a picture through the utilization of applicable filters. The engineering plays out a superior fitting to the image dataset because of the decrease in the quantity of boundaries included and reusability of loads. As such, the organization can be prepared to comprehend the refinement of the image better.

8.1.1.2 Cloud Computing

Enormous image and text data generated by the proposed system needs sufficiently large space to get stored and retrieved for future usage. Cloud computing can be seen as quite

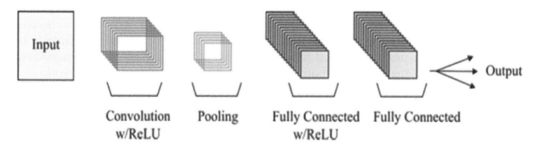

FIGURE 8.2
Work flow of convolutional network.

possibly the most feasible innovation for taking care of the big data and giving the framework as services and these services ought to be continuous. This computing is one of the practical procedures for capacity and examination of big data. The cloud helps in processing and analyzing data faster, leading to insights that can improve the product or service.

8.1.2 Literature Review

In this paper, [24] proposed a system for designing the license plate recognition system by using deep CNN. It is proposed for detecting the character, recognize plates, and segment the characters of that plate. It takes the initiative for controlling the traffic and toll management in smart cities. In this paper, they start with preprocessing of license plate of a vehicle; for this processing, they use gray scale image of the number plate as an input and then detect the edges of that plate. After takes the input sharp the image and apply this image to the first layer to the CNN. In this paper, it uses nine layers of convolution neural network for text identification and classifies it by using ConvNet. Contribution for development this architecture is the production of CNN model by defining the feature selection and filtering for identification of license or nonlicense plate. It used heuristic technique for the detection of image based on CNN technique. For outliers of image, it used linear filtering and symmetric kernel. By using this technique, it detected the boundaries of the image. For this image analysis and enhancing the image, it used the horizontal and vertical clipping for improving the quality of the system. In this paper, the experimental results define the accuracy of the recognition of the plate that is completely different with the old recognition system. It used Relu activation function and SoftMax regression for improving the accuracy. The limitation of this paper is unrecognized or misdetection of images [25].

In Paper [26], the authors focused on intelligent systems for recognizing the plate detection using convolution neural network method. Intelligent systems are used to solve the problem of rising vehicles on the road, so some problems are raised to heavy traffic such as rule of traffic violated, undefined number of accidents, and number of traffic crimes. So Intelligent system plays an important role in finding the number plate recognition from cloud by using deep learning technique. In this paper, we focused on the perceiving and identify the numbers from the number plate in any language that is perceived from cloud. To identify each number from number plate, we trained the network by using ML system. They followed the several steps are preprocessing, find the regions, resolution techniques, apply segmentation on number plate for character identification and extract each feature of that plate. In pre-processing, first portion that we extract from image of the vehicle by matching of template and it consist of three activities that is convert the image from low to high resolution. Then it divides in to number of segments and extract the alphabets and numbers by using Convolution neural network. The pattern matching method used to find the region from the image of the vehicle and matched from the target and find out the accuracy in similarity. For increasing the accuracy use the super resolution technique for betterment of the image resolution and higher the accuracy.

In Paper [27], LPR system is a big achievement for controlling traffic, toll management and scrutiny in border. Entire system of plate recognition is divided in to number of parameters that includes data procurement, data enhancement, analyzing of data from the cloud with feature extraction related with ML approaches. There are many approaches of ML those are used for character segmentation like as neural network, support vector machine, PCA (Principal component analysis) and Random Forest. The suggested solution has two parts: a cloud-based training dataset for plate recognition and testing data for license plate verification. Acquire data using varied, high-quality camera pictures. This document includes photographs of indoor and outdoor parking, and vehicles on the road in Dhaka. The quality of licensed plate photos is the main reason. After picture capture and data preprocessing, it split the image into 32*32 pixels for post processing. In this paper, use the convolution neural network for trained the data and enhance the quality of the model that is capable to perform the better image recognition not only 2d, 3d also. The proposed models use the Relu model for deal the problem of gradient descent problem and train the network for minimizing the error and improve the quality of the model. The experimental approach of this paper, it uses 1750 training data sample from the pool and 350 as testing data sets and it uses 16 different classes for data preparation with the characterization from 0 to 9. That is observed the Bangla licensed plates for better quality and performance.

In this paper [28] Recognition of the license plate system is the way of extracting the image and identified the numbers from that plate. It requires the first step of pre-processing so we have to normalize that image, scale that image for improvement and process data by using techniques named as neural network and support vector machine using cloud computing network. These images are apprehension by the high impact cameras and scale that picture in a large scale. For improving the success rate of the image some edge detection algorithms are used purposely. Perceived images are putted in to the system named as convolution neural network and Support Vector Machine used as classifier for these images. The success rate by using this classifier is very high. In this paper, Perceive the image then convert this image in to plain text that is uploaded in to cloud then check the identification of the numbers of the plate then take the decision on that it is same that exist in cloud or it is new or there is any type of fraud. So, these types of activities identified with these images. Train the network of car licensed plate by using Convolution neural network and first learn the network to perform the edge rectification of these licensed plate database and then use multiclass SVM for train the network. Use the Combination of CNN-SVM classifier by using cameras of self-driving cars. That trained database verified with existing database and find whether it is driven individual is better or hazardous. This process is repeated till the entire database is completed.

In Paper [29], in the current scenario the technological development in all the fields increased day by day that means demand of technology in the market is high. By seeking this environment and easier work of human and betterment in the technology of controlling traffic, toll management, Design the system name as Anti vehicle theft using number plate recognition that is betterment for the user. The entire database taken from cloud and design the efficient system to identification of number plates that is create the boundary from the theft of the vehicle. The aim of this paper is to design a system that provides the help to the user and implemented on public places, toll plazas. That not only better for users but also provide help for police The system divides in to four major parts, first is automobile recognition for this in this use moving object detection, second is extract the number from that number plate by using optical character recognition and then compare with the existing cloud database. Each and every detail of vehicle and the user easily fetched from cloud server. In this paper the laser camera and high security registration plate is used for better recognition of the number plate. Cloud service provider is used for provide the API's and it is installed in the computer. By using this system check the registration details and finds it is fake or actual. If it is fake and the laser code is not matched then pop up the alert message to the RTO.

In this paper [30], proposed a new concept of vehicle license plate recognition, this is used image segmentation technique with sliding window concept in character recognition. Collect the number of images from the camera, one thing is very important at the time of image clicking it is angle and distance from the vehicle. In this paper, for experimental setup taking 1334 images of different backgrounds. These images are properly segmented with 1287 segments over 1334 images so it is approximated 96.5% images are segmented. After this process use the character recognition system with two-layer probabilistic neural network that is formulated as 108–180–36 and with respect to this performance of the system is 89.1%. In this paper, the network is trained by using probabilistic neural network for identification of alphanumeric characters from the license plates. In this the license plate visualization as the text of the images in irregular views. In this one very famed technique is us for segmentation named as SCW. This is developed for describe the irregular images so use some statistics calculate in the form of standard deviation and mean values. The algorithm SCW was implemented with two steps: (1) There are two homocentric windows are taken of different pixels and from that create first pixel of the image and (2) calculate the statistical formations of two windows in the form of standard deviation and mean value. The paper completely divides in to three parts: (1) License plate segmentation (2) license plate processing (3) character Recognition. At the time of recognition of image, the main problem is that so images are classified properly and some images are misclassified due to some misclassifications those cases are "0" recognize as "o" and "1" recognize as "l". These character misclassification problems are varied from country to country. So, these problems create the major issue, the solution of this problem solved by a priori algorithm and some rule-based methods are also incorporated.

8.2 Proposed Model

This chapter proposes a model using deep learning technique capable of detecting and recognizing number plates of vehicles in India. Figure 8.3 shows the proposed model.

In brief, flow of the proposed model constitutes of capturing of the target vehicle through phone or camera. This image is then preprocessed using various image processing operations like flipping, cropping, color augmentation, smoothing for a clearer picture. Once a refined image is achieved, segmentation is applied to it followed by optical character recognition process. Now, these characters are passed to a CNN model for final classification through a pre-trained network.

Following part of the section discusses the model in detail.

8.2.1 Image Acquisition

First step in the model is to acquire the image. Image acquisition can be done either using mobile phone or camera installed at various places. This step is very important because the quality of the captured image plays an imperative role in locating and recognizing the number plate in subsequent steps.

8.2.2 Horizontal Flipping

Flipping means to reverse the pixels of the image horizontally or vertically. This is similar to mirror effect. For example, in horizontal flipping, pixel with coordinate (x, y) will have coordinate (width −x −1, y) in the new image.

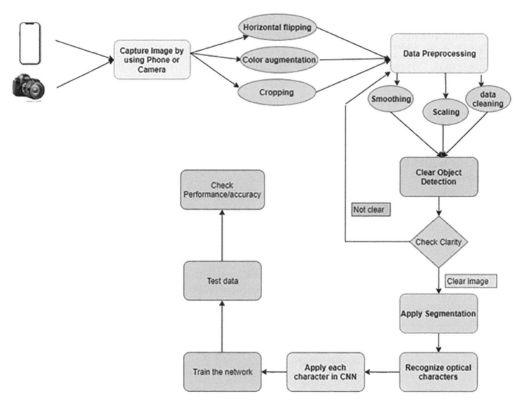

FIGURE 8.3
Proposed model.

8.2.3 Color Augmentation

Changing an image's pixel values changes its color characteristics. Color augmentation uses statistical principles to superimpose one image's colors on another. The greatest results are obtained by combining color enhancement with geometric alteration.

8.2.3.1 Brightness

Changing picture brightness may enhance colors. The original picture is darkened or lightened.

8.2.3.2 Contrast

A picture's contrast may be described as the distance between the darkest and lightest portions. Additionally, the image's contrast may be altered.

8.2.3.3 Saturation

It is the separation of colors in a picture that is called saturation.

8.2.3.4 *Hue*

The shade of a color in a picture is what is meant by the term "hue."

8.2.4 Cropping

Image Cropping is the demonstration of working on a photograph or picture by eliminating the pointless parts. The cycle typically comprises of the evacuation of a portion of the fringe region of a picture to eliminate incidental junk from the image, to work on its outlining, to change the aspect ratio, or to highlight or separate the topic from its background.

8.2.5 Data Pre-Processing

The point of pre-processing is an improvement of the image information that smothers reluctant mutilations or upgrades some picture highlights significant for additional handling. For the most part mathematical changes of pictures (for example rotation, scaling, translation) are characterized among pre-processing techniques.

8.2.5.1 *Smoothing*

Smoothing is used to reduce noise or to produce a less pixilated image. In order to get this effect, blurring is used. Using blurring as a pre-processing step for the removal of minor features, noise reduction may be achieved. Smoothing can be achieved by Linear Filters (Mean Filters) and Order Statistics (Non-linear) filters.

8.2.5.2 *Scaling*

Image scaling is the process of resizing a digital image. Scaling a photograph greater than its original proportions might make it blurry.

8.2.5.3 *Data Cleaning*

Data cleaning is the most common way of fixing or eliminating mistaken, tainted, inaccurately designed, copy, or deficient information inside a dataset. While joining numerous information sources, there are numerous open doors for information to be copied or mislabeled. In the event that information is inaccurate, results and calculations are questionable, despite the fact that they might look right. There is nobody outright method for recommending the specific strides in the data cleaning process in light of the fact that the process will change from dataset to dataset.

8.3 Segmentation

Picture segmentation reduces the complexity of a digital image to make future processing or analysis easier. Segmentation labels pixels. All pixels in the same category are labeled. Let's say a photo is needed for object recognition. Instead of the complete picture, a segmentation algorithm might feed the detector a section. This reduces inference time by preventing the detector from analyzing the whole picture.

Image Segmentation divides a digital image into groupings called image sections to enable future handling or investigation easier. Labeling pixels is segmentation. All picture components or pixels in a comparable class have a standard mark. Let's say a picture is needed for object identification. Instead of addressing the whole image, a segmentation algorithm might choose a region for the identification. This will reduce inference time by preventing the locator from processing the complete picture along these lines.

8.3.1 Segmentation Approaches

1. **Similarity approach:** This method uses pixel similarity to form a fragment based on a threshold. ML algorithms like clustering rely on this method of picture sectioning.

2. **Discontinuity approach:** This relies on picture pixel values. Line, Point, and Edge Detection use this method to produce transitional division data that may be used to segment the final picture.

8.3.2 Segmenting Images

- Sectioning on the Basis of Threshold
- Segmentation Based on the Edge
- Segmentation by Geographic Area
- Segmentation based on clustering
- Segmentation using an ANN

8.3.3 Segmentation Based on Thresholds

When it comes to separating images, one of the easiest methods is known as picture thresholding. Setting a threshold feed on the pixels of the original picture data allows for the creation of an RGB image. Edge Based Segmentation.

This category of segmentation depends with respect to edges found in an image utilizing different edge detection techniques. These edges mark image areas of discontinuity in gray levels, texture, color, and so forth. At the point when we move starting with one region then onto the next, the gray level might vary. So in the event that we can observe that irregularity, we can track down that edge. An assortment of edge detection techniques are accessible however the subsequent picture is an intermediate partition result and ought not be mistaken for the last segmented picture.

8.3.4 Segmentation Based on Location

By recursively incorporating adjacent pixels that are comparable and related to the seed pixel, we may build areas. If the gray levels in an area are uniform, we may use similarity metrics like the difference in gray levels to compare them. Connectivity is a tool we employ to keep sections of a picture from being linked together. Segmentation by clustering.

It is a technique for pixel-by-pixel segmentation of an image. This method of segmentation involves grouping together similar pixels. The Segmentation by clustering may be done in two different ways.

- Merging to Create Clusters
- Divisive clustering

8.3.5 Clustering by Merging

The pixel nearest to the cluster is assigned in this method, which follows the bottom-up technique. The agglomerative clustering method is as follows:

- Each point should be treated as a distinct cluster.
- Indefinitely, or until clustering is adequate, depending on the number of epochs.
- Combine the two groups that have the shortest distance between them (WCSS).
- Repeat the above step

8.3.6 Divisive Splitting or Clustering by Division

- In this method, we allocate the cluster-closest pixel. Agglomerative clustering algorithm.
- Create a single cluster that contains all of the points.
- Indefinitely, or until clustering is adequate, depending on the number of epochs.
- Consider dividing your data set into two groups based on their distance from one another.
- Re-enact the preceding procedure.

8.4 Segmentation Using an Artificial Neuronal Network

Segmentation methods based on neural networks have been widely used because of their signal-to-noise independence and capacity to provide findings in real time, according to a large body of research.

8.5 Optical Character Recognition

OCR turns images containing text into machine-readable text data. OCR digitises documents automatically, without human data input. Traditional OCR has three stages: picture pre-processing, character recognition, and post-processing.

Image pre-processing removes image noise and increases text-to-background contrast, improving text identification. At this phase, the OCR computer turns the document to a black and white version and then analyses it for the existence of bright and dark regions. Light parts are recognised as the backdrop, whereas dark portions are identified as characters to be processed.

Feature detection and pattern recognition methods are used to identify a single character. Pattern or feature detection methods are used to identify characters.

- Pattern recognition is a technique that uses the system's embedded fonts and formats to identify matches between the picture text and the text samples stored in the system. Fonts that are not part of the system cannot be used with this approach, which is best used with typescript.

- To identify new characters, the system uses criteria based on each character's unique characteristics. Slanted, crossing, or curving lines in the comparison sign are examples of these traits.

Most often, OCR programs with feature detection use classifiers based on ML or neural networks to process characters. Classifiers are used to compare image features with stored examples in the system and select the closest match. The feature detection algorithm is good for unusual fonts or low-quality images where the font is distorted.

Post processing: Once a symbol is identified, it is converted into a code that can be used by computer systems for further processing. We should mention that the output of any OCR and OCR-related technology/algorithm has a lot of noise and false positives. It makes it difficult to use OCR's output directly, so we have to:

- Filter out noisy outputs and false positives
- Combine recognized entities with their extracted meaning
- Check for possible mistakes and prevent output to the user if any

The system can identify OCR problems based on statistical data, such as similar letters and phrases. This step corrects defects to increase OCR output quality.

OCR using ML/CV: Computer vision tasks include OCR. Computer vision lets computers view real-world objects and distinguishes messages against complicated backdrops. Early versions of OCR required character pictures and could only function with one typeface. Modern ML methods improve text recognition accuracy for most typefaces and input data types.

Advances in ML have boosted OCR's development and applications. With appropriate training data, OCR ML may be used to any real-world identification and text transformation situation. Receipt scanning, text scanning with voice synthesis, traffic sign recognition, license plate identification, etc.

8.6 Convolutional Neural Networks

Many individuals believe OCR has been "solved" OCR doesn't need deep learning, according to related sources. Deep learning is required for better, more generic answers.

After the words have been scanned, the written or printed character is compared with the similar character stored within the predefined class, for the classification of every character. This stage uses CNN for classification of characters recognized from number plate. A CNN is a multi-layered neural network with a specific architecture to identify complex features in data. It can be applied to classify the contents of various images. The images can be provided as an input into the model. CNNs are able to classify images by extracting features, much like how the human brain searches for features to identify the objects. The CNN has set of convolutional layers and max pooling layers. The nth pooling layer is connected to fully connected layer. It carries few back propagation steps in learning phase in order minimize the loss. It finally uses some activation function to generate the output [14].

Proposed model will be trained using CNN to identify the recognized characters with training dataset and then will be tested using test dataset. Final step is to check the accuracy and efficiency of the proposed model using certain parameters which are given in the next section.

8.7 Evaluation Parameters for the Proposed Model

Most common parameter to evaluate the performance of the proposed model accuracy, definition of which is as follows:

$$\text{Accuracy} = (\text{Count of accurately classified images}/ \atop \text{Count of testing images}) * 100 \tag{8.1}$$

Few other parameters can be Precision, f1 score, recall/sensitivity etc.

8.8 Conclusion

The summarization of this work is that to solve the license car plate recognition problem that is beneficial for the traffic management, fraud analysis, toll management and security related issues. Click the automobile picture acquired by the camera, then remove the number plate and apply segmentation to identify each character. After segmentation, the CNN identifies each picture character and vehicle city type. Convolution neural network provides a huge set of features for the classification of the images with highest accuracy. This exploration used the number of techniques for better recognition and provide the highest accuracy in the work in experimental results. The main techniques those are used to solve this problem with highest accuracy those are Support vector machine and convolution neural network. These models provide the good platform for cloud-based connectivity for collecting the databases as a centralized system with high storage capacity for analysis the data in an effective way. The implementations of this system provide the help on the number of variable activities and improve the quality of work.

8.9 Future Work

License plate recognition system plays an important role in the current research for extracting the major key points like toll management, security related problems and traffic management. The operation of an automated recognition is the main motive to solve these key points that term in the aspect of software and hardware. This operation is divided in two phases: one is the license plate segmentation and the second option is the processing and character recognition. License plate recognition is the vehicle identification so that is solve the problem of surveillance. It is an important era of computing techniques of cloud. Cloud computing expended the view of computation for enhancing the storage mechanism. In this detection logic is highly applicable in self-driving cars so that send only captured images and reduce the processing cost by the cloud servers. This provides the help for load sharing and resource planning with reduced the cost of processing. Two methods named as edge computing and Fog computing are implemented to reduce the stress in cloud computing unit. For enhancing the identification process by using the SCW method for image enhancement in the binary logic format with the conjunction of Probabilistic neural network. For inspection of vehicle plate after the trained the network compare the predicted number plates with the existing number plate from the database and calculate the results by using statistical rules named as standard deviation and mean value.

References

1. V. Pandey, J.P. Patra, S. Choubey, A. Choubey, Light weighted convolutional neural network for license plate recognition. *Turkish Journal of Computer and Mathematics Education*, 12(12), 2021, 4119–4125.
2. I. V. Pustokhina, D. A. Pustokhin, J. P. C. Rodrigues, D. Gupta, A. Khanna, K. Shankar, C. Seo, G. P. Joshi, Automatic vehicle license plate recognition using optimal k-means with convolutional neural network for intelligent transportation systems. *IEEE Access*, 8, 2020, 92907–92917. https://doi.org/10.1109/ACCESS.2020.2993008.
3. N. do Vale Dalarmelina, M. A. Teixeira, R. I. Meneguette, A real-time automatic plate recognition system based on optical character recognition and wireless sensor networks for ITS. *Sensors*, 20(1), 2020, 55. https://doi.org/10.3390/s20010055.
4. A. Siti Norul Huda Sheikh, et al. Comparison of feature extractors in license plate recognition. *First Asia International Conference on Modelling & Simulation (AMS'07)*, 2007, 502–506. https://doi.org/10.1109/AMS.2007.25.
5. S. Humayun Karim, D. I. Ye Zhang, A. K. Sulehria, Vehicle number plate recognition using mathematical morphology and neural networks. *WSEAS Transactions on Computers*, 7(6), 2008, 581–590.
6. H. K. Sulehria, Y. Zhang, D. Irfan, Mathematical morphology methodology for extraction of vehicle number plates. *International Journal of Computers*, 1(3), 2007, 69–73.
7. C. T. Hsieh, Y.-S. Juan, Wavelet transform based license plate detection for cluttered scene. *WSEAS Transactions on Computers*, 4(1), 2005, 40–44.
8. M. M. Shaifur Rahman, M. Mostakim, M. S. Nasrin, M. Z. Alom, Bangla license plate recognition using convolutional neural networks (CNN). In: *2019 22nd International Conference on Computer and Information Technology (ICCIT)*, 2019, 1–6, https://doi.org/10.1109/ICCIT48885.2019.9038597.
9. K. Premaa, P. Arivubrakanb, V. Suganyac, Automatic number plate recognition using deep learning. *Turkish Journal of Computer and Mathematics Education*, 12(9), 2021, 265–267.

10. B. Yousif, M. M. Ata, N. Fawzy, M. Obaya, Toward an optimized neutrosophic k-means with genetic algorithm for automatic vehicle license plate recognition (ONKM-AVLPR). *IEEE Access*, 8, 2020, 49285–49312.

11. M. Z. Alom, M. Hasan, C., Yakopcic, T. M. Taha, Inception recurrent convolutional neural network for object recognition. *arXiv preprint arXiv:1704.07709*, 2017. https://doi.org/10.48550/arXiv.1704.07709.

12. B. Kokila, S. Pattabiraman, M. Praveena, H. Thabass, Smart system for Indian license plate detection and recognition using deep learning techniques, *International Journal of Science, Engineering and Technology*, 9(2), 2021, 1–9.

13. K. Kishor, R. Sharma, M. Chhabra, Student performance prediction using technology of machine learning. In: Sharma D.K., Peng SL., Sharma R., Zaitsev D.A. (eds) *Micro-Electronics and Telecommunication Engineering. Lecture Notes in Networks and Systems*, vol. 373. Springer, Singapore, 2022. https://doi.org/10.1007/978-981-16-8721-1_53

14. K. Kishor, Communication-efficient federated learning. In: Yadav S.P., Bhati B.S., Mahato D.P., Kumar S. (eds) *Federated Learning for IoT Applications. EAI/Springer Innovations in Communication and Computing*. Springer, Cham, 2022. https://doi.org/10.1007/978-3-030-85559-8_9.

15. J. Schmidhuber, Deep learning in neural networks: An overview. *Neural Networks*, 61, 2015, 85–117.

16. K. Kishor, Personalized federated learning. In: Yadav S.P., Bhati B.S., Mahato D.P., Kumar S. (eds), *Federated Learning for IoT Applications. EAI/Springer Innovations in Communication and Computing*. Springer, Cham, 2022. https://doi.org/10.1007/978-3-030-85559-8_3.

17. K. Kishor, D. Pandey, Study and development of efficient air quality prediction system embedded with machine learning and IoT. In: Gupta D. et al. (eds), *Proceeding International Conference on Innovative Computing and Communications. Lecture Notes in Networks and Systems*, vol. 471, Springer, Singapore, 2022. https://doi.org/10.1007/978-981-19-2535-1.

18. B. K. Rai, S. Sharma, G. Kumar, K. Kishor, Recognition of different bird category using image processing. *International Journal of Online and Biomedical Engineering (iJOE)*, 18(07), 2022, 101–114. https://doi.org/10.3991/ijoe.v18i07.29639.

19. A. Sharma, N. Jha, K. Kishor, Predict COVID-19 with chest X-ray. In: Gupta D., Polkowski Z., Khanna A., Bhattacharyya S., Castillo O. (eds) *Proceedings of Data Analytics and Management. Lecture Notes on Data Engineering and Communications Technologies*, vol. 90. Springer, Singapore, 2022. https://doi.org/10.1007/978-981-16-6289-8_16.

20. S. Gupta, S. Tyagi, K. Kishor, Study and development of self sanitizing smart elevator. In: Gupta D., Polkowski Z., Khanna A., Bhattacharyya S., Castillo O. (eds) *Proceedings of Data Analytics and Management. Lecture Notes on Data Engineering and Communications Technologies*, vol. 90. Springer, Singapore, 2022. https://doi.org/10.1007/978-981-16-6289-8_15.

21. A. Jain, Y. Sharma, K., Kishor, Financial supervision and management system using ML algorithm. *Solid State Technology*, 63(6), 2020, 18974–18982. http://solidstatetechnology.us/index.php/JSST/article/view/8080.

22. M.T. Vasumathi, M. Kamarasan, An effective pomegranate fruit classification based on CNN-LSTM deep learning models. *Indian Journal of Science and Technology*, 14(16), 2021, 1310–1319. https://doi.org/10.17485/IJST/v14i16.432.

23. S. Dwarkanath Pande, P. Pandurang Jadhav, R. Joshi, A. Dattatray Sawant, V. Muddebihalkar, S. Rathod, M. Navnath Gurav, S. Das, Digitization of handwritten Devanagari text using CNN transfer learning – A better customer service support. *Neuroscience Informatics*, 2(3), 2022. https://doi.org/10.1016/j.neuri.2021.100016.

24. R. Polis Hetty, A next-generation secure cloud-based deep learning license plate recognition for smart cities, *2016 15th IEEE International Conference on Machine Learning and Applications*, 2016.

25. B.G. Geetha, Cloud based anti vehicle theft by using number plate recognition. *International Journal of Engineering Research and General Science*, 2(2), 2014, ISSN 2091-2730.

26. Nur-A-Alam. *Intelligent System for Vehicles Number Plate Detection and Recognition Using Convolutional Neural Networks*, MDPI Technologies.

27. M.M. Shaifur Rahman, Bangla license plate recognition using convolutional neural networks (CNN), In: *2019 22nd International Conference on Computer and Information Technology (ICCIT)*, https://doi.org/10.1109/ICCIT48885.2019.9038597.
28. B. D. Dayana, Autonomous vehicular surveillance using license plate recognition over cloud computing architecture. *International Journal of Engineering and Advanced Technology (IJEAT)*, 9(1), 2019, ISSN: 2249-8958 (Online).
29. L. Wang, B. K. P. Horn, Time-to-contact control for safety and reliability of self-driving cars. *2017 International Smart Cities Conference (ISC2)*, 2017. https://doi.org/10.1109/isc2.2017.8090789.
30. C.-S. Ahn, B.-G. Lee, S.-S. Yang, S.-C. Park, Design of car license plate area detection algorithm for enhanced recognition plate. In: *2017 4th International Conference on Computer Applications and Information Processing Technology (CAIPT)*, 2017.
31. C. N. E. Anagnostopoulos, I. E. Anagnostopoulos, V. Loumos, E. Kayafas, A license plate-recognition algorithm for intelligent transportation system applications, *IEEE Transactions on Intelligent Transportation Systems*, 7(3), 2006, 377–392. https://doi.org/10.1109/TITS.2006.880641.

9

Sentimental Analysis Using Cloud Dictionary and Machine Learning Approach

Sansar Singh Chauhan, Satya Prakash Yadav,
Shashank Awashthi, and Mahaveer Singh Naruka
GL Bajaj Institute of Technology and Management

CONTENTS

9.1 Introduction

Every customer-facing sector (retail, telecom, banking, etc.) wants to know whether customers like or dislike them. Python sentiment analysis determines a text's latent sentiment. Combining machine learning and NLP does this (NLP). Sentiment analysis analyses text emotions. Sentiment analysis or opinion mining analyses human opinions, feelings, emotions, and attitudes regarding goods, services, topics, events, themes, and their attributes [1–3]. Sentiment analysis can follow public opinion and create relevant data. This knowledge may also explain and predict social dynamics (). Sentiment research helps businesses establish a strategy and get customer insight. In today's customer-focused society, understanding the consumer is crucial [4–6].

Figure 9.1 demonstrate the flow chart of the steps involved in building the sentimental analysis model using a dictionary-based approach, According to the figure first tweet is taken using scrapper as input text for data processing and the sentence is broken into the smallest unit which is word or tokens followed by removal of stop words to transform it into a list which contains words which are useful in performing sentimental analysis and finally emotion is classified using the Dictionary which contains words as key and emotion as the value of the key.

The Internet has changed how people exchange ideas. It is primarily done via blogs, forums, product review sites, social media, and other means. Millions of individuals use Facebook, Twitter, Google Plus, and others to express feelings, debate ideas, and share everyday opinions [7]. Online communities provide interactive media where customers educate and influence others. Social media produces sentiment-rich data via tweets, status updates, blog posts, comments, and reviews. Social media helps firms to advertise to customers. Internet user-generated content influences many choices. People will research a product or service online and on social media before buying it. Normal users can't read end-user-generated stuff. Automation is needed. Textual information retrieval techniques analyse, discover, and understand facts. There are factual facts, yet subjective literary elements. Sentiment Analysis includes opinions, feelings, evaluations, attitudes, and emotions (SA). Due to the profusion of online material through blogs and social media, designing new apps is tough. SA may predict product suggestions from a recommendation platform based on favourable or negative remarks. Sentiment analysis covers extraction, classification, subjective categorization, opinion summarizing, and spam identification. It examines how people feel about products, people, subjects, organizations, and services [8–9].

Figure 9.2 is the Pictorial Representation of the types of basic emotion present in the text or words in a conversation which are positive, neutral, and negative.

The three levels of sentiment categorization are Document level, Sentence level, and Aspect or feature level. The objective at the document level is to categorize the entire document into a good or bad category. Sentence-level sentiment categorization divides sentences into three classes: positive, negative, and neutral. The polarity of each word in

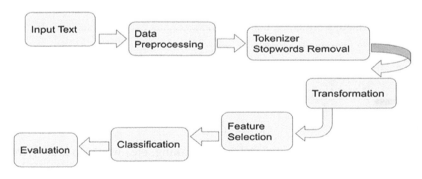

FIGURE 9.1
Flow chart of sentimental analysis.

SENTIMENTS

POSITIVE   **NEUTRAL**   **NEGATIVE**

FIGURE 9.2
Segments of sentimental analysis.

a sentence is decided first, followed by the overall mood of the statement. Before categorizing, aspect or feature-level sentiment classification pulls product characteristics from source data. Most sentiment analysis uses machine learning and dictionaries. A machine learning-based technique categorizes text using an SVM or neural network. A dictionary-based method compares opinion phrases to data to detect polarity. Give positive, negative, and objective word sentiment ratings [9].

9.2 Literature Review

There have already been a lot of studies done on sentiment analysis in the past. The most recent study in this area focuses on doing emotional analysis of any type of text, sentence, paragraph, or someone's voice, with the majority of the data coming from social media platforms such as Facebook, Twitter, and Amazon. Emotional analysis research, in particular, is focused on machine learning algorithms, to determine whether a given text encourages or opposes recognizing text divisions. In this part, you'll get an in-depth look at one of the most useful research activities: sentiment analysis. The following are some examples of research in sentiment analysis using various techniques [10].

They were the pioneers in the area of sentiment analysis. Their major goal was to categorize material based on overall sentiment rather than simply topic, for example, good or negative movie reviews. They use a movie review database to test machine learning algorithms, and the findings show that these algorithms outperform human-made techniques. They employ Nave-Bayes, maximum entropy, and Support vector machines as Machine Learning Algorithms. They also end by looking at a variety of characteristics that make sentiment categorization difficult. They reveal the root of sentiment analysis is supervised machine learning algorithms.

Proceedings of the ACL-02 Workshop on Effective Tools and Methodologies for Teaching Natural Language Processing and Computational Linguistics, vol. 1, 63–70, 2002. Loper/Bird [11].

NLTK is a collection of software modules, structured files, tutorials, problem sets, statistical algorithms, machine learning classifiers, and other tools. Natural language processing is one of NLTK's basic functions. It analyses human language data. NLTK's corpora train classifiers. Developers update outdated components, programmes become structured, and datasets provide sophisticated results.

Almatrafi, Parack, Chavan [12], According to the researcher sentiment, sentimental analysis is the process of extracting sentiment from a text unit from a specific location using Natural Language Processing (NLP) and machine learning approaches. They look at a variety of location-based sentiment analysis applications using a data source that permits data to be obtained from numerous locations easily. A script may easily access a feature of Twitter called tweet location, which allows data (tweets) from a given location to be obtained for the aim of detecting trends and patterns. The following illustration aims at providing an insight into more popular algorithms used in sentiment analysis:

9.2.1 Machine Learning Approach

Machine learning educates computers to learn from experiences like humans and animals. Machine learning algorithms "learn" data without a model. Machine learning educates computers to learn from experiences like humans and animals. Machine learning algorithms "learn" data without a model [13,14].

The sentiment analysis machine learning approach has four parts.

9.2.2 Supervised Learning

Supervised learning trains a computer system on input data labelled for a given output [15,16].

9.2.3 Decision Tree Classifier

Each node in the decision tree classifier represents an attribute test [17,18].

9.2.4 Linear Classification

A linear classifier is a model that uses a linear combination of explanatory factors to categorize a set of data points into a discrete class.

9.2.5 Support Vector Machine (SVM)

Support-vector machines are supervised learning models with associated learning methods [19].

Figure 9.3 demonstrates the different ways of using the machine learning approach for sentimental analysis.

9.3 Lexicon-Based Approach

Using a pre-prepared sentiment lexicon, the Lexicon-based approach aggregates the sentiment ratings of all the words in a text. The sentiment lexicon should contain a term's sentiment score.

Figure 9.4 demonstrates the various case used in the lexicon-based approach for sentimental analysis.

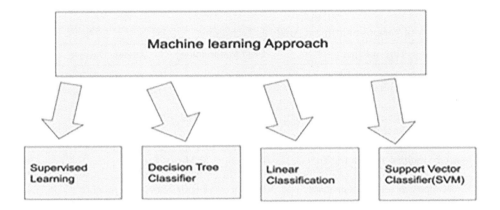

FIGURE 9.3
Flow chart of machine learning approach.

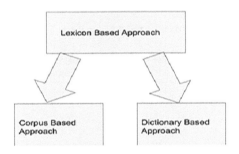

FIGURE 9.4
Flow chart of lexicon-based approach.

Corpus-based approach: The corpus-based approach to language instruction is based on genuine and authentic occurrences of language as it is spoken, written, and used by native speakers in a variety of settings.

Dictionary-based sentiment analysis measures the reader's feelings about a text. Sentiment may be good or negative but also fear, grief, rage, joy, etc.

Table 9.1 presents the various works and techniques in the field of sentiment analysis with accuracy. Referring to the table, an ML algorithm's methodology, i.e.; Naïve Bayes has been used to review the "Open Rank Hotel" in the proposed paper "A framework for Sentiment Analysis" with hotel review is shown with an accuracy of 83.5%. Many more works are also mentioned in the above table.

9.4 Methodology

9.4.1 Dictionary Based Approach

We reviewed the strategy used in performing the execution of the study and the algorithm utilized in the sentimental analysis using scrapper to extract tweets for text data. System's process flow chart is given in Figure 9.5.

TABLE 9.1

Contrasted Study of Various Sentiment Analysis Techniques

S. No	Title of Paper	Used Methodology	Review Dataset	Accuracy
1)	SVM and co-reference resolution in a feature-based approach for sentiment analysis (2017)	Resolution based on SVM and co-reference	Product review dataset for training	73.6%
2)	Sentiment analysis on twitter using neural networks (2015)	Feed-forward neural networks	Data from Twitter	74.15%
3)	Twitter sentiment analysis using python machine learning algorithms (2015)	Maximum Entropy, Naive Bayes, SVM	Data from Twitter	86.4% 73.5% 88.97%
4)	A new approach: sentiment analysis using neural networks (2018)	Neural network with convolution	Review of product data on Twitter	74.15% 64.69%
5)	Twitter corpus sentiment analysis in relation to AI assistants (2018)	(VADER) Valence aware dictionary for sentiment reasoning	Electronic product reviews	87.4%
6)	A framework for sentiment analysis with hotel review opinion mining (2018)	Naive Bayes	Opin Rank hotel reviews.	83.5%
7)	Sentiment analysis on e-commerce data at the aspect level (2018)	SVM, Naive Bayes	Review data of Amazon customer	90.423% 83.43%
8)	Sentiment analysis at the document level from news (2017)	Approaches of machine learning	Dataset from BBC News	57.7%

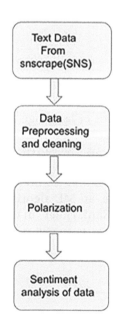

FIGURE 9.5

Methodology for sentiment analysis using NLP.

There are various steps involved in the methodology of the first proposal from the text data to the sentimental analysis of that text data. As we discussed above that Text data are taken as input from snscrape which is scrapping tool, and data are processed after breaking a big sentence into individual words or tokens and removing the stop words or unnecessary words from that list, the next step is polarization, which involves the nltk or natural language processing to give the score of the sentiment under class like pos, neg, neu, compound using Sentiment IntensityAnalyzer function, and the final step is to analyze the sentiment based on the score.

9.4.1.1 Text Data from Snscrape (SNS)

Text data are taken from Scraper for social networking services, snscrape (SNS). It scrapes user profiles, hashtags, and tweets and returns the items found, such as related postings.

9.4.2 Data Pre-Processing

The unanalyzed data are handled in preprocessing for feature extraction. It is further broken down into the following steps:

9.4.2.1 Tokenization

A phrase is broken down into words by removing white spaces, symbols, and special characters.

9.4.2.2 Stop Words Removal

Some words like article, adjective, etc., are removed using NLTK corpus library, which does not have any kind of emotion.

9.4.2.3 Case Normalization

The entire documents are converted into lower case.

9.4.3 Data Polarization

The element's sentiment polarity controls the direction of the reported emotion, whether it is positive, negative, or neutral. The main motive of sentimental analysis is to examine a body of text to determine the viewpoint communicated. We usually measure this feeling with a positive or negative polarity value. The polarity score's sign is usually used to assess whether an emotion is positive, neutral, or negative.

9.5 Machine Learning Based Approach

The methodologies utilized in the execution of the study and the Binary text Classifier algorithm that are employed in the class prediction using sentiment analysis are explained in this model. The flow chart of the approach used in this article is shown below.

The steps involve under the propose-4 in Figure 9.6 are as follows: first csv file or dataset is taken from the Kaggle, which have more than 14,000 tweets of us-airline sentiment and then huge dataset is converted and cleaned using pandas which make dataset of more than six column into two column, which are text and airline sentiment and binary text classifier algorithm is used with LSTM to predict the class.

9.5.1 Dataset: Contains

More than 14,000 tweet data samples are included in the collection, which are classified into three groups: positive, negative, or neutral (Figure 9.7).

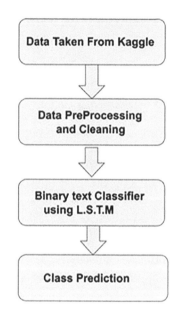

FIGURE 9.6
Methodology for sentiment analysis using binary text classifier.

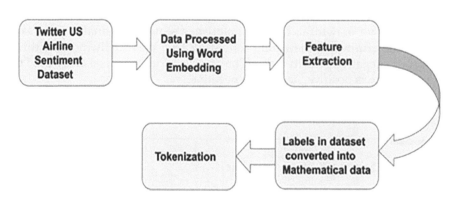

FIGURE 9.7
Flow chart of data pre-processing and cleaning.

Utilized the US Airline Twitter Dataset, which comprises over 15,000 tweets, in this work. The dataset initially contains parameters such as twitter id, airline sentiment, text, airline sentiment, confidence, airline, and name, which are then reduced to two attributes, airline sentiments and text, using feature extraction. In this paper, we used a binary text classifier that gives 0 and 1 for negative and positive classes for column airline sentiment.

9.5.2 Data Pre-Processing and Cleaning

We have used binary text classifier which only takes two classes as we don't need neutral reviews from the dataset; therefore, it has been removed from the dataset.

This dataset's labels are categorical. Only numeric data are understood by machines. So, using the factorize () function, transform the category data to numeric values. This gives you an array of numeric numbers as well as a category index.

```
(array([0, 1, 1, ..., 0, 1, 1], dtype=int64),
    Index(['positive', 'negative'], dtype='object'))
```

The 0 signifies good feeling and the 1 represents negative sentiment, as you can see.

Here's the crux of python sentiment analysis. The supplied text must be machine-readable. Thus, the text has been vector embedded. Word embeddings show word relationships in a text. We replace each unique word with its allocated number.

Before continuing with python sentiment analysis, tokenize the text using Tokenizer. In tokenization, we split the text into little tokens. Fit on texts () links words with numbers. The tokenizer stores this relationship as a dictionary. Indexing word. Replace words with integers using text-to-sequence ().

The sentences in the dataset are not all the same length. To make the sentences equal in length, use padding.

9.6 Binary Classifier Using LSTM

Our sentiment analysis model uses LSTM layers. Our model has three layers: embedding, LSTM, and dense. Dropout between LSTM layers reduced overfitting.

In Figure 9.8 explains the mathematical working of the long-short-term neural network.

LSTM stands for long-short-term memory networks. It is RNN-based. RNNs analyse text and audio sequentially. Embedding matrices keep each word's meaning and accompanying calculations (hidden states) [20]. RNNs can't maintain all calculations in memory if a word's reference is used after 100 words. RNNs can't learn long-term dependencies. Dropout regularises. Overfitting is avoided. Dropout randomly removes neurons. The layer takes a 0–1 argument reflecting the chance of losing neurons. This prevents model overfitting.

9.6.1 Class Prediction

Train the sentiment analysis model for five epochs on the complete dataset with a 32-batch size and 20% validation split.

We have defined a function to predict sentiment that takes the input as a sentence and classifies it into one of the two-class that is Positive and Negative. The accuracy of the

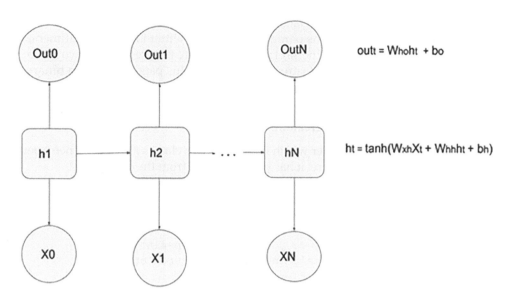

FIGURE 9.8
Long-short-term neural network.

model is approximately 94.0% as we see that the test_sentence1 which seems to be negative is also predicted negatively by our text classifier model and text_sentence2 which seems to be positive is also predicted correctly by our text classifier model.

9.7 Result and Discussion

Table 9.2 illustrates the comparison and similarities between the two proposed approaches in this paper using the strength and challenges given as follows:

We successfully constructed a sentiment analysis model in Python. We created a binary text classifier in this machine learning project that divides tweet sentiment into positive and negative categories. On validation, we got more than 94% accuracy. Let's use matplotlib to plot these metrics. Matplotlib is a visualization tool that uses a low-level graph plotting toolkit written in Python.

In Figure 9.9 the orange line in the graph shows the training accuracy is approx. to 96% and testing accuracy approx. to 94% respectively.

Now, we have compared the both Dictionary based approach and the text-classifier approach for the given tweet and the following results are obtained (Figure 9.10).

9.8 Conclusion

This work is divided into two sections. The first part of the project focuses on sentimental analysis using a dictionary-based technique, while the second portion focuses on

TABLE 9.2

Strength and Challenges of Proposed Approaches

	Approach	Strength	Challenges
Dictionary based approach	This approach requires a reference dictionary to categorize each individual word/sentence/dataset.	1. This method is mostly Utilize with unsupervised Data sets. 2. This technique does not require any prior Dataset Training. 3. This method works well with datasets with few Dimensions. 4. Because this technique works with fewer datasets, it is faster to execute and has greater Accuracy. 5. This method requires less computation because no prior training or Modeling is necessary. 6. This method is less risky since it has been tried and tested.	1. This method is incapable of learning. 2. This is a rule-based strategy that necessitates the creation of rules by an Expert at initially. 3. This method has issues with high-dimensional data sets. 4. Because this technique is not sensitive to the kind of document being coded, it is not ideal for all types of documents.
Machine learning based approach	For classification of dataset this approach requires supervised and un-supervised machine learning approaches.	1. This method is applicable to both supervised and unsupervised datasets. 2. This method does not necessitate the use of a dictionary. 3. This method achieves the maximum classification accuracy regardless of the size of the dataset. 4. Unlike dictionary-based approaches, the efficiency of this technique is not dependent on any single rule. 5. This method works well with any multidimensional data set. 6. This method is capable of learning.	1. A classifier that has been trained in one domain does not function on texts from other domains. 2. Unbalances generated by classes and other language variances have an impact on this method. 3. In certain rare circumstances, this technique may provide contradicting results for the same input.

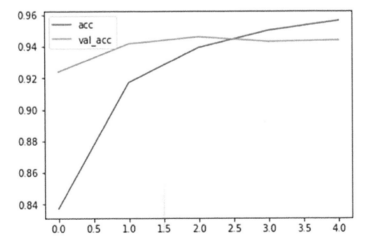

FIGURE 9.9
Accuracy function of the model.

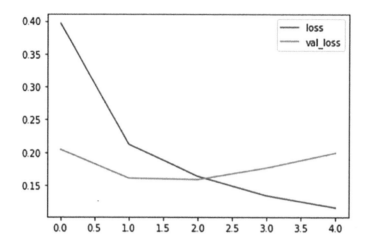

FIGURE 9.10
Loss function of the model.

sentimental analysis using a machine-learning approach. After comparing both, it was determined that the second propose advised the correct sentiment for a particular tweet with a testing accuracy of 94% our second proposal, a machine learning technique, has certain limitations. Therefore, if the provided tweet contains terms that are not included in the dataset, the class prediction may be incorrect for a few tweets as input.

References

1. A. Pak and P. Paroubek, Twitter as a corpus for sentiment analysis and opinion mining. In *Proceedings of the Seventh Conference on International Language Resources and Evaluation*, 2010, pp. 1320–1326.
2. G. Vinodhini and R. M. Chandrasekaran, Sentiment analysis and opinion mining: A survey. *International Journal of Advanced Research in Computer Science and Software Engineering*, 2(6), June 2012. ISSN: 2277 128X.
3. Z. Zhai, B. Liu, H. Xu and H. Xu, *Clustering Product Features for Opinion Mining, WSDM'11, Hong Kong, China*, February 9–12, 2011. Copyright 2011 ACM 978-1-4503-0493-1/11/02…$10.00.
4. Singh and V. Kumar, A clustering and opinion mining approach to socio-political analysis of the blogosphere. In *Computational Intelligence and Computing Research (ICCIC), IEEE International Conference*, 2010.
5. C. Li and R. Li, Lexicon construction: A topic model approach. In *International Conference on Systems and Informatics (ICSAI)*, IEEE, pp. 2299–2303, 2012.
6. M. Karamibekr and A. Ghorbani, Sentiment analysis of social issues. In *International Conference on Social Informatics (Social Informatics)*, IEEE 2012, December 2012.
7. Z. Madhoushi, A. R. Hamdan and Zainuddin, Sentiment analysis techniques in recent works. *Science and Information Conference (SAI)*, IEEE, 2015.
8. A. Mukwazvure and K.P. Supreethi, A hybrid approach to sentiment analysis of news comments. Reliability. In *4th International Conference on Infocom Technologies and Optimization (ICRITO) – Trends and Future Directions*, IEEE, 2015.

9. I. M. Jha, N. Shenoy, K. R. Venugopal and L. Patnaik, HOMS: Hindi opinion mining system. In *IEEE 2nd International Conference on Recent Trends in Information Systems (RTIS) M*, 2015.

10. P. Pang, L. Lee and S. Vaithyanathan, et al. Thumbs up? In P. Pang, L. Lee, and S. Vaithyanathan. *Proceedings of ACL-02 Conference on Empirical Approaches in Natural Language Processing*, vol. 10, pp. 79–86, 2002.

11. E. Loper and S. Bird, NLTK: The natural language toolkit. In *Proceedings of ACL-02 Workshop on Effective Tools and Methodologies for Teaching Natural Language Processing and Computational Linguistics*, vol. 1, pp. 63–70, 2002.

12. O. Almatrafi, S. Parack and B. Chavan, Application of location-based sentiment analysis using Twitter for identifying trends towards Indian general elections 2014. In *Proceedings of the 9th International Conference on Ubiquitous Information Management and Communication*, 2015.

13. K. Kishor, R. Sharma and M. Chhabra, Student performance prediction using technology of machine learning. In Sharma D.K., Peng S.L., Sharma R., Zaitsev D.A. (eds) *Micro-Electronics and Telecommunication Engineering. Lecture Notes in Networks and Systems*, vol. 373. Springer, Singapore. 2022. https://doi.org/10.1007/978-981-16-8721-1_53.

14. K. Kishor, Communication-efficient federated learning. In Yadav S.P., Bhati B.S., Mahato D.P., Kumar S. (eds) *Federated Learning for IoT Applications. EAI/Springer Innovations in Communication and Computing*. Springer, Cham, 2022. https://doi.org/10.1007/978-3-030-85559-8_9.

15. K. Kishor, Personalized federated learning. In Yadav S.P., Bhati B.S., Mahato D.P., Kumar S. (eds) *Federated Learning for IoT Applications. EAI/Springer Innovations in Communication and Computing*. Springer, Cham, 2022. https://doi.org/10.1007/978-3-030-85559-8_3.

16. S. Gupta, S. Tyagi and K. Kishor, Study and development of self sanitizing smart elevator. In Gupta D., Polkowski Z., Khanna A., Bhattacharyya S., Castillo O. (eds) *Proceedings of Data Analytics and Management. Lecture Notes on Data Engineering and Communications Technologies*, vol. 90. Springer, Singapore, 2022. https://doi.org/10.1007/978-981-16-6289-8_15.

17. K. Kishor and D. Pandey, Study and development of efficient air quality prediction system embedded with machine learning and IoT. In Gupta D. et al. (eds), *Proceeding International Conference on Innovative Computing and Communications. Lecture Notes in Networks and Systems*, vol. 471, Springer, Singapore, 2022. https://doi.org/10.1007/978-981-19-2535-1.

18. B. K. Rai, S. Sharma, G. Kumar and K. Kishor, Recognition of different bird category using image processing. *International Journal of Online and Biomedical Engineering (iJOE)*, 18(07), 101–114, 2022. https://doi.org/10.3991/ijoe.v18i07.29639.

19. A. Sharma, N. Jha and K. Kishor, Predict COVID-19 with chest X-ray. In Gupta D., Polkowski Z., Khanna A., Bhattacharyya S., Castillo O. (eds) *Proceedings of Data Analytics and Management. Lecture Notes on Data Engineering and Communications Technologies*, vol. 90. Springer, Singapore, 2022. https://doi.org/10.1007/978-981-16-6289-8_16.

20. A. Jain, Y. Sharma and K. Kishor, Financial supervision and management system using Ml algorithm. *Solid State Technology*, 63(6), 18974–18982, 2020. http://solidstatetechnology.us/index.php/JSST/article/view/8080.

10

Impact of Cloud Computing on Entrepreneurship, Cost, and Security

Kaushal Kishor

ABES Institute of Technology

CONTENTS

10.1 Introduction

IBM and Apple released PCs in the 1980s, spurring global acceptance. IT includes all data-related technologies. IT impacts all sorts of organizations and is a critical tool. IT innovation boosts globalization. Disintegrated language and geographical borders make communication simpler, cheaper, and more efficient [1]. Businesses may build new worldwide marketplaces. Staff can save, retrieve, and analyze information more effectively

DOI: 10.1201/9781003213895-10

and automate boring tasks using IT advancements [2]. Virtualization, system resource management, and Internet connectivity lead to cloud computing. "Cloud computing" is a metaphor for the Internet. Cloud computing employs real-time networked computers (usually the Internet). Businesses, individuals, and governments are expected to use cloud computing. This new paradigm may meet business needs. Businesses may access computer resources and apps online. Third-party hardware, software, and data may be used. Cloud computing may also foster innovation, support new business models, and boost organizational cooperation and effectiveness. It may improve healthcare and education [3].

Cloud computing is transformational but risky. Because cloud computing links several devices, the delivered data may be worrying. Cloud computing challenges include data security, privacy, and vendor lock-in [3]. Cloud computing is still young; yet, it's already changed how governments, industries, and enterprises use IT. Cloud computing affected work habits [4]. Many expect cloud computing to effect companies as the Internet did in the 1990s [5]. Pervasive cloud computing unknowingly, we utilize cloud services. Cloud services include email and storage. Businesses like cloud computing. Researchers, scientists, and academicians are conducting research and surveys to explain how its adoption might boost economic growth and value. Cloud computing in wireless and machine learning (ML) domain A distributed system includes autonomous computers connected by a network and distribution middleware, which enables them to coordinate their operations and share system resources so users experience it as a single, integrated computing facility [6,7]. Mobile nodes like a robot or smartphone are connected to the Internet by a Wi-Fi access point, base station, or satellite. Mobile cloud computing is confined to infrastructure-based communication technologies and cannot be deployed in mobile ad hoc scenarios. Mobile ad hoc cloud computing uses several mobile devices to construct a virtual supercomputing node. Mobile nodes communicate across a mobile ad hoc network that supports network discovery, monitoring, and routing. Cloud middleware controls resources, failures, mobility, communications, and tasks. It hides complexity and delivers a unified system view to users and applications [8–10].

ML, a subset of AI, seeks to design systems/machines that can automatically learn from data patterns and experiences and improve their predictions without being explicitly programmed. ML involves the study of algorithms and design of self-training computer systems [11–13]. Applying ML approaches (decision tree, logistic regression, linear regression, support vector machine, K-nearest neighbour, etc.) to enormous amounts of data may be tricky. Traditional ML libraries don't manage big datasets, so new strategies were required [14–16]. ML was out of reach for small- and medium-sized organizations as it was costly to implement ML technology and solutions. Cloud computing enhances and extends ML applications. "Intelligent cloud" is ML in the cloud. Cloud machine learning boosts the capabilities of both the cloud and ML algorithms [17,18].

10.1.1 Theoretical Background

Cloud computing is an IT innovation. It improves efficiency and saves money for businesses. It affects how corporations obtain PCs [19]. Computing as a product is being replaced by computing as a service [19]. 2011:126 Growing tech. International Data Corporation (IDC) expects 2015 public IT cloud sales of $72.9 billion [20]. Microsoft, Google, and Amazon provide cloud services. Cloud computing will look different in 10–15 years [21]. Cloud computing has altered computer and Internet usage in organizations. This affects app data storage. Cloud computing stores files on the "cloud" rather than PCs. The cloud is Internet-accessible computers and servers [22]. Online users may access files, apps, and documents. Users can now participate from everywhere, not just from their desktop PCs [23]. Companies cut IT expenses. Many start by combining IT processes and leveraging virtualization technologies to host server's on-premises. Cloud computing saves money by improving usage, decreasing infrastructure and administrative expenses, and shortening deployment cycles. Dynamic resource pools, high availability, and virtualization [24]. Cloud computing is a platform and software. User and organization data are on cloud servers. Cloud computing configures and distributes PCs. Online applications are meant. Powerful computers in data centres host cloud applications [25]. Cloud computing maximizes hardware and software investments. Physical boundaries between systems are removed and their management is centralized. Virtualized data centre technologies [25]. Cloud computing's advantages and hazards must be weighed before adoption [26]. Cloud computing has sceptics. Security worries temper economic optimism [27] says cloud computing cost and security research has conflicting results. Uncertain business benefits [20]. Cost and security uncertainties require further investigations. Current research focusses on cloud computing cost advantages and security problems for enterprises but overlooks the dangers and rewards. Research lacks mitigating ideas. This endeavour addresses research shortages.

1. What are cloud computing's financial advantages and risks for businesses?
2. What are cloud computing risks and benefits?

This chapter discusses cloud computing's economic and security implications for enterprises, as well as its advantages and concerns. This research seeks to explain that modern society has abundant water, power, gas, and telecommunications. Because they're essential, anybody can acquire them instantaneously and pay as they go. Recent advances in ICT (information and communications technology) may make the computer a fundamental requirement like water, electricity, gas, and phone. Computing utility will supply computing resources as services, which are consumed depending on our requirements and supplied in a similar fashion to other utilities: users don't know about the underlying hosting infrastructure or how services are given to them [28]. Leonard Kleinrock stated that computer networks were in their infancy when he launched ARPANET in 1969. As "computer utilities" expand and become more sophisticated, they may serve homes and companies throughout the nation like electric and phone utilities (2005). In recent decades, cluster, grid, and cloud computing have been created to achieve this aim. Cloud computing isn't new; it's been utilized in the business for years. Many companies didn't know what was it or how it might help them. Numerous technologies underpinning cloud computing were in the rudimentary phases of development; thus, their full potential could not be harnessed until today [29]. Microsoft said in 2012 that the cloud "stops being a jargon or future objective and becomes part of your strategy, today" [30]. Cloud computing began with virtualization, distributed computing, utility computing, networking, and online and software services [31]. Cloud computing is the consequence of the growth and maturation of two independent streams: the first is the enhancement of internet services, which became more reliable, efficient, and widely accessible, along with virtualization methods and shared computing provisioning, and the second stream involves on-demand self-service computer capability [32–36].

10.1.2 Cloud Computing

Since cloud computing's emergence, researchers have defined it. There's no general term that fully explains this phenomenon. Since researchers study business, education, etc., several meanings exist. The most important aspect in describing cloud computing is whether the paradigm is accurately described. The National Institute of Standards and Technology's definition is generally accepted:

Cloud computing enables ubiquitous, accessible, on-demand network access to a shared pool of customizable computing resources (network, servers, storage, applications, and services) that can be instantly supplied and released with minimum administrative effort or service provider contact [37]. This definition defines cloud computing clearly and succinctly, covering its fundamental features and aspects and synthesizing most of the generated definitions.

Cloud computing offers unique deployment and delivery methods. Understanding cloud computing as a service requires studying these properties and paradigms. The latter refers to cloud price and security problems.

On-demand self-service, wide network access, resource pooling, fast adaptability, and quantifiable service make cloud computing appealing [38]. 2009 Cloud Security Alliance Consumers may obtain server time, network storage, and applications without contacting a service provider [38]. 2009 Cloud Security Alliance As these capabilities are network based, they may be accessed from anywhere on several platforms, in-house devices, PCs, and mobile devices like smartphones and tablets. Since mobile devices gained power and capabilities, cloud computing has helped organizations enhance mobility. Next, cloud providers must deploy and manage cloud services. Storage, memory, computing, virtual machines, and network bandwidth are shared by the provider in a multi-tenant arrangement [38]. 2009 Cloud Security Alliance These materials are supplied dynamically to customers. They're also delivered elastically, so the user gets as much as he/she needs [24]. 2009 Cloud Security Alliance Cloud computing flexibility allows providers to quickly increase computer capacity. Cloud services are metered in that cloud systems optimize, control, monitor, and report automatically "resource utilization by applying a metering capability at some level of abstraction relevant to the sort of service." 2009 Cloud Security Alliance Both vendors and consumers can see and forecast the service. It also enables users to assess their long-term need for computer resources by evaluating real-time use.

Public, private, community, and hybrid cloud deployments exist [38]. 2009 Cloud Security Alliance Their differences stem from cloud infrastructure location, maintenance, and control. This implies a user's control over data and security. A public cloud is when an organization's cloud infrastructure is exposed to the public [38]. 2009 Cloud Security Alliance It's appropriate for situations when data confidentiality isn't crucial. The most closed kind is the private cloud, where a single organization uses on-premise or off-premise infrastructures managed by the corporation or a third party (Cloud Security Alliance, 2009). 2009 Cloud Security Alliance Since the cloud is not shared, enterprises have ultimate control over their data and its security [39]. (2010) Community clouds let enterprises share cloud resources. Mission, policy, security, and compliance infrastructures are shared. These companies or third parties manage on- or off-site storage. A hybrid cloud combines two or more cloud infrastructures (private, public, or communal) to ease data and application mobility [38]. This model combines the finest of the previous ones.

Software as a service (SaaS), platform as a service (PaaS), and infrastructure as a service (IaaS) supply cloud computing (IaaS). Cloud control and security differ. How a company tackles security issues depends on its delivery strategy. SaaS consumers can only utilize applications running on the provider's cloud infrastructure. They can't manage the network, servers, storage, or operating systems. This also applies to individual programme capabilities, with limited user-specific configurable options. High-security integration is the supplier's responsibility; this leaves customers powerless. Security. PaaS allows customers to deploy applications on cloud infrastructure. He/she can only manage applications in the cloud. The user may add additional protection compared to using SaaS. IaaS provides cloud security and resources. He/she manages storage, networks, CPUs, OSs, and apps. This strategy has the least integrated security as the provider protects the infrastructure. Operating systems, applications, and data are the customer's responsibility.

This section describes cloud computing advantages. Both deployment and delivery influence cloud user control, data, and security. How a corporation tackles security issues. Cloud computing adopters must understand cloud models and security tradeoffs. Next, we'll cover cloud computing costs and security benefits and risks.

10.2 The Technical Part of the Cloud

The cloud computing model has five distinguishing features. Understanding these cloud attributes is crucial for businesses and individuals. Below are their characteristics:

1. **On-demand self-service:** Cloud consumers can provision computing resources without interacting with the provider.
2. **Ubiquitous network access:** Smartphones, tablets, laptops, etc. can access computing resources over the Internet.
3. **Location-independent resource pooling:** Cloud consumers don't know the exact location of resources. Using virtualization and multi-tenancy, cloud providers share computing resources to provide cloud services to customers.
   Cloud users can quickly scale up or down their computing capacity. Automatic scaling up or down is possible.
4. **Measured service:** Customers are charged based on the computing resources (storage, computing power, bandwidth, etc.) they actually use (pay-per-use or charge-per-use model).

SaaS, PaaS, and IaaS are the three layers of cloud computing (IaaS). These types have different uses and customer needs (Figure 10.1).

10.2.1 SAAS (SaaS)

Cloud users can access applications running on the cloud provider's infrastructure via the Internet. Therefore, the user doesn't need to install or update software. The supplier automatically updates end-user versions. In the SaaS model, companies don't pay for a licence since costs are based on what you use, which may reduce the overall cost [40]. Organizations use SaaS for certain services or processes (e.g. emailing, customer management systems, etc.). In SaaS, users cannot control or maintain cloud infrastructure, with few exceptions. Google Apps (Gmail and Drive), Microsoft Office 365, Salesforce (CRM), LinkedIn, Exact-online, and Dropbox are SaaS.

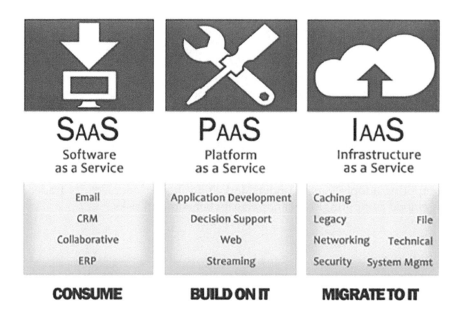

FIGURE 10.1
Layers of cloud computing.

10.2.2 PAAS (PaaS)

Consumers may design, install, manage, and execute applications on the provider's infrastructure using cloud-delivered services. Cloud providers provide multiple programming languages, libraries, and proprietary tools to make development simpler, quicker, and cheaper. Cloud consumers may control deployed applications and occasionally the hosting environment parameters. Google App Engine, Microsoft Azure, Amazon EC2, Engine Yard, and GridGain are PaaS.

10.2.3 IAAS (IaaS)

Cloud service providers provide customers with a virtual data centre with storage, servers, bandwidth, networks, and other computer capabilities. Amazon, Rackspace, and CloudVPS and Amazon, Mozy, and Rackspace are IaaS providers.

Other services have emerged recently, such as business process as a service (BPaaS). BPaaS is a SaaS progression. Businesses use BPaaS to outsource HR, payroll, and supply chain management to a third-party vendor [41].

Figure 10.2 shows different cloud deployment methods. Private Cloud: A single entity owns or leases the cloud infrastructure, which might be on- or off-premises.

Cloud Community. The cloud infrastructure is shared by a particular community of companies with similar interests (e.g. purpose, security needs, etc.) and may be on- or off-premises.

10.2.4 Public Cloud

An organization offers cloud services to the public or significant industry group for open usage.

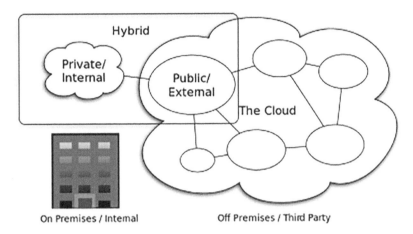

FIGURE 10.2
Cloud computing types.

10.2.5 Hybrid Cloud

The cloud infrastructure combines private, communal, and public deployment strategies with standardized or proprietary technologies [42].

10.3 Case Studies Abroad

Cloud services may be utilized in everyday life and businesses. Unknowingly, we may be utilizing cloud services. SaaS is the end-user-friendly cloud computing paradigm. Cloud services include email and storage. Cloud services may make our everyday lives simpler and timesaving and also save money and improve corporate efficiency.

Social networking services like Facebook, LinkedIn, and Twitter leverage cloud computing. Social networking platforms offer social values, but firms can utilize them to engage with consumers, market goods, and collaborate internally. Cloud-based email systems provide freedom and mobility since emails may be viewed anywhere. Because email is so vital, some of the largest cloud services are web-based emails. Google Docs users may modify online documents, share them, and work simultaneously, boosting cooperation and teamwork. Finally, online storage services like Dropbox or Syncplicity make backing up and accessing information from several devices straightforward [43]. Several worldwide cloud service providers provide a range of cloud services and solutions to people and businesses. Amazon, IBM, Google, Oracle, Dell, Cisco, HP, Intel, etc. The following companies provide cloud services. Social and commercial dynamics influenced the corporations' selection [44].

10.3.1 Google.com

Google's cloud apps (Gmail, Google Drive, Google Calendar, etc.), Picasa, and Google Reader may be accessed from any Internet-connected device, at any time. These SaaS cloud

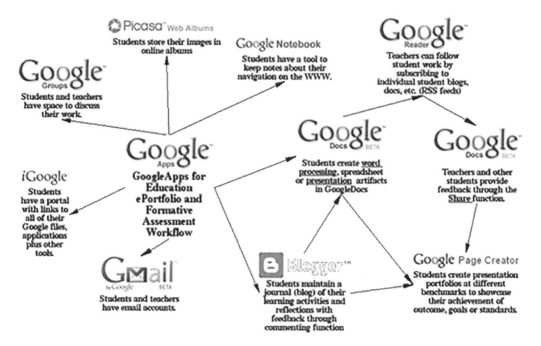

FIGURE 10.3
Example of Google cloud services used in the area of education.

services don't need users to install software or store data on their PCs. Google's data centres house apps and data. Figure 10.3 shows Google's educational SaaS cloud offerings.

Developers may create and execute apps on Google's infrastructure using Google App Engine. Google App Engine supports several programming languages and makes it simple to construct scalable, easy-to-maintain apps.

10.3.2 Amazon.com

Amazon EC2 provides a resizable cloud computing capability. Amazon EC2 lets users scale their computer capacity up and down in minutes. Customers may instantaneously commission as many server instances as they need, and the application can scale up or down as demand fluctuates. Amazon EC2 offers multiple instance types for different uses. These may vary from tiny, cheap instances for low-volume applications to cluster computing instances for high-performance workloads. Virtualization lets developers choose between operating systems, instance kinds, and software packages. These services provide elasticity, control, flexibility, security, and on-demand pricing with no long-term obligations or upfront payments. Amazon S3, DynamoDB, and Simple Queue Services are other Amazon services.

10.3.3 Microsoft

Microsoft offers all three cloud tyers. It provides public and commercial SaaS services, a PaaS platform for creating and deploying applications, and an IaaS infrastructure. Microsoft offers end-users and businesses SaaS services. Cloud services include Bing,

Hotmail, and MSN sites. Office 365 suite, Exchange online, Outlook online, Microsoft Dynamics CRM online, collaboration tools, etc. are commercial services.

Windows Azure and SQL Azure are prominent PaaS services for hosting and storage, respectively. Developers may host their apps on Windows Server 2008, so they can utilize Windows Azure in the same manner as in an on-premise environment. .NET, Java, PHP, and Python are supported.

Microsoft SQL Azure delivers database features including synchronization, backups, etc.

10.3.4 Apple

Apple wanted to give its gadget users a unique cloud service. iCloud, Apple's latest cloud storage and cloud computing service, stores data such as programmers and music for download to iOS-based devices or personal PCs. It syncs iOS emails, contacts, calendars, and notes.

10.3.5 Adoption of Cloud Computing in Europe

IDC surveyed 1556 companies from nine European nations online. United Kingdom, Sweden, Czech Republic, France, Germany, Hungary, Spain, Poland, and Italy participated in the November–December 2011 poll. 1–9, 10–99, 100–249, and 250+ personnel were questioned [45]. According to the report, European firms' cloud usage and preparedness vary. Organizations that utilize the cloud may be divided into those that do so in more than one application area, those that do so in just one, and those that have restricted or experimental usage. Organizations not utilizing the cloud may be categorized as those preparing to adopt, those considering adopting but not yet planning, and those not using or not intending to use it. Figure 10.6 shows various adoption phases.

About 64.5% of firms in the study sample employ cloud services. More firms will use cloud computing and public cloud services. In 2011, public cloud software services in Europe reached €3.5 billion and hardware services €1.1 billion. IDC estimates 2014 public cloud sales to exceed €11 billion (Figure 10.4).

In 2011, public cloud services were 1.6% of enterprise IT expenses. Due to quick developments, it will reach 3.6% of the IT market in 2014.

10.3.6 Potential Benefits of Cloud Computing

The word "cloud computing" is frequently too ambiguous for companies and organizations in order to really appreciate the advantages and potentials that lay behind it. Cloud computing experts say clients sometimes see just the tip of the iceberg in terms of future benefits [3]. Companies often overestimate new technologies' short-term impacts while underestimating their long-term advantages [34]. The cloud computing utility model reduces IT expenses and simplifies IT operations. Using the cloud eliminates the need for upfront hardware, servers, and other IT expenses. Companies may shift capital costs into operating costs. Cost varies on consumption as there are no upfront commitments (pay-per-use model). Cloud users don't pay for system maintenance or updates since cloud service providers handle it [46]. The low cost of certain cloud services for data storage and processing power might be enticing when a customer needs a change quickly.

Directly, cloud technologies save IT costs, but indirectly, they enable companies to concentrate on their core operations and what's most essential. Focus on what you're doing,

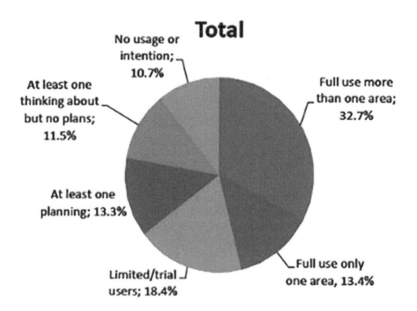

FIGURE 10.4
Cloud adoption in levels.

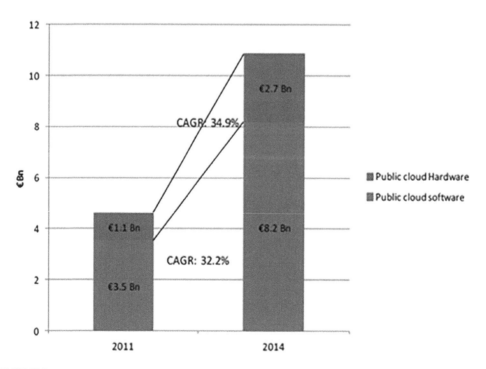

FIGURE 10.5
Public cloud market in EU 2011–2014.

not how. By lowering IT complexity, it frees up time and resources and fosters business agility so companies can concentrate on what matters most. It accelerates business outcomes, improves business processes, and enhances the company overall.

Concerning IT scalability and flexibility, cloud users don't have to worry about overprovisioning as computer resources may be dynamically accessed. Companies may meet peak demands by employing cloud resources and only paying for what they use. Cloud services make app development easy, rapid, and efficient. Traditional IT requires weeks or months to acquire and deploy servers and create an application. Customers may purchase cloud services with a credit card and use them immediately.

The cloud also improves a company's external capabilities, such as cooperation with external partners, and helps enterprises to adapt their processes, goods, and services to suit market requirements.

Cloud computing has a big influence on IT and telecom, but it may also be crucial in media, healthcare, education/research, industry, and government (Figure 10.6).

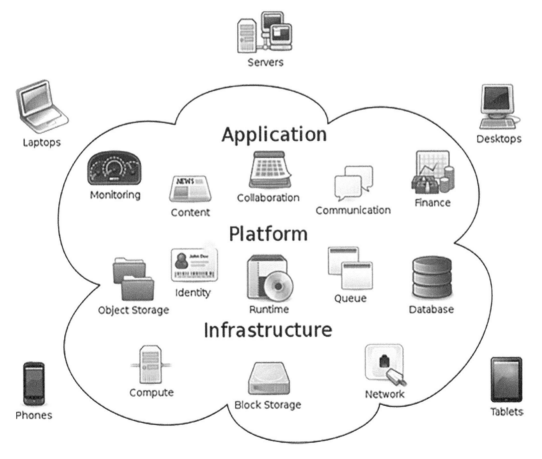

FIGURE 10.6
Potential use of cloud in different industries.

10.4 Concerns and Challenges

As with any new technology, the cloud has issues and worries. These difficulties delay its adoption and need attention and methods to overcome.

Security and privacy concerns make many firms hesitant to utilize cloud computing. Customers' data may be kept and shared over several servers, discouraging organizations with sensitive data from embracing cloud computing [47]. Cloud providers invest in superior hardware and software to handle this problem. Enterprises may keep critical data inside while most servers are on the cloud using a hybrid cloud [35].

Another worry is vendor lock-in, which might make switching cloud providers difficult. Switching prices may be expensive and cloud migration difficult. The lack of standards might prevent cloud interoperability. Institutional lock-in is also conceivable when cloud services become part of an enterprise's habits and operations.

10.4.1 Cost Benefits

Cloud computing's popularity among businesses stems from its cost savings. Researchers focus on cost benefits when studying cloud computing's cost impact on organizations. This section discusses the cost benefits of cloud computing. As cloud computing is a relatively new technology, there are numerous untried situations that pose economic concerns for depending on or outsourcing certain activities utilizing cloud computing services. Existing research is flawed because it ignores organizations' cost risks. This study examines cost risks. Cloud computing reduces hardware expenses, first [24]. Cloud services eliminate the need for powerful, expensive machines to operate cloud applications. Reduced processing and storage demands cause this. Cloud apps use less RAM than conventional software. No-installation software means smaller hard drives. Buying cheaper PCs helps firms save expenditures. Cloud computing reduces IT infrastructure investments. This affects bigger businesses. IT departments may utilize cloud computing to replace or upgrade internal computer resources instead of buying a large number of powerful servers. Miller [24] says, like, that businesses no longer need to buy new equipment to address computational power peaks and valleys. Cloud servers manage computational peaks.

The cloud reduces software expenses. Companies no longer purchase separate software for each machine. Instead, only the app's users may access it. Installing and maintaining the software on each machine is also cheaper. Organizations don't have to pay for software upgrades to get the newest apps [1]. The supplier automatically upgrades all cloud-based apps. Maintenance expenditures may be reduced. Hardware and software upkeep. Fewer PCs and servers reduce maintenance expenses. All software in businesses is on the cloud and managed by the cloud provider. We suggest that software costs rely on cloud deployment and delivery strategies. This implies that software expenses vary with control and maintenance levels. Public clouds and SaaS have the lowest software expenses, but private clouds and IaaS do not. Security expenditures are similar.

From a customer's standpoint, cloud computing may boost efficiency and effectiveness, which increases profitability. Computing power boosts a company's productivity. According to Miller [24] (p. 26), businesses may "perform supercomputing-like operations using hundreds of computers and servers." This increases their production and efficiency. Predictable earnings and a larger client base are the key cost advantages for providers [48]. Cloud computing reduces administrative expenses and offloads three administrative tasks [49]. First, it offloads infrastructure management, such as hardware maintenance, infrastructure software, adding new computers, and replacement of parts. Second, the provider conducts the backup policy. Once installed, the app is accessible to authorized users. Organizations must handle security risks when transitioning to the cloud, despite its economic advantages. Next, we'll discuss this.

10.4.2 Cost Impact

Cloud computing's appeal lies in its cost effectiveness and cost reductions, according to the previous study. Cloud computing flexibility reduces costs. Even though cloud services are more costly than a server for comparable activities and time, the flexibility makes them cheaper [23]. A and D cited elasticity as a reason for moving to the cloud. Cloud computing features a flexible pricing model that enables enterprises to pay only for the time and scale they utilize (Respondent D).

The previous study cites hardware, software, and infrastructure cost reductions [24,48]. The absence of upfront hardware expenditures is a huge financial advantage since enterprises no longer need to buy expensive machines to operate cloud-based apps. Respondent B says firms don't need powerful servers to calculate. Respondents C and E agree. Organizations may utilize cloud-based software instead of installing it on their own devices. Respondent A says cloud outsourcing can save half the cost of each application. Reducing hardware, software, and infrastructure reduces maintenance expenses. Respondent C said that reducing internal servers reduces maintenance expenses (Respondent C). All possible costs may be employed for marketing and innovation, resulting in better revenues.

Other elements boost an organization's revenue by boosting productivity and effectiveness. The previous study has shown enhanced processing power, simpler group collaboration, universal document access, operating system compatibility, and document format compatibility. Empirical evidence adds elements. Increased cloud stability, accountability, and predictability boost cost effectiveness and competitiveness (Respondent F).

Previous studies showed that hardware, software, and infrastructure are the key cost reductions, but actual data suggest that personnel reduction is the main cost saving now. Respondent A says that currently, personnel costs more than hardware and software. Cloud computing saves enterprises' money by decreasing operational and administrative expenses (Respondents A, B, and G).

Cost-wise, cloud computing is best for small- and medium-sized businesses. This is due to cheap starting costs, decreased resource ownership costs, and the removal of software administration [48]. Smaller firms lack the capacity to construct and manage their own data centres and applications. Large enterprises pay more for cloud services than for in-house data centres. Respondents have similar views. Small- and medium-sized businesses profit from not needing their own infrastructure, software, and IT teams (Respondents A, C, and F). Private cloud expenditures are only viable for big enterprises with significant power demands (Respondents B and E). Cloud computing is beneficial for providers but expensive for small businesses (Respondent G).

Few studies have examined the financial implications cloud computing poses to businesses. The analysis highlighted many cost hazards. The lack of precise and advanced cost models in the cloud market is the biggest cost concern. This risk complicates cloud computing's cost calculation. The market isn't developed enough to set a market-conform price for cost projections (Respondent D). Organizations struggle to decide whether to shift to the cloud. This risk varies. First, it's hard for firms to evaluate the return on their early cloud expenditures, particularly long term (Respondents A and E). Moving to another cloud might be costly for organizations currently using cloud computing. According to respondent E, switching clouds costs more. Second, cloud service prices vary by application and use case, making precise client calculations difficult. This and the expanding number of suppliers make estimating the best provider's offering challenging (Respondent F). Third, provider cost calculations are complex. Providers estimate what a consumer really consumes from total service usage without an appropriate cost model. This complicates consumer billing (Respondent G). Some cloud apps may have less capability than their traditional counterparts. The firms couldn't save money on software (Respondent C); thus, they may have to run more costly apps.

IT experts' empirical results indicate ways to prevent the aforementioned cost issues. New, realistic pricing models are needed to help users calculate cloud service prices (Respondent F). We need better business and cost models to calculate service and user expenses (Respondent G). Competition in the cloud market should be encouraged to decrease cloud service rates (Respondent F). Before switching to the cloud, companies should assess if cloud apps offer the same capabilities as regular software (Respondent C).

10.5 Security Risks

Security issues are the main hurdle to cloud migration, notwithstanding economic advantages. Pearson [50] says corporations are most concerned about cloud computing security. Abstraction of infrastructure causes a lack of awareness and an inability to incorporate many basic security measures, particularly at the network layer. Cloud Security Alliance. On the other side, argues that these concerns stem from a misunderstanding about who is accountable for particular components of cloud API security. Organizations' deployment and delivery methodologies affect security vulnerabilities. Risk management must comprehend deployment and delivery strategies, and security trade-offs. Organizations may face security threats from cloud computing. These threats include data security and confidentiality. Organizations employing third-party cloud apps must safeguard the data they handle, store, and transport.

Due to poor data management and protection by cloud providers, data may be lost, acquired, and utilized by unauthorized parties [50]. Service-level agreements (SLAs) between a supplier and client can pose a risk. Some don't include security services. These agreements lack security provisions. As the terms of service favour the cloud provider, "if something goes wrong, the consumer is frequently accountable." This happens when a customer's delivery methodology shifts a security risk to the supplier. As not all hazards may be transferred, cloud customers may be liable. In such instances, an organization needs significant financial strength to defend itself legally, which is challenging for tiny groups. Pearson [50] adds that customers may wish to check if service agreements have been completed, but cloud infrastructure may not give the necessary information or analysis.

Cloud data security requires access management. This control may be insufficient. Unauthorized individuals may get access to private information and steal or compromise data. Governments, cloud provider IT workers, data thieves, cybercriminals, and cloud service users may be involved. Customers may do so owing to insufficient data segregation. Multi-tenancy in the cloud, where one software application serves several client businesses in a SaaS environment, causes this risk. If the software fails to isolate data, a tenant may access and jeopardize other tenants' data. The administration interface might jeopardize data. This applies to public clouds when the administration interface is accessible remotely through the Internet and a web browser. Remote access vulnerabilities put client data at risk.

Insufficient interoperability standards threaten cloud data. Different cloud providers produced incompatible architectural standards (Open Virtualization Format, Open Cloud Computing Interface, Security Assertion Markup Language, etc.). Incompatibility hinders standardizing cloud security frameworks. Customers can't easily switch cloud providers or bring data in-house. We propose that avoiding security risks by moving to a better data protection provider is difficult.

Inadequate data erasure is another cloud computing security problem. Customers want to know that erased data are unrecoverable. Cloud companies don't offer proof and rely on faith. Multiple backups of the data on various systems and locations make its deletion more difficult since some are kept by other businesses. The supplier may not wish to delete other customers' data. Data backups may potentially be susceptible, leading to lost, compromised, and unrecoverable data.

Cloud computing security threats and advantages must both be considered. Existing research fails to address the security advantages for enterprises. In the Conclusions chapter, this study discusses possible security advantages. The Conclusions chapter shows the financial risks and security advantages of cloud computing, along with implications and ideas for avoiding the dangers. The next chapter explains how this study was done.

10.5.1 Security Impact

The previous study shows that cloud computing security is an issue [50]. The previous study has addressed many security threats related to major concerns of firms using cloud computing: data loss and breach. Unwanted access to sensitive information, poor data erasure, management interface compromise, backup weaknesses, and isolation failure are security threats. Organizations fear critical company data exposed on the cloud and copied, stolen, lost, or hacked. Cloud risk is greater than in-house (Respondents C and F).

The empirical results vary from earlier studies addressing real security issues. According to respondent D, cloud computing's main security danger isn't data loss. A data breach is always a possibility but not data loss, he says.

Gaps in security, vendor lock-in, lacking assurance and transparency, and poor monitoring are further security threats. When a cloud provider is responsible for security, bad security management and a lack of provisions assuring the degree of security supplied are risks. According to A and B, this leads to another cloud computing obstacle: trust. They say that a lack of confidence and honesty prevents firms from using cloud services, not security problems. As their firms have never confronted cloud security concerns, they consider them promising, but distrust remains where client data is held and how it's managed and safeguarded is unclear (Respondent A). Cloud clients don't understand their legal responsibility for data protection or whether they'll be paid in a catastrophe (Respondent E).

Empirical evidence shows a major security concern. There are no supranational regulatory frameworks for cloud computing legal agreements, security, and interoperability. Different national laws heighten security issues, which inhibit or preclude certain cloud clients from migrating. As cloud computing crosses national borders, espionage and hacking by foreign companies and governments are a concern for data confidentiality (Respondents C and F). Recent leaks and hacking incidents raise questions about cloud providers' and governments' integrity and how these concerns will be dealt supranationally. That makes cloud computing security more important.

Little study has been done on cloud computing security advantages for businesses. This study explored them and found various security advantages. Cloud computing improves data security. Respondent D says client data is backed up on many servers, allowing for speedy restoration in a crisis. B says clouds are safer than in-house data centres and servers. Most companies that create in-house data centres can't afford enough servers to ensure data security. Empirical data demonstrate that firms get security advantages. First, cloud computing centralization improves PaaS and IaaS security. Instead of managing numerous servers independently, clients consolidate their security efforts. SaaS clients have no security obligations. Cloud computing centralization also improves cloud providers' security mechanisms (Respondents B, C, D, and G). Second, cloud services reduce risk management, security maintenance, and support costs (Respondents A, D, and E). Cloud providers vary in their security maintenance and support. SaaS clients have no financial obligations. Third, security software and maintenance are enhanced over older systems (Respondent C). Thus, a cloud provider has greater security control tools than a data centre owner. Cloud services speed up data transit and recovery. Cloud computing firms don't spend money and time waiting for data to be recovered or moved in case of breach (Respondents E and F).

Empirical evidence suggests ways to prevent the aforementioned security issues. Organizations should analyze which data should be kept in the cloud to prevent data loss and maintain confidentiality. This necessitates analyzing a provider's security trade-offs. Cloud providers should strengthen data encryption and firewalls (Respondents G and A). Small- and medium-sized enterprises should use a hybrid cloud as a compromise between sensitive data and cost savings, according to experts. Transparency is essential to increase cloud computing confidence. This refers to cloud providers' security measures and customers' rights; thus, they must design user-friendly SLAs. Organizations require supplier data (Respondent F). Without interoperability and international regulatory frameworks for security standards, cloud computing security issues are difficult to overcome (Respondent C). This implies supranational law should create cross-national interoperability and security standards.

10.6 Data Collection

Crawford (1997) believes that in data collection, the examination of existent research precedes empirical data collection. This study evaluates what scholars have explored and found before collecting empirical data. According to Bryman and Bell [51], earlier research is increasingly important in business and management studies. Existing research evaluation is an essential aspect of qualitative research with several benefits. Researchers can acquire a better understanding of the phenomenon; thanks to the existing study [52]. The summary of prior studies offers a clear knowledge of how cloud computing influences enterprises. This enhances data-gathering preparation, leading to more relevant and successful results. Literature research is faster than empirical research [52].

This study utilized papers, journals, books, and website materials. Relevant material search has two goals. First, given the study field is large, discover concentrated literature that best matches the issue. The second goal was to locate enough material to show that existing research fails to address cost concerns, security advantages, and alternative solutions. The literature was then compiled and analyzed to identify relevant outcomes for data analysis. Cloud computing cost advantages and security threats for enterprises.

10.7 Cloud Computing on Investments

Starting a business needs enormous financial costs, and getting investors is one of the major hurdles entrepreneurs face, particularly in the early stages. Due to the necessity and difficulty of getting startup money, this chapter discusses cloud computing's function.

Fundraising requires careful deal-making. Investors want a return that compensates for risk and entrepreneurs' finance. During new business funding, information challenges arise due to the asymmetry between the entrepreneur and financier. Investors may have greater knowledge about economic worth than entrepreneurs have regarding technical quality. Financiers don't know the entrepreneur's ability and devotion; thus, they want real proof to lessen startup uncertainty. Instead of committing money upfront, staged funding is reliant on performance standards (milestones).

Cloud computing has revolutionized how IT businesses are founded and funded. The cloud allows businesses to easily construct infrastructure and test new concepts. Starting up is simpler and cheaper technically than ever. Entrepreneurs need less funding to design prototypes, test them, offer the first product, recruit customers, and get feedback. This means that businesses can start consumer validation and show investors how their ideas work sooner and are simpler and cheaper. Investors face less early-stage risks, and certain technical and product concerns may be managed [53].

Venture funders and entrepreneurs want to focus on their business strategy, not their technical infrastructure. Startups may employ cloud technologies to launch their ideas quickly and cheaply, unlike older alternatives. Using prior technological solutions, prototyping a new system required the purchase, installation, and setup of new hardware and software. Now, cloud solutions may be used instead.

In a World Economic Forum report, a venture investor says, "We no longer support startups based on PowerPoint pitches. We finance live, cloud-based applications." In the same research, venture capitalists said that they wouldn't invest in IT startups without cloud ambitions [3].

Cloud computing is appealing to venture capitalists and angel investors because it enables entrepreneurs to develop low-capital-expense business plans, which in turn makes cloud services attractive to these types of investors. The risk profile of a new company could change as a result of using cloud computing.

10.8 Conclusions

The effects of cloud computing on enterprises, both financially and in terms of their level of safety, have been investigated in this chapter. Previous studies have shown that the primary allure of cloud computing for businesses is the significant reduction in operating expenses that it affords, but the primary cause for worry is the dangers that it poses to data security. However, there has not been a significant amount of work made into doing an in-depth analysis of the financial risks and security advantages of adopting cloud computing. As a consequence of this, the study that has already been done is problematic due to the fact that it does not address these difficulties. This study has addressed these challenges by identifying the cost risks and security advantages that companies face when employing cloud computing. These cost risks and security benefits are exclusive to cloud computing. In the present cloud market, there is a lack of accurate and sophisticated cost models, which has been highlighted as the primary source of potential financial risk. Increased data safety, security centralization, reduced financial commitments for risk management, improved security software mechanisms and maintenance, and faster data recovery and transfer are some of the security benefits that have been identified. Other benefits include lower financial commitments for security maintenance and support. The findings of this investigation have shown various significant consequences. To begin, in today's business world, businesses see a decrease in employees, as well as the commensurate reduction in the expenses of operations and administration that it provides, as the single most important cost advantage. The second benefit of cloud computing is that it is more suitable for small- and medium-sized businesses. In addition, the hybrid cloud deployment model is seen to be the most suitable cloud deployment model for them since it strikes the ideal balance between concerns over sensitive data and the need to reduce costs. Third, the avoidance of the cost risks for organizations necessitates the development of new and more accurate cost models for the exact calculation of the charges for cloud services, as well as the stimulation of greater competition in the cloud market. Fourth, organizations can reduce their exposure to the potential security threats posed by cloud computing by conducting in-depth research to determine which types of data should be kept in the cloud, advancing the state of the art in terms of data protection mechanisms and increasing the level of transparency regarding the security precautions taken by cloud service providers. An additional condition for a cloud computing environment to be considered safe is the establishment of international regulatory frameworks, as well as interoperability and security standards on a supranational level. In conclusion, given what we've covered in this chapter, we can assert that businesses operating in the cloud have the ability to take a number of advantages. Nevertheless, making use of this technology does not ensure any level of success, and the "war" is not over even after new technologies have been implemented. The best way for entrepreneurs to increase their chances of success is to embrace innovation and new ideas, utilize new technology as a tool, attempt new things, and learn from their mistakes. According to the findings of the research, there are strong indicators that the adoption of cloud technologies led to an astonishing number of new startup firms as well as a significant rise in investments. Cloud computing has the ability to offer up a whole new universe of chances for company development and new prospects for corporate growth in the nation. It has the ability to improve the whole startup ecosystem by lowering the entry barriers in certain areas and making those markets more accessible to new businesses. However, just like any other recent innovation in technology, the usage of cloud computing has its own unique set of obstacles and potential threats, all of which need to be managed and avoided to the greatest extent possible. The obstacles that prevent people from using cloud technology may be different in different parts of the world (for example, Europe and Asia) and for different kinds of users (governments, businesses, etc.). Data security, privacy concerns, challenges with compliance, and the fear of being locked in by a vendor are some of the most serious threats.

References

1. Pieterson, M. N. B. (2009). *Benefits of IT (Information Technology) in Modern Day Business.* Retrieved March 19, 2014, from http://www.modernghana.com/news2/242392/1/benefits-of-it- information-technology-in-modern-da.html

2. Acevedo, L. (n.d.). *Business Benefits of Information Technology*. Retrieved March 16, 2014, from http://smallbusiness.chron.com/business-benefits-information-technology-4021.html.

3. Gordon, J. & Hayashi, C. (2010). *Exploring the Future of Cloud Computing: Riding the Next Wave of Technology-Driven Transformation*. World Economic Forum Report in partnership with Accenture, 2010. Available online at: http://www.accenture.com/SiteCollectionDocuments/PDF/Accenture_The_Future_of_Cloud_Computing.pdf

4. Guo, D. & Koufakou, A. (2017). How cloud computing is addressed for software development in computer science education. In: Kurosu, M. (eds) *Human-Computer Interaction. User Interface Design, Development and Multimodality*. HCI 2017. Lecture Notes in Computer Science, vol. 10271. Springer, Cham. https://doi.org/10.1007/978-3-319-58071-5_31.

5. Chan, W., Leung, E. & Pili, H. (2012). *Enterprise Risk Management for Cloud Computing*. The Committee of Sponsoring Organizations of the Treadway Commission (COSO), Chicago. http://www.coso.org/documents/Cloud%20Computing%20Thought%20Paper.pdf.

6. Kishor, K., Nand, P. & Agarwal, P. (2017). Subnet based ad hoc network algorithm reducing energy consumption in MANET. *International Journal of Applied Engineering Research*, 12(22), 11796–11802.

7. Kishor, K., Nand, P. & Agarwal, P. (2018). Secure and Efficient Subnet Routing Protocol for MANET. *Indian Journal of Public Health*, 9(12), 200. https://doi.org/10.5958/0976-5506.2018.01830.2.

8. Kishor, K., Nand, P. & Agarwal, P. (2018). Notice of retraction design adaptive subnetting hybrid gateway MANET protocol on the basis of dynamic TTL value adjustment. *Aptikom Journal on Computer Science and Information Technologies*, 3(2), 59–65. https://doi.org/10.11591/APTIKOM.J.CSIT.115

9. Kishor, K. & Nand, P. (2013). Review performance analysis and challenges wireless MANET routing protocols. *International Journal of Science, Engineering and Technology Research (IJSETR)*, 2(10), 1854–1855, ISSN 2278-7798.

10. Kishor, K. & Nand, P. (2014). Performance Evaluation of AODV, DSR, TORA and OLSR in with respect to end-to-end delay in MANET. *International Journal of Science and Research (IJSR)*, 3(6), 633–636, ISSN 2319-7064.

11. Kishor, K., Sharma, R. & Chhabra, M. (2022). Student performance prediction using technology of machine learning. In: Sharma D.K., Peng SL., Sharma R., Zaitsev D.A. (eds) *Micro-Electronics and Telecommunication Engineering*. Lecture Notes in Networks and Systems, vol. 373. Springer, Singapore. https://doi.org/10.1007/978-981-16-8721-1_53

12. Kishor, K. (2022). Communication-efficient federated learning. In: Yadav S.P., Bhati B.S., Mahato D.P., Kumar S. (eds) *Federated Learning for IoT Applications. EAI/Springer Innovations in Communication and Computing*. Springer, Cham. https://doi.org/10.1007/978-3-030-85559-8_9.

13. Kishor, K. (2022). Personalized federated learning. In: Yadav S.P., Bhati B.S., Mahato D.P., Kumar S. (eds) *Federated Learning for IoT Applications. EAI/Springer Innovations in Communication and Computing*. Springer, Cham. https://doi.org/10.1007/978-3-030-85559-8_3.

14. Gupta, S., Tyagi, S. & Kishor, K. (2022). Study and development of self sanitizing smart elevator. In: Gupta D., Polkowski Z., Khanna A., Bhattacharyya S., Castillo O. (eds) *Proceedings of Data Analytics and Management*. Lecture Notes on Data Engineering and Communications Technologies, vol. 90. Springer, Singapore. https://doi.org/10.1007/978-981-16-6289-8_15.

15. Kishor, K. & Pandey, D. (2022). Study and development of efficient air quality prediction system embedded with machine learning and IoT. In: Gupta D. et al. (eds), *Proceeding International Conference on Innovative Computing and Communications*. Lecture Notes in Networks and Systems, vol. 471, Springer, Singapore. https://doi.org/10.1007/978-981-19-2535-1.

16. Rai, B. K., Sharma, S., Kumar, G. & Kishor, K. (2022). Recognition of different bird category using image processing. *International Journal of Online and Biomedical Engineering (iJOE)*, 18(07), 101–114. https://doi.org/10.3991/ijoe.v18i07.29639.

17. Sharma, A., Jha, N. & Kishor, K. (2022). Predict COVID-19 with chest X-ray. In: Gupta D., Polkowski Z., Khanna A., Bhattacharyya S., Castillo O. (eds) *Proceedings of Data Analytics and Management*. Lecture Notes on Data Engineering and Communications Technologies, vol. 90. Springer, Singapore. https://doi.org/10.1007/978-981-16-6289-8_16.

18. Jain, A., Sharma, Y. & Kishor, K. (2020). Financial supervision and management system using ML algorithm. *Solid State Technology*, 63(6), 18974–18982. http://solidstatetechnology.us/index.php/JSST/article/view/8080.

19. Tyagi, D., Sharma, D., Singh, R., & Kishor, K. Real Time 'Driver Drowsiness'& Monitoring & Detection Techniques. *International journal of Innovative Technology And Exploring Engineering*, 9(8), 280–284, JUNE 2020, .DOI - 10.35940/ijitee.H6273.069820

20. Balobaid, A. & Debatosh, D. (2020) An Effective Approach to Cloud Migration for Small and Medium Enterprises (SMEs). *2020 IEEE International Conference on Smart Cloud (SmartCloud)*, 7–12.

21. IDC. (2013). *IDC Cloud Research*. http://www.idc.com/prodserv/idc_cloud.jsp. Retrieved date April 15, 2013.

22. Velte, A. T., Velte, T. J. & Elsenpeter, R. (2010). *Cloud Computing: A Practical Approach*. McGraw-Hill Education (India) Private Limited, New Delhi.

23. Armbrust, M., Fox, A., Griffith, R., Joseph, A, D., Katz, R., Konwinski, A., Lee, G., Patterson, D., Rabkin, A., Stoica, I. & Zaharia, M. (2009). *Above the Clouds: A Berkeley View of Cloud Computing*. Electrical Engineering and Computer Sciences, University of California at Berkeley.

24. Rochwerger et al., "The Reservoir model and architecture for open federated cloud computing," in IBM Journal of Research and Development, vol.53, no.4, pp.4:1–4:11, July 2009, doi: 10.1147/JRD.2009.5429058.

25. Boss, G., Malladi, P., Quan, D., Legregni, L. & Hall, H. (2007). *Cloud Computing*. IBM White Paper, 2007. http://download.boulder.ibm.com/ibmdl/pub/software/dw/wes/hipods/Cloud_computing_wp_f inal_8Oct.pdf.

26. Hosseini, A. K., Sommerville, I. & Sriram, I. (2010). *Research Challenges for Enterprise Cloud Computing*. Unpublished, http://arxiv.org/abs/1001.3257.

27. McAfee, A. (2011). *What Every CEO Needs to Know About the Cloud*. Harvard Business Review.

28. Buyya, R., Yeo, C. S., Venugopal, S., Broberg, J. & Brandic, I. (2009). Cloud computing and emerging IT platforms: Vision, hype, and reality for delivering computing as the 5th utility. *Future Generation Computer Systems*, 25(6), 599–616. https://doi.org/10.1016/j.future.2008.12.001.

29. Carlin, S. & Curran, K. (2012). Cloud computing technologies. *International Journal of Cloud Computing and Services Science*, 1(2), 59–65.

30. Yuen, E. (2012). *Microsoft: 2012 – The Year Cloud Moves from a Buzzword to Reality*. Retrieved from http://vmblog.com/archive/2011/12/12/microsoft-2012-the-year-cloud-moves-from-a-buzzword- to-reality.aspx#.U16V4lV_vw5.

31. Vouk, M. A. (2008). Cloud computing – Issues, research and implementations. *Journal of Computing and Information Technology*, 235–246. https://doi.org/10.1109/ITI.2008.4588381.

32. Willcocks, L., Venters, W. & Whitley, E. (2011a). *Cloud and the Future of Business: From Costs to Innovation, Part One:* Promise Accenture/LSE Outsourcing Unit London, UK.

33. Willcocks L.P, Venters W., and Whitley E.A. (2011b). Cloud and the Future of Business: From costs to innovation five reports: Promise, challenges, impact, innovation and management, Accenture and the Outsourcing Unit [www document] https://www.academia.edu/3012942/Cloud_and_the_Future_of_Business_From_Costs_to_Innovation

34. Greenhalgh T, Robert G, Macfarlane F, Bate P, Kyriakidou O. Diffusion of innovations in service organizations: systematic review and recommendations. Milbank Q. 2004;82(4):581–629. doi: 10.1111/j.0887-378X.2004.00325.x. PMID: 15595944; PMCID: PMC2690184.

35. Willcocks, L.P., Venters, W. and Whitley, E.A. (2013), "Cloud sourcing and innovation: slow train coming? A composite research study", Strategic Outsourcing: An International Journal, Vol. 6 No. 2, pp. 184–202. https://doi.org/10.1108/SO-04-2013-0004

36. Venters, W., & Whitley, E. A. (2012). A Critical Review of Cloud Computing: Researching Desires and Realities. Journal of Information Technology, 27(3), 179–197. https://doi.org/10.1057/jit.2012.17

37. Mell, P. & Grance, T. (2011). The NIST Definition of Cloud Computing Recommendations of the National Institute of Standards and Technology. https://nvlpubs.nist.gov/nistpubs/legacy/sp/nistspecialpublication800–145.pdf

38. Cloud Security Alliance. (2009). *Security Guidance for Critical Areas of Focus in Cloud Computing.* https://cloudsecurityalliance.org/csaguide.pdf. Retrieved date: 24-05-2012.

39. Velte AT, Velte TJ, Elsenpeter RC. Cloud Computing: a Practical Approach / Anthony T. Velte, Toby J. Velte, Robert Elsenpeter. 1st edition. McGraw-Hill Education; 2010.

40. Gong, C., Liu, J., Zhang, Q., Chen, H. & Gong, Z. (2010). *The Characteristics of Cloud Computing,* 2010 39th International Conference on Parallel Processing Workshops, 275–279.

41. Schaeffer, C. (2014). *What Is Cloud Computing and Why Does Your Small Business Need It?* Retrieved April 29, 2014, from http://www.hyphenet.com/blog/cloud-computing-for-your-small-business/. Schwab, K. (2013). *The Global Competitiveness Report 2013–2014 Full Data Edition,* 198–199.

42. Joton, S. (2009). *Diagram Showing Three Main Types of Cloud Computing (Public/External, Hybrid, Private/Internal).* Retrieved March 10, 2014, from http://en.wikipedia.org/wiki/Cloud_computing. Kleinrock, L. (2005). *A Vision for the Internet,* 2(1), 4–5.

43. Gordon, M. & Marchesini, K. (2010). *Examples of Cloud Computing Services.* Retrieved March 15, 2014, from http://www.unc.edu/courses/2010spring/law/357c/001/cloudcomputing/examples.html.

44. Danchev, S., A. Tsakanikas, and N. Ventouris. "Cloud computing: A driver for Greek economy competitiveness." Iobe_cloud computing (2011).http://iobe.gr/docs/research/en/RES_05_F_25112011.pdf

45. Cattaneo, G., Kolding, M., Bradshaw, D. & Folco, G. (2012). *Quantitative Estimates of the Demand for Cloud Computing in Europe and the Likely Barriers to Take-up.* Retrieved from https://www.eurocloud.fr/doc/idc-smart-2011.pdf

46. Yeo, C. S., Buyya, R., Assunção, M. D. de, Yu, J., Sulistio, A., Venugopal, S. & Placek, M. (2006). *Utility Computing on Global Grids,* ArXiv, abs/cs/0605056, 1–26.

47. Krikos, A. (2010). *Disruptive Technology Business Models in Cloud Computing.* Massachusetts Institute of Technology. http://dspace.mit.edu/handle/1721.1/7582.

48. Goncalves, V. & Ballon, P. (2011). Adding value to the network: Mobile operators' experiments with software-as-a-service and platform-as-a-service models. *Telematics and Informatics,* 28(-2011), 12–21.

49. Rosenthal, A., Mork, P., Li, M., Stanford, J., Koester, D. & Reynolds, P. (2009). Cloud computing: A new business paradigm for biomedical information sharing. *Journal of Biomedical Informatics.* http://www.sciencedirect.com/science/article/pii/S1532046409001154.

50. Pearson, S. (2012). *Privacy, Security and Trust in Cloud Computing.* Springer. ISBN: 978-1-4471-4189-1.

51. Bryman, A. & Bell, E. (2007). *Business Research Methods.* Second edition, Oxford University Press, Oxford, cop. 2007, ISBN: 9780199284986, 0199284989.

52. Crawford, I. (1997). *Marketing Research and Information Systems.* Food and Agriculture Organization of the UN. Retrieved date May 26, 2012 http://www.fao.org/docrep/W3241E/W3241E00.htm.

53. Padnos, C. (2012). *How Cloud Computing Changes Startup Investing.* Retrieved April 25, 2014, from http://sandhill.com/article/how-cloud-computing-changes-start-up-investing/.

11

Green Cloud Computing

Amit Kumar

IMS Engineering College

CONTENTS

11.1 Introduction

As of Wikipedia, cloud computing is a combination of lots of computing technologies that uses real-time communication across hundreds of machines to give users the impression that they are using a large amount of resources at once. Numerous services are offered by cloud computing, including Web data repositories, vast computer resources, and data processing servers.

Amazon introduced cloud computing in 2002 with the launch of its Amazon Web Services (AWS) and Elastic Compute Cloud services (EC2). Other major Web companies including Google and Yahoo have joined through this system since 2009, with the advent of Web 2.0 [1] (Figure 11.1).

DOI: 10.1201/9781003213895-11

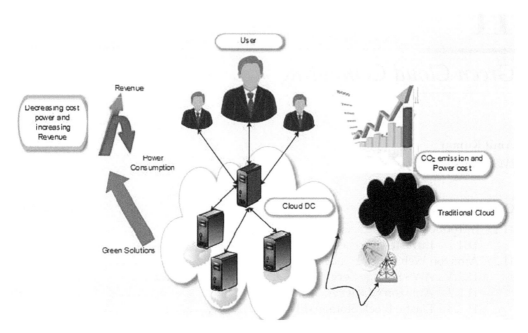

FIGURE 11.1
Clouds and its environment.

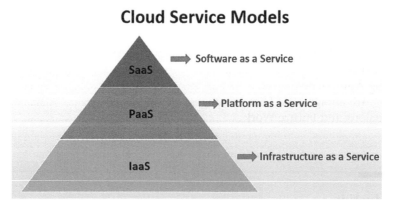

FIGURE 11.2
Cloud service models.

Service model of cloud computing (CC) provides services (Figure 11.2). These services are [2]:

- Software as a service (SaaS),
- Platform as a service (PaaS), and
- Infrastructure as a service (IaaS).

11.1.1 Infrastructure as a Service (IaaS)

Large-scale enterprise customers utilise this complete platform. IaaS gives developers access to infrastructure like limitless storage and processing capacity without requiring any on-site physical gear. The infrastructure-as-a service (IaaS) cloud providers primarily deal with virtual machines, storage, servers, networks, and load balancers at this core layer of cloud computing. In order to build an IaaS cloud, all you need is a virtual machine monitor (VMM), a hypervisor, and a public or private networking architecture. The requirement for a data centre and on-site hardware maintenance is reduced thanks to IaaS. IaaS might be mistaken for hardware-as-a-service (HaaS).

An example of a Web service is AWS.

11.2 Amazon Web Services

AWS is a cloud computing platform that offers a variety of online computing services [3]. Netflix, NASDAQ, SmugMug, Pinterest, and WeTransfer are examples of well-known clients who profit from AWS. Principal elements of AWS are:

11.2.1 AWS Storage Services

AWS storage services offer dependable, secure, and affordable infrastructure for storing and retrieving data [4].

11.2.2 Amazon Glacier

Amazon Glacier is a low-cost storage option since it scales with user needs and allows for both massive and little data sets to be stored. Amazon's distinctive features include data storage reliability and Amazon Simple Storage Service.

Amazon Glacier eliminates the need for businesses to do any kind of computation, and instead charges them based on their actual use, taking into account factors like company size, computing requirements, and available resources. Any data can be virtually stored. Amazon merely keeps track of the data stored in whatever format by the client in order to bill them [5].

Amazon Simple Storage Service (S3): An online file storage structure is provided by a Web service called Amazon Simple Storage Service (S3) [6]. It can be stored and access enormous amounts of data through Web services interfaces like SOAP, REST, and BitTorrent. It strives to deliver high availability, scalability, and affordable infrastructure while managing data with object storage architecture. It is essential for backup, archiving, disaster recovery, and content delivery and storage.

11.2.3 Elastic Block Storage (EBS)

Elastic Block Storage (EBS) is a virtualised SAN. Amazon employs RAID storage since it's redundant. As the name suggests, it exposes raw block devices for EC2 instances. EBS supports snapshotting and cloning. EBS volumes may be 1TB and use mirrored back-end storage and redundancy. EBS volumes should be used for block-level data updates. It's virtualised, allowing users to utilise given storage space and connect to servers through

API. Binding the volume to an instance is necessary because users may use it like an actual hard disc [7]. EBS has standard volumes and provisioned IOPS volumes. Both quantities' performance and cost differ. Open data sets may be used with AWS cloud-based applications to make data sets easier to access.

11.2.4 AWS Computing Service

Computing, a service provided by Cloud, allows for scalable computation, automated parallelization, and work scheduling. Amazon Elastic Compute Cloud (EC2) is a web service that offers a virtual computing environment that may be used to launch an Amazon Machine Image (AMI) or "instance" [8]. AMI is essentially accumulating of operating system, related system configuration settings, libraries, data, and application software. Using static IP addresses, AMIs can be utilised to provision several instances. The instances can be scaled up or down in response to variations in demand and come with persistent storage.

11.3 Platforms as a Service (PaaS)

With the help of PaaS, users may access a computing platform that primarily comprises of tools like an operating system, programming language, database, and Web server and that instantly grows to accommodate application demand. Here, in this architecture, programmers use unique APIs to construct programs that work in specific environments and further control software deployment and configuration choices. The program can only be utilised on the platform for which it was designed. PaaS shrinks the expense and complexity of application deployment by removing the need to buy, maintain, and provide hosting resources for the underlying hardware and software [9–11].

Deployment models [12] of cloud computing are:

- Public cloud,
- Private cloud,
- Community cloud, and
- Hybrid cloud.

11.3.1 Public Cloud

Anyone can buy computing power thanks to public clouds. A public cloud is often shared by many people. Private cloud, on the other hand, refers to cloud-based services that are housed on a company's own private servers [12,13].

The "public cloud" deployment model utilises computer resources that are owned and controlled by a provider and made accessible to several tenants through the Internet. A public cloud extends a company's IT infrastructure by using a virtualised environment, allowing it to host parts of its services and infrastructure used by virtual servers that are off-site and are controlled by another party. The advantages of public cloud service providers are numerous, and they provide a variety of services and fee structures. Companies who are thinking about moving to the public cloud should carefully weigh their provider options, if a long-term contract will bind them. With vigilant preparation, monthly cloud service prices can be reduced; nonetheless, businesses with erratic public cloud usage may find it difficult to stay within their spending limits on public cloud services when demand spikes [14–16].

Security in the public cloud is another factor that IT managers will want to consider because computers in the cloud exchange data from several businesses. Data encryption is a fantastic technique to provide greater security, but not all encryption solutions are compatible with both public and private clouds, which is what is known as a hybrid cloud. Every time data is transferred between a private data centre or private cloud and a public cloud, there is an inherent security risk [17–19].

The position of your public cloud service provider is one more thing to think about. Numerous nations have laws requiring the local storage of specific categories of data. These regulations regularly change, so it's a good idea to pick a cloud service provider based in your nation who can vouch for the locality and legal compliance of the servers hosting your data. Another problem is latency; if your data is being stored on another continent, it can take longer than if it were nearby [20,21].

11.3.2 Private Cloud

A single-user organisation has exclusive access to a private cloud's infrastructure. A private cloud may be hosted in a company's data centre, a third-party colocation facility, or by a private cloud provider, who may or may not also provide public shared multi-tenant cloud architecture. As with a typical infrastructure, the end-user organisation runs a private cloud, which requires maintenance, updates, OS patches, middleware, and application software management. Private cloud solutions demand more IT skills than public cloud but provide greater control and security.

The same security and control are provided by private clouds as by conventional on-premises infrastructure. The following list of factors influences why businesses choose private cloud computing.

11.3.2.1 Security

Since an organisation's own transactions are often the only ones sent to a private cloud, security is improved. Public cloud providers must manage simultaneous traffic from millions of users and transactions, increasing the likelihood of fraudulent traffic. The enterprise has superior control over server, network, and application security because private clouds are composed of dedicated physical infrastructure.

Workload performance is predictable and unaffected by other businesses sharing infrastructure or bandwidth since the hardware is dedicated.

11.3.2.2 Long-Term Savings

Although setting up the infrastructure to enable a private cloud might be expensive, in the long term, it could pay off. A private cloud can be significantly less expensive in the long run than paying monthly fees to use someone else's servers on the public cloud if an organisation already possesses the gear and network needed for hosting.

Cost predictability: Public cloud fees can vary greatly depending on consumption, storage costs, and data egress costs. No matter what workloads an organisation runs or how much data is transported, private cloud prices are the same every month.

11.3.2.3 Regulatory Governance

Where data is stored and where computation takes place may be determined by regulations like the EU's GDPR. A private cloud can be necessary in those areas where public cloud providers are unable to provide service. In order to guarantee that they are completely in charge of any personally identifiable or sensitive data, enterprises with sensitive data, such as financial or legal firms, may choose private cloud storage.

The consolidation of resources from different data centres into a single pool of resources is known as private cloud architecture. Organisations improve the effectiveness and use of their private cloud infrastructure by virtualising the hardware components. Leading software providers like VMware, Microsoft, and others offer private cloud solutions, while Red Hat, OpenStack, and other providers offer enterprise-grade open-source alternatives.

Through the use of virtual machines and software-defined networking (SDN), private cloud solutions enable businesses to design data centres (VMs). An international colocation facility or numerous server locations can be leased as part of a private cloud that spans the entire world's network.

11.3.3 Community Cloud

This idea aims to eliminate the need for a decentralised cloud infrastructure by enabling numerous users to collaborate on community-owned projects and applications. In other words, community cloud is a distributed infrastructure that integrates the services offered by many kinds of cloud solutions to address the unique problems faced by various business sectors.

In their cloud contacts, the communities interested in these projects—such as tenders, corporate organisations, and academic groups—concentrate on related concerns. Concepts and guidelines pertaining to security and compliance issues, as well as the project's objectives, may be of interest to both of them.

Community cloud solutions have been created by cloud providers, and some businesses are already reaping the rewards. Some of the key community cloud model scenarios that benefit the participating organisations are listed below.

Processing systems from many government agencies that conduct transactions with one another can share infrastructure. The tenants can save money with this set-up, and it may also result in less data traffic.

Community cloud is available to American government organisations that have identical standards for security measures, audits, and privacy. Users feel comfortable enough to invest in the platform for their ideas because it is community-based. A certain system or application hosted via cloud services could be required by numerous businesses. The cloud provider can let different users connect to the same environment and logically divide their sessions. A system like this eliminates the requirement for separate servers for every client with identical goals.

Instead of using a public cloud, agencies can utilise this model to test apps with advanced security requirements. This could be an opportunity to test aspects of a public cloud offering given the regulatory procedures connected with community clouds.

11.3.4 Hybrid Cloud

A combined computing, storage, and service environment known as a hybrid cloud is comprised of on-premises infrastructure, private cloud services, and a public cloud such as AWS or Microsoft Azure, along with orchestration across the various platforms. If you utilise a combination of computing done on-site (on-premises), private clouds, and public clouds inside your data centre, you have what's known as a hybrid cloud infrastructure. Although cloud services have the potential to save costs, the primary way in which they bring value is by facilitating the rapid digital transformation of businesses. The information technology agenda and the business transformation agenda are the two primary aims of any organisation that focuses on technology management. Historically speaking, cost reduction has been at the forefront of the IT agenda. However, the agendas for the digital transformation of companies are focused on the financial rewards that may be made from investments.

The hybrid cloud is more adaptable. A digital company is required to swiftly adapt and alter its direction. It's possible that your company may wish to integrate public, private, and on-premises resources in order to increase its agility.

A company's on-site data centre was converted into a private cloud and combined with public cloud environments hosted off-site by a public cloud provider in the early stages of hybrid cloud architecture. Using a public cloud service, this was accomplished (e.g. AWS, Google Cloud Services, IBM Cloud, Microsoft Azure). Using business middleware like Red Hat OpenStack or unified management tools to monitor, allocate, and administer those resources from a central interface (referred to as a "single pane of glass"), this was made possible.

For a number of different use cases, a common IT architecture was developed. Regulatory conformity and safety: Use the resources of the public cloud for workloads and data that are less sensitive, and use the resources of the private cloud for data that is sensitive and for activities that are regulated. Make use of public cloud computing and cloud storage in order to respond rapidly, automatically, and cost-effectively to spikes in traffic while protecting private cloud applications from disruption (this is known as "cloud bursting"). It is possible to adopt or migrate to the most recent software-as-a-service (SaaS) solution without first constructing new infrastructure on-premises. Make use of public cloud services in order to enhance already existing applications or increase the number of devices compatible with them (Figure 11.3).

According to the National Institute of Standards and Technology (NIST), cloud computing's primary goal is to maximise or improve the shared resources, but it also has a disadvantage because of its pricey infrastructure and high power consumption.

High power use and CO_2 emissions have been a major cause for concern because they accelerate global warming.

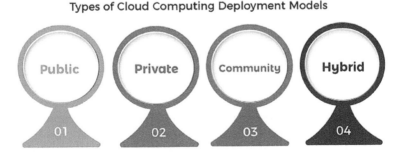

FIGURE 11.3
Types of deployment model of cloud computing.

We need to protect our planet and ecology from groups including the Climate Savers Computing Initiative, Greenpeace, and the US Environmental Protection Agency (EPA).

Researchers were forced to develop concepts for a green cloud computing flavor of cloud computing due to the ever-increasing acceptability and use of cloud computing and the expanding worldwide public awareness of the use of environmentally friendly resources.

The cloud uses hundreds of data centres to process or address user requests, and running these data centres requires a significant amount of power for procedures such as cooling. Green cloud computing works to lower the power application, helping to address the problems as they are progressively getting worse each year. To reduce this expense, numerous methods and algorithms are employed [2].

11.4 Literature Review

The application of green cloud computing has grown significantly during the recent few years. Numerous researches have been carried out recently to improve the use of green cloud in real-world situations with the aid of numerous criteria.

In data centres, energy use has greatly increased.

Cavdar et al. [3,21] have given some methods for increasing usage of less energy in data centres.

The Green Grid is recommending various factors, including thermal design power (TDP) [3], data centre efficiency (DCE) metrics [7], and power usage effectiveness (PUE) [22]. The typical parameter is PUE. PUE, which ranges from 1.0 to infinity, is a measure of how successfully a computer data centre uses its electricity, according to Wikipedia. When the PUE is 1.0, all of the power is being used efficiently and to its full capacity.

Corporations now use more energy than is necessary, for example, if data centres demand 1 kWh but companies use 1.5 kWh. Therefore, 0.5 WH of energy was lost while producing nothing useful for cooling, CPU use, or other tasks. Google's PUE is 1.13.

Table 11.1 explains some suggested data centre settings. PUE can rise to 3.0 or higher in many data centres, but with proper design, 1.6 levels would be possible [23]. The PUE values of the 22 data centers examined in this estimate, undertaken at Lawrence Berkeley National Labs [7] varied from 1.3 to 3.0.

Reduced energy use in data centres is another area of interest for Fumiko Satoh et al. [5]. However, for the purpose of developing an energy management system for the cloud, they combine an improved VM allocation tool with a sensor management function. According to the results, this solution will contribute to a 30% reduction in energy use across many data centres. This technique is also utilised to cut down on carbon emissions' energy content.

Another significant problem that uses a lot of energy in data centres is cooling. In the past, cooling was accomplished by utilising mechanical refrigerators that provided cooled water for IT equipment. Today, pre-cooling, sometimes referred to as no-cost cooling, is used. No-cost cooling lowers the need for cooling. Similar to when Facebook erected their data centre in the cold, dry country of Sweden. For rapid cooling, Microsoft puts its servers outdoors. Google also uses river water to cool its data centre [21]. To reduce energy usage, many hardware technologies, such as virtualisation, and software technologies, such as efficient algorithms for software, are used.

TABLE 11.1

Measurement of Green Metrics Power [3,21]

Metric	Explanation	Formula
Power usage effectiveness (PUE)	It is the ratio of the total energy used by a data centre's operations to the total energy used by its IT equipment.	Overall energy facility/IT equipment of energy
Carbon usage effectiveness (CUE)	It is a computation of the data centre's output of greenhouse gases (CO_2, CH_4) into the environment.	(Total CO_2 emission from total energy used for service of data centre)/total energy consumed by IT equipment
Water usage effectiveness (WUE)	It calculates how much water the data centre uses annually for things like cooling and electricity production.	Annual usage of water/total energy used by IT equipment
Energy reuse factor (ERF)	It computes the reusable energy utilised by data centres, such as hydropower and solar power	Use of reused energy/overall energy used by IT equipment
Energy reuse effectiveness (ERE)	This parameter calculates the financial benefit of reusing data centre energy.	Overall energy – reused energy/overall energy used by IT equipment
Data centre infrastructure efficiency (DCiE)	This variable is used to determine a data centre's energy efficiency.	(Overall IT equipment power/overall facility power)*100
Data centre productivity (DCP)	It determines how much of a contribution the data centre makes.	Overall useful work/overall resource used to do this work
Compute power efficiency (CPE)	It establishes how much electricity is actually used for computation overall.	IT equipment utilisation energy

Rasoul Beik et al. propose a software architectural layer that computes data centre energy usage and delivers energy-efficient services. In order to make the cloud more environmentally friendly in terms of energy efficiency, Bhanu Priya et al. provided several metrics. Various energy models are explored in this study in order to cut down on power usage and CO_2 emissions. Virtualisation, workload dispersion, and software automation are the three factors that contribute to a cloud becoming more environmentally friendly. Pay-per-use and self-service, which have been shown to be crucial for reducing energy use, are two additional factors to make clouds greener that are also investigated.

Kliazovich and Pascal Bouvry [11] say cloud data centre costs are rising. This study focuses on load distribution across data centres so energy consumption may be tracked at the packet level. This approach uses packets. The simulator, such as the green cloud NS2 simulator and the only one for clouds dubbed "CloudSim," has been used to simulate energy at the packet level. "Two-tier, three-tier, and three-tier high-speed data centre designs" are the three levels of this simulation.

After Kaur and Singh et al. [2], the author suggests a technique for calculating the energy used to produce various environmental gases. Completed the various issues in the field of energy cloud computing. The virtualisation concept in green cloud is included in the proposed model along with numerous fields for data, analysis, recording, put on guard, and restraint in order for environmental health and energy efficiency.

Hosman and Baikie et al.'s [24] new difficulty in the field of cloud computing was the fact that data centres use a lot of energy and that energy is always available. As a result, the author in his article discusses solar energy. Solar power's involvement in data centre energy usage is a hot issue. The author proposes a small-scale cloud data centre that includes "reduced power consumption platform, energy-efficient cloud computing, and DC power distribution." Owusu et al. [12] surveyed the level of cloud computing energy efficiency. They skilfully bring up the contentious topic of energy efficiency in relation to cloud computing. The energy efficiency of cloud computing is one contentious topic that is covered in this chapter.

Yamini and others [13] have done an excellent job of explaining the essential ideas of green cloud computing, such as virtualization, resource conservation, material reuse, and telecommuting. This paper's main objective is to lower the high energy consumption in green cloud computing through task and resource consolidation or scheduling. The good results presented in the research apply potential electricity reserve in sizable cloud data centres rather than the immediate extreme energy minimisation.

Buyya [14] argues that the increased demand for cloud services is accompanied by excessive energy usage and gas emissions that are hazardous to health and a major driver of rising cloud-operating costs. Buyya provided a clear and convincing study of the literature on the many cloud members that affect total energy usage. In this work, the cloud's structure is addressed in relation to the usage of green cloud computing.

Buyya et al. [25] carbon green cloud construct, which emphasises the notion of a second party, is made up of two distinct directories of the "green offer" and "carbon emission" types. These directories enable us to offer and make use of green services from both users and suppliers. Green brokers use a directory of green offers to access services, and they arrange services based on those with the lowest CO_2 emissions. Virtual machines are the main topic of Beloglazov and Buyya et al.'s [25] study on how to consume less energy. In order to save significant energy in the actual data centres of cloud computing, a publisher suggests the dynamic reallocation strategy for VMs and turns off the idle servers.

The goal is to develop a green cloud environment using the virtualisation concept; Nimje et al. [26] examined the security of cloud data centres. The study uses a number of techniques to address security and power consumption reduction. Here, virtualisation entered the picture since it eases the burden on data centres and allows for the quick deployment, administration, and distribution of resources. In order to provide virtualisation and achieve a high security standard for green cloud computing, Nimije integrated a hypervisor environment.

11.5 Existing Approaches

Buyya et al. [25] carbon's green cloud design emphasises a third party and comprises of green offer and carbon emission directories. These directories allow consumers and providers to offer and utilise green services.

"Green Offer Directory" lists registered suppliers' services. The green broker classified these services by price, time, and CO_2 emissions. Carbon Emission Directory stores data on cloud services' energy and cooling efficacy. Green broker used latest service knowledge.

Green broker receives user service requests. Using these directories, the green broker picks the green offer, accumulates energy efficiency statistics, and provides help to the private cloud. Using this directory approach, Hulkury et al. [27] and Garg et al. [28] propose the integrated green cloud architecture (IGCA), shown in Figure 11.4. Client-oriented cloud middleware uses QoS and budget to prove cloud computing is better than local.

This design has client and server sides. The management and users are on the client side, where the task will be done, while the server side contains green cloud middleware,

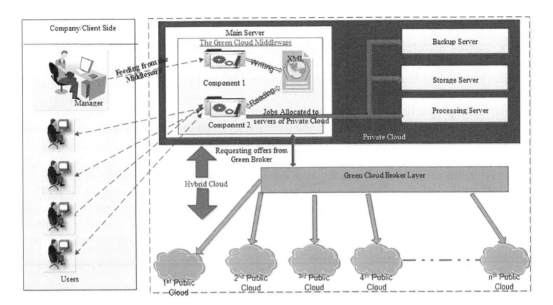

FIGURE 11.4
Integrated green cloud architecture.

a green broker, and processing and storage servers. The IGCA's green broker layer uses the directory idea to organise public cloud data and deliver green services [27].

Green cloud middleware has two pieces. Managers control one element and keep middleware data. Computer use, private cloud servers, data, and server frequencies of high, medium, and low. Middleware addresses energy consumption, storage capacity, and other data.

Manager got it when customer asked. The request is divided into jobs and supplied to users, while the component stores job information. Users may calculate how much energy and carbon are used when a job is run on a client's PC, a public cloud using a green broker, or a private cloud utilising servers. The management picks the greenest offer while considering job security. The specifics of management's decisions are saved in an XML file.

Every user connects to component 2 to read XML. This file contains the complete job. The file lists job locations, and they run based on the addresses. If the work isn't in the file, the client's PC or private cloud will be utilised. Three locations are involved. First, if the job is done LOCALLY (on the requester's side), the data is stored on the client side; thus, middleware is not utilised [29].

This file gets the job's private cloud address and server name. If it's a public cloud, we'll contact a green broker for the best green choice. Middleware knows three sites. Middleware accounts for workers' decision-making energy [30].

Processing speed, energy usage, bandwidth, and other factors define the best work execution site. The program will compute and analyse the three sites using all parameters. The IGCA provides employment balance, stability, and high-quality service. The manager distributes tasks and the greenest solution by location (public, private, local host).

In this system, the manager assigns responsibilities and makes choices. If the manager fails, the whole structure collapses.

11.5.1 Advantages and Disadvantages

Every existing architecture, as we've already discussed, has some positive and negative aspects. Buya et al. [14] provided the architecture for green clouds, and the CO_2 emission directory is its key benefit. This directory measures the best suitable services that give less carbon emission, and because carbon dioxide emission and energy consumption are both directly proportionate to one another, it immediately suggests that energy will also decrease. Similar to the disadvantage, the drawback is that quality provisioning, security, and other factors should be taken into account in addition to CO_2 emissions and energy use [31].

By taking into account additional components that search services on the private cloud first, followed by the public cloud, Hulkary et al. [27] cover these elements as well. This saves time and yields superior results when compared to Buya Architecture. The system's manager serves as the primary point of communication, so if he or she crashes, the entire system would disintegrate. In addition, the manager's decision-making isn't clever, and everything has been done by hand [26,29,32].

These are a few of the benefits and drawbacks that can be improved upon for next projects in relation to these present designs.

11.6 Conclusions and Future Work

In this article, we covered the topics of conventional cloud computing and the use of green cloud while also shedding light on new advancements in the area of green cloud computing with the purpose of creating a world that is both healthier and friendlier to the environment. As a result of this, we offered a comparative study on the subject of environmentally friendly cloud computing. In future, research may be done in a number of different locations. In the process of resolving the problem of developing an efficient method for extracting results from the cloud in order to bring into practice all of the topics covered in the article, we will also be tackling this issue. In addition, we may be able to computerise the manager of the green cloud, who is responsible for making all decisions pertaining to the services.

References

1. D. Cavdar and F. Alagoz, (Eds.), "A Survey of Research on Greening Data Centers", *Proceedings of the IEEE Global Communications Conference (GLOBECOM)*, December 3–7; Anaheim, CA (2012).
2. A. Jain, M. Mishra, S. Kumar Peddoju and N. Jain, (Eds.), "Energy Efficient Computing-Green Cloud Computing", *Proceedings of the International Conference of the Energy Efficient Technologies for Sustainability (ICEETS)*, April 10–122; Nagercoil (2013).
3. T. Vinh T. Duy, Y. Sato and Y. Inoguchi, (Eds.), "Performance Evaluation of a Green Scheduling Algorithm for Energy Savings in Cloud Computing", *Proceedings of the IEEE International Symposium of the Parallel & Distributed Processing, Workshops and PhD Forum (IPDPSW)*, April 19–23; Atlanta, GA (2010).

4. F. Satoh, H. Yanagisawa, H. Takahashi and T. Kushida, (Eds.), "Total Energy Management System for Cloud Computing", *Proceedings of the IEEE International Conference of the Cloud Engineering (IC2E)*, March 25–27; Redwood City, CA (2013).

5. R. Beik, (Ed.), "Green Cloud Computing: An Energy-Aware Layer in Software Architecture", *Proceedings of the Spring Congress of the Engineering and Technology (S-CET)*, May 27–30; Xian (2012).

6. S. Greenberg, E. Mills, B. Tschudi, P. Rumsey and B. Myatt, (Eds.), "Best Practices for Data Centres: Results from Benchmarking 22 Data Centres", *Proceedings of the ACEEE Summer Study on Energy Efficiency in Buildings*, April, pp. 3-76–3-87 (2006).

7. T. Kgil, D. Roberts and T. Mudge, (2006). Pico server: Using 3D stacking technology to build energy efficient servers, *Three Dimensional Integrated Circuit Design*, 4(16), 219–260.

8. N. Rassmussen, (Ed.), "Electrical Efficiency Modelling of Data Centres", *American Power Conversion (APC) White Paper #113*, October, pp. 1–18 (2007).

9. B. Priya, E. S. Pilli and R. C. Joshi, (Eds.), "A Survey on Energy and Power Consumption Models for Greener Cloud", *Proceeding of the IEEE 3rd International Advance Computing Conference (IACC)*, February 22–23; Ghaziabad (2013).

10. D. Kliazovich and P. Bouvry, (Eds.), "Green Cloud: A Packet-level Simulator of Energy-aware Cloud Computing Data Centers", *Proceeding of the IEEE Global Telecommunications Conference (GLOBECOM)*, December 6–8; Miami, FL (2010).

11. M. Kaur and P. Singh, (Eds.), "Energy Efficient Green Cloud: Underlying Structure", *Proceeding of the IEEE International Conference of the Energy Efficient Technologies for Sustainability (ICEETS)*, April 10–12, Nagercoil (2013).

12. F. Owusu and C. Pattinson, (Eds.), "The Current State of Understanding of the Energy Efficiency of Cloud Computing", *Proceeding of the IEEE 11th International Conference of the Trust, Security, Privacy in Computing and Communications (TrustCom)*, June 25–27; Liverpool (2012).

13. R. Yamini, (Ed.), "Power Management in Cloud Computing Using Green Algorithm", *Proceeding of the IEEE-International Conference on Advances in Engineering, Science and Management (ICAESM)*, March 30–31; Nagapattinam, Tamil Nadu (2012).

14. S. K. Garg and R. Buyya, "Green Cloud Computing and Environmental Sustainability", S. Murugesan and G. R. Gangadharan, (Eds.), *Wiley-IEEE Press Ebook*, Edition 1, no. 3, pp. 76–87 (2012).

15. D. H. Heo, X. Liu and T. Abdelzaher, (Eds.), "Integrating Adaptive Components: An Emerging Challenge in Performance-Adaptive Systems and a Server Farm Case-Study", *Proceeding of the IEEE 28th International Conference of the Real-Time Systems Symposium (RTSS)*, December 3–6; Tucson, AZ (2007).

16. K. Kishor, P. Nand and P. Agarwal (2017). Subnet based ad hoc network algorithm reducing energy consumption in MANET. *International Journal of Applied Engineering Research*, 12(22), 11796–11802.

17. K. Kishor, P. Nand and P. Agarwal (2018). Secure and efficient subnet routing protocol for MANET, *Indian Journal of Public Health*, 9(12), 200. https://doi.org/10.5958/0976-5506.2018.01830.2.

18. K. Kishor, P. Nand and P. Agarwal (2018). Notice of retraction design adaptive subnetting hybrid gateway MANET Protocol on the basis of dynamic TTL value adjustment. *Aptikom Journal on Computer Science and Information Technologies*, 3(2), 59–65. https://doi.org/10.11591/APTIKOM.J.CSIT.115.

19. K. Kishor and P. Nand (2013). Review performance analysis and challenges wireless MANET routing protocols. *International Journal of Science, Engineering and Technology Research (IJSETR)*, 2(10), 1854–1855, ISSN 2278-7798.

20. K. Kishor and P. Nand (2014). Performance evaluation of AODV, DSR, TORA and OLSR in with respect to end-to-end delay in MANET. *International Journal of Science and Research (IJSR)*, 3(6), 633–636, ISSN 2319-7064.

21. "Green Grid Metrics—Describing Data Centres Power Efficiency", *Technical Committee White Paper by the Green Grid Industry Consortium* (2007).

22. C. Belady, (Ed.), *How to Minimize Data Centre Utility Bills, US* (2006).

23. L. Hosman and B. Baikie, (Eds.), *Solar-Powered Cloud Computing Datacenters*, vol. 2, no. 15 (2013).

24. M. N. Hulkury and M. R. Doomun, (Eds.), "Integrated Green Cloud Computing Architecture", *Proceedings of the International Conference on Advanced Computer Science Applications and Technologies (ACSAT)*, Washington DC, USA (2012).

25. S. K. Garg, C. S. Yeo and R. Buyya, (Eds.), "Green Cloud Framework for Improving Carbon Efficiency of Clouds", *Proceedings of the 17th International European Conference on Parallel and Distributed Computing (EuroPar)*, August–September. Bordeaux, France (2011).

26. A. R. Nimje, V. T. Gaikwad and H. N. Datir, (Eds.), "Green Cloud Computing: A Virtualized Security Framework for Green Cloud Computing", *Proceeding of the International Journal of Advanced Research in Computer Science and Software Engineering* (2013).

27. K. Kishor, P. Nand and P. Agarwal, (2017). Subnet based ad hoc network algorithm reducing energy consumption in MANET. *International Journal of Applied Engineering Research*, 12(22), 11796–11802.

28. L. Wang and G. Von Laszewski, "Scientific Cloud Computing: Early Definition and Experience", *Proceedings of the 10th IEEE International Conference on High Performance Computing and Communications* (2008).

29. P. Mell, and T. Granc, *The NIST Definition of Cloud Computing*, National Institute of Standards and Technology (NIST) (2011). [Online]. Available: http://csrc.nist.gov/publications/nistpubs/800-145/SP800-145.pdf.

30. S. Pal and P. K. Pattnaik, (2012). Efficient architectural framework for cloud computing, *International Journal of Cloud Computing and Services Science (IJ-CLOSER)*, 1(2), 66–73.

31. C. S. Yeo, R. Buyya, M. Dias de Assunção, J. Yu, A. Sulistio, S. Venugopal, and M. Placek, "Utility Computing on Global Grids", Chapter 143, H. Bidgoli (ed.), *The Handbook of Computer Networks*, John Wiley & Sons, New York, 2007, ISBN: 978-0-471-78461-6.

32. A. Berl, E. Gelenbe, M. Di Girolamo, G. Giuliani, H. De Meer, M. Quan Dang and K. Pentikousis (2009). Energy-efficient cloud computing, *The Computer Journal*, 53, 1045–1051.

12

Study of Issues with Cloud Security

Amit Kumar Singh Sanger

KIET Group of Institutions

CONTENTS

12.1 Introduction

12.1.1 Cloud Computing

Computing services, including virtual machine (VM), memory, connectivity, software, and offerings, are pooled and made available through the Internet, making "cloud computing" a viable option for rapidly provisioning a wide range of services from any location with no upfront investment. The symbol of the cloud is used to represent the Internet. To describe the infrastructure, storage services, and delivery of software over the Internet, cloud computing is used. This is not a new technology, but rather the lack of computational resources based on long-established technologies such as server virtualization [1]. In simple words, cloud computing is a place or ability where users can store their data, and they can process it and access it from anywhere in the world.

12.1.2 The Cloud Model Consists of Five Key Features

1. **Demand-driven self-service:** This enables the user to rapidly and automatically access resources without requiring further human interplay.

2. **Access to a wide area network:** It enables users to use the offerings using any typical gadget that can establish a network connection, such as desktop computers, notebooks, mobiles, or tabs.

3. **Resource pooling:** Through a multi-tenant paradigm, the service provider pools its computing resources to provision several customers, allocating and reallocating various hardware and software resources on the fly to meet fluctuating demands.

4. **Rapid elasticity:** This enables rapid reduction of cloud capabilities at the national user domain level.

5. **Metering:** This involves monitoring and controlling the level of resource utilization or cost of utilization.

12.2 Literature Survey

Cloud computing is one of the hot areas of research. In the last few years, there has been a significant amount of effort put in by researchers in cloud computing. Some research papers that focus on cloud computing have been discussed below:

In [2], the authors published a document. NIST Technical Series publications are written by or for NIST and published by the NIST Research Library. In this special publication, NIST defines cloud computing. NIST has also elaborated services and deployment models for cloud computing.

In [3], the authors explored various problems in cloud computing. The focus of their research is to optimize the use of energy in data centres. The authors also suggested few areas of concern such as security, energy consumption in the cloud, and data storage. Further, the authors also pointed out the need for a framework that can coordinate to combine various approaches.

In [4], the authors evaluated the two commercial cloud platforms. The authors evaluated the performance of different HPC standards on Amazon Web Services and Microsoft Azure. Their primary concentration was on computer instances. According to their results, the AWS compute instance in raw computing was affordable, while Azure offered low-cost bandwidth.

In [5], the authors studied the essential security issues in the area of cloud computing. His results included a study of a number of cloud computing security concerns, with an emphasis on three key cloud computing security dimensions (computer security, network security, and information security). Theoretically, security concerns from outsider and insider threats were addressed in this paper, as well as potential solutions. These solutions may be used to improve security in future.

In [6], the authors studied the issues and challenges in the cloud. The authors also discussed the security and privacy concerns related to cloud computing use. Further, possible countermeasures were also suggested for securing the data used over the cloud. In the concluding remarks, the author suggested the need to develop a secure model that can solve security issues.

In [7], the authors worked on reviewing the difficulties faced by the organizations in migrating on the cloud. The authors found in their study that to migrate on the cloud it was necessary to define challenges in the adoption process and to build a precise strategy model that will effectively migrate to the cloud. The authors proposed a theoretical cloud adaptation framework based on the facts and findings during their research. This framework will help to examine challenges during migration and adopting a cloud.

In [8], the authors worked on securing data sharing in the cloud. During his study, the author found that cloud users were unwilling to share their vulnerable data on an unreliable cloud server. For supporting data sharing in a secure and efficient way, the author proposed a method that modified RS-IBE scheme proposed in [9] and analysed the top three cloud companies (AWS, Azure, and GCP).

The analysis was done to compare the performance and the tools provided by all the three cloud providers. The authors also summarized the features and results of comparison that will help the users to select suitable cloud providers as per their requirements.

In [10], the authors reviewed cloud computing security issues in this paper. The authors presented the cloud service model and discussed the issues and challenges. The authors also explored a few of the issues in greater depth such as network and data protection, data confidentiality, data integrity, data availability, and backup disaster recovery. The authors also suggested ways to deal with these security issues. In the final remark, the author also indicated the need for continuous improvement in security mechanisms.

12.3 Cloud Models and Their Security Issues

12.3.1 Service Models

These models are basically the kind of service offered by the cloud. These services are divided into further modules [11] and are depicted in Figure 12.1.

a. **Software as a service:** The user is offered the option to use cloud-based services from the provider that can be accessed from various user devices using a simple user interface, like a Web browser. To put it another way, according to this paradigm, a complete program is made available to the customer as a service that may

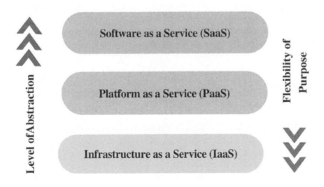

FIGURE 12.1
Cloud service models.

be requested. An excellent illustration of this would be making use of a browser to access one's email through a service such as that offered by Microsoft, Yahoo, or Google [12].

b. **Platform as a service:** The user can upload programs they have developed themselves or purchased via the vendor's assisted development tools to the cloud architecture. The user manages the implemented programs and potentially the parameters of the software hosting platform, however not the network, servers, operating systems (OS), or memory that makes up the core cloud platform [12].

c. **Infrastructure as a service (IaaS):** The user has the ability to create and run any kind of programme, including operating systems (OS) and installed applications, and he has control over the provisioning of essential computer functions like as computation, memory, and networking. The user does not administer or control the fundamental cloud architecture, but the user does have access to the OS, memory, and software that have been implemented [12]. The user may also have partial access to some network elements.

12.3.2 Deployment Models

Figure 12.2 depicts a high-level overview of cloud deployment models. Public, private, and hybrid cloud deployment options are listed below.

a. **Public cloud:** It offers the general public a shared platform that may be accessible by anybody who has Internet access. It works under the pay-per-use model and is administrated by the third-party cloud service provider. In this, multiple users can use the same storage simultaneously. It is utilized, administered, and run by enterprises, institutions, or federal agencies, or intermingling of these three types of organizations.

b. **Private cloud:** It is generally known as the "in-house cloud" or "business cloud". Rather than serving the wider public, it serves a private internal network and its

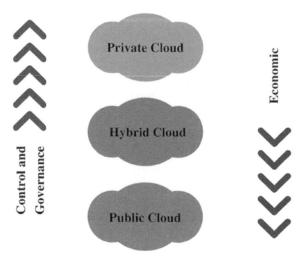

FIGURE 12.2
Cloud deployment models.

authorized customers. With the assistance of firewalls and internal hosting, the private cloud is capable of providing an increased amount of data privacy and secrecy. It also ensures that the operational and sensitive information cannot be accessed by third-party vendors. Some examples of private clouds are Microsoft, Ubuntu, and HP data centres.

c. **Hybrid cloud:** An amalgamation of public and private clouds is what's known as the hybrid cloud. For the development of a unified, automated, and well-managed IT environment, these clouds (public and private) are combined into a hybrid cloud. The public cloud works on the non-critical activities, and the private cloud works on the critical activities. A hybrid cloud is used in health care, finance, and academia. Some hybrid cloud provider companies are Amazon, Google, Cisco, and Microsoft.

12.4 Cloud Security Issues

Cloud technology has the potential to pose a significant number of security risks and issues, despite the fact that it has introduced a wide range of helpful services. Various weaknesses can be abused by nefarious actors due to the fact that a large amount of data is sent via the network and kept in certain cloud services. As shown in Figure 12.3, concerns regarding cloud computing security can be divided into the two primary classes that are listed below:

12.4.1 Deployment Models Security Issues

The following is a list of problems that can arise when

i. **Considering a public cloud [13]**

a. When storing data on the cloud, it can be challenging to guarantee its safety because the security measures are within the cloud provider's control. Therefore,

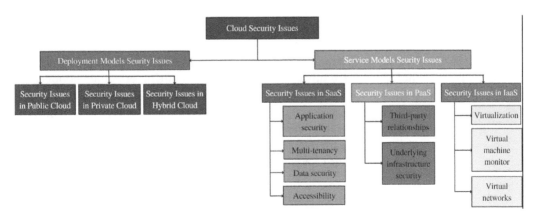

FIGURE 12.3
Cloud security issues.

in order to secure information throughout its lifespan during the many phases of operation, achieving the fundamental security standards, which are known as consistency, reliability, and secrecy, becomes a challenging issue.

b. Because a public cloud is used by multiple users, there is an increased risk that sensitive data could be compromised. Therefore, the provider of the service must be selected thoughtfully in order to prevent such dangers.

c. If a cloud provider uses a third-party vendor, the consumer should review the service-level agreements (SLAs) and risk mitigation in the event of any disruptions [14].

d. SLAs and the degrees of encryption and authentication that will be used to safeguard data against nefarious attackers should be confirmed in order to avoid insider assaults.

ii. **A private cloud is considered [15]**

a. As a result of the methodologies used for virtualization, VMs may connect with the incorrect VMs, which will result in a variety of security vulnerabilities. Implementing the appropriate cryptographic procedures is the best way to stop something like this from happening.

b. The OS that is behaving as the host should be protected from any malicious software attack in order to prevent any potential risks. Additionally, communication among the guest VMs and the host OS should take place through the use of physical interfaces rather than directly.

c. Customers of private clouds have the ability to exercise control over a portion of the cloud's architecture and make use of it through an hypertext transfer protocol (HTTP) endpoint or a Web interface. In such a scenario, the interfaces require to be created appropriately, and a variety of HTTP requests require to be guarded by making use of common Web-based software security mechanisms.

d. A security protocol should not only be employed to provide the basic level of security but it should also be utilized to avoid assaults that originate from within the business [16].

iii. **Using hybrid cloud**

a. In order to keep the system security consistent throughout the entirety of the network, it is necessary to implement good architecture policies. This strategy should include identification process, Intrusion Prevention System (IPS) signatures, and firewall policies.

b. It is challenging to guarantee that a hybrid cloud complies with public and private cloud provider requirements while also ensuring adequate cooperation across the two types of providers.

c. It is critical to have proper security monitoring in place whenever a hybrid system includes both public and private cloud computing. As a result, pre-existing rules, such as authentication, authorization, and identification control, require revision in order to adequately address the sophisticated integration problems at hand.

d. Because hybrid clouds are required to handle operations that span numerous domains, they are susceptible to a variety of dangers because not many administrators have the necessary experience and skills to do so.

12.4.2 Service Models Security Issues

i. **Security issues in SaaS**

    a. **Application security:** Generally speaking, these apps are provided to users through the Internet and a browser. On the other hand, security holes in Web apps could make the software-as-a-service (SaaS) providers more susceptible to attack. Adversaries have been utilizing the Internet to infect the systems of consumers and carry out other nefarious operations including stealing confidential material [17]. The Open Web Application Security Project (OWASP) has determined which ten dangers pose the greatest danger to the protection of Web-based applications [16]. Although there are still other security concerns, this is an excellent starting point for the process of safeguarding online apps.

    b. **Multi-tenancy:** SaaS systems can be categorized into competency models based on qualities such as flexibility, customizability through XML, and multi-tenancy [17]. These frameworks can be identified by the underlying attributes. A single instance caters to the needs of multiple tenants at the same time in multi-tenancy. This strategy allows for highly effective utilization of the available resources; yet, it has restricted scalability. Due to the fact that it is probable that information from numerous tenants will be maintained in the same database, there is a high potential for data leakage among those tenants. It is essential to have security measures in place to guarantee that the information of one client is not shared with the information of another consumer [18].

        Data security: Data security is a common concern for any new technology, but it becomes a serious challenge for SaaS customers because they require to rely on their providers for appropriate safety [18]. In the case of SaaS, authorized data is routinely converted into plaintext and then stored in the cloud. The provider of the SaaS is the one who is responsible for maintaining the confidentiality of the data while it is being accessed, used, and stored [17].

    c. **Accessibility:** Utilizing a browser to access Web-based services enables users to view those apps from any system, like open PCs and mobile phones. Nonetheless, this throws up the possibility of additional security risks. A study has been distributed by the Cloud Security Alliance (CSA) [19] that depicts the current predicament of portable trying to sign up and the top risks here. These dangers include data attempting to take portable malware, unverified devices (Wi-Fi), and security flaws discovered in the system OS and authority applications, ambiguous business areas, and proximity-based hacking.

ii. **Security issues in PaaS**

    a. Third-party relationships: In addition, platform as a service (PaaS) provides not just standard program development language but also Web services techniques provided by third parties, including middleware. This means that PaaS can facilitate third-party partnerships. The term "middleware" refers to the process of combining components from multiple sources into a single cohesive entity. As a result, PaaS models are also a solution to the security challenges that are associated with mashups, such as the security of data and networks [18]. In addition, consumers of PaaS have to rely on the safety of Web-hosted design tools in addition to the solutions provided by third parties.

b. **Underlying infrastructure security:** Although software developers typically do not have exposure to the core layers in PaaS, it is the responsibility of the service providers to ensure that both the architecture and the software are secure [18]. Even in situations in which programmers have full control over the safety of the programs they create, they do not have any guarantee that the resources of the development platform that are offered by a PaaS provider are secured.

iii. **Security issues in IaaS**

a. Virtualization: The term "virtualization" refers to a technology that enables users to create copies of virtual computers, start sharing them with other users, migrate them, and transfer them back again, which in turn allows users to run a variety of applications [20]. In any case, because there is an added element that needs to be validated, it furthermore opens up new potential entryways for criminals [18]. The safety of VMs becomes just as important as the safety of physical servers, and any flaws in either type of security could potentially have an effect on another. However, cybersecurity is a more significant challenge since virtualization involves more objectives of section and more interconnections that have a multidimensional character. Virtualized environments are vulnerable to a wide variety of attacks that are designed for conventional systems. Unlike actual servers, VMs have two types of limitations: physical and virtual [21].

b. **Virtual machine monitor:** The virtual machine monitor (VMM) is responsible for the separation of VMs. As a consequence, if the VMM is compromised, it is possible that the VM it manages will also be compromised. The VMM is low-level programming that monitors and manages its VMs; hence, just like any other traditional programming, it contains security flaws [20].

c. **Virtual networks:** Due to the sharing of assets, different residents of the network share different segments of the system. As was said earlier, sharing assets gives attackers the ability to carry out cross-occupant assaults more effectively. The strategy that uses dedicated physical channels to connect each VM with its own host offers the highest level of protection. However, the majority of virtual servers make use of VMs to connect VMs in order to communicate in a more acceptable and effective manner. For instance, the majority of virtualization platforms, such as Xen, give users two distinct ways to organize VMs: spanned and managed to steer. Despite the fact that these processes increase the probability of carrying out certain attacks, such as intercepting and imitating virtual systems [18], these options are provided by most virtualization platforms.

12.5 Countermeasures

In prior sections, we covered a variety of different exploits and assaults that can be used against a system. In this section, we will go over various preventative steps that can be taken in order to prevent those problems. Nevertheless, the primary purpose of this chapter is to draw attention to the safety concerns connected to virtualization that are present in the cloud architecture. As a result, protective actions are not described in this subsection in a manner that is exhaustive and detailed.

Some of the countermeasures related to threats are illustrated in Figure 12.4.

Threats	Countermeasures
Hijacking of service or account	Identity and Access Management Guidance Dynamic credential
Data scavenging	Service-level agreements (SLAs) should be updated with destruction strategies
Data leakage	FRS techniques Digital Signatures Encryption Homomorphic encryption
Denial of service	Only limited computational resources should be offered
Customer-data manipulation	Web application scanners
VM escape	HyperSafe TCCP (Trusted Cloud Computing Platform) TVDc (Trusted Virtual Datacenter)
VM image creation	Mirage
Insecure VM migration	PALM TCCP (Trusted Cloud Computing Platforms VNSS
Sniffing/spoofing virtual networks	Virtual network framework based on Xen
Abuse and nefarious use of cloud computing	Customer CSC's network traffic introspection VM monitoring.
Malicious insiders	Supply chain audit including human resource hiring procedure, Security certification, Audits, use of trusted Cloud computing platform (TCCP)
Shared technology issues	VM monitoring and cloud audit, Access control, SLA enforcement for patching and vulnerability remediation
Unknown security profile	Security certification, Audits, SLA monitoring

FIGURE 12.4
Threats and countermeasures in cloud.

12.6 Conclusion

The concept of cloud technology is getting traction, but alongside with that, security is becoming an increasingly important component for delivering a dependable infrastructure. Investigators will have a better knowledge of the problem at hand, allowing them to create potential solutions, if the risks and threats are systematically organized.

Although cloud technology is an offshoot of numerous other innovations, it also carries with it the risks associated with those technologies' parent companies. We have modelled potential security risks based on different service models in cloud technology, including SaaS, IaaS, and PaaS, respectively. Additionally, a classification has been depicted in aspects of security flaws, corresponding risks, and their probable countermeasures based on the different research that is available concerning the security issues and their alternatives in cloud technology. This classification was derived from the various sources of information. Although substantial solutions have been presented but have not yet been put into practical execution, advanced innovations such as virtualization in cloud platform, cloud identification operations, and cloud security employing cryptofunctions can be built to make cloud systems that are more resilient.

References

1. Bhamare, D., T. Salman, M. Samaka, A. Erbad, and R. Jain. "Feasibility of supervised machine learning for cloud security," In: *2016 International Conference on Information Science and Security (ICISS)*, pp. 1–5. IEEE, 2016.
2. P. Mell, and T. Grance, *NIST Definition of Cloud Computing*, Special Publication (NIST SP), National Institute of Standards and Technology, Gaithersburg, MD [online], 2011. Doi: 10.6028/NIST.SP.800-145 (Accessed December 14, 2022).
3. A. Kaur, V. P. Singh and S. Singh Gill, "The future of cloud computing: Opportunities, challenges and research trends," In: *2018 2nd International Conference on I-SMAC (IoT in Social, Mobile, Analytics and Cloud) (I-SMAC)*, Palladam, India, pp. 213–219, 2018, doi: 10.1109/I-SMAC.2018.8653731.
4. C. Kotas, T. Naughton and N. Imam, "A comparison of Amazon web services and Microsoft Azure cloud platforms for high performance computing," In: *2018 IEEE International Conference on Consumer Electronics (ICCE)*, Las Vegas, NV, USA, pp. 1–4, 2018, doi: 10.1109/ICCE.2018.8326349.
5. X. Sun, "Critical security issues in cloud computing: A survey," In: *2018 IEEE 4th International Conference on Big Data Security on Cloud (Big Data Security), IEEE International Conference on High Performance and Smart Computing, (HPSC) and IEEE International Conference on Intelligent Data and Security (IDS)*, Omaha, NE, USA, pp. 216–221, 2018, doi: 10.1109/BDS/HPSC/IDS18.2018.00053.
6. C. Kumari, G. Singh, G. Singh and R. Singh Batth, "Security issues and challenges in cloud computing: A mirror review," In: *2019 International Conference on Computational Intelligence and Knowledge Economy (ICCIKE)*, Dubai, United Arab Emirates, pp. 701–706, 2019, doi: 10.1109/ICCIKE47802.2019.9004361.
7. M. Shuaib, A. Samad, S. Alam, and S.T. Siddiqui, Why adopting cloud is still a challenge? A review on issues and challenges for cloud migration in organizations. In: Hu Y.C., Tiwari S., Mishra K., Trivedi M. (eds) *Ambient Communications and Computer Systems. Advances in Intelligent Systems and Computing*, vol. 904. Springer, Singapore, 2019. doi: 10.1007/978-981-13-5934-7_35.
8. K. Lee, Comments on "secure data sharing in cloud computing using revocable storage identity-based encryption", In: *IEEE Transactions on Cloud Computing*, vol. 8, no. 4, pp. 1299–1300, 2020, doi: 10.1109/TCC.2020.2973623.
9. M. Saraswat and R. C. Tripathi, "Cloud computing: Comparison and analysis of cloud service providers – AWs, Microsoft and Google," In: *2020 9th International Conference System Modeling and Advancement in Research Trends (SMART)*, Moradabad, India, 2020, pp. 281–285, doi: 10.1109/SMART50582.2020.9337100.

10. A. Bansal, A.K. Bairwa, and S. Hiranwal, Security issues in cloud computing: A review. In: Purohit S., Singh Jat D., Poonia R., Kumar S., Hiranwal S. (eds) *Proceedings of International Conference on Communication and Computational Technologies. Algorithms for Intelligent Systems.* Springer, Singapore, 2021. doi: 10.1007/978-981-15-5077-5_4.

11. K. Kishor, P. Nand, P. Agarwal, Secure and efficient subnet routing protocol for MANET, *Indian Journal of Public Health*, 9(12), 200 (2018). doi: 10.5958/0976-5506.2018.01830.2.

12. O.-A. Isaac, M. Ananya, F. Agono, and R. Goddy-Worlu. "Cloud computing architecture: A critical analysis," In: *2018 18th International Conference on Computational Science and Applications (ICCSA)*, pp. 1–7. IEEE, 2018.

13. A. Poniszewska-Marańda, Selected aspects of security mechanisms for cloud computing-current solutions and development perspectives. *Applied Computer Science* 8, 35–49 (2014).

14. L. Juhnyoung, A view of cloud computing. *International Journal of Networked and Distributed Computing* 1(1), 2–8 (2013).

15. R. Bhadauria, and S. Sanyal, Survey on security issues in cloud computing and associated mitigation techniques. *arXiv preprint arXiv: 1204.0764* (2012).

16. J. Jang-Jaccard and S. Nepal, A survey of emerging threats in cyber security. *Journal of Computer and System Sciences* 80(5), 973–993 (2014), ISSN: 0022-0000. doi: 10.1016/j.jcss.2014.02.005.

17. J. Ju, Y. Wang, J. Fu, J. Wu, and Z. Lin, "Research on key technology in SaaS." In: *2010 International Conference on Intelligent Computing and Cognitive Informatics*, pp. 384–387. IEEE, 2010.

18. K. Hashizume, D. G. Rosado, E. Fernández-Medina, and E. B. Fernandez. An analysis of security issues for cloud computing. *Journal of Internet Services and Applications*, 4(1), 1–13 (2013).

19. Cloud Security Alliance (2012) Security guidance for critical areas of Mobile Computing. Available: https://downloads.cloudsecurityalliance.org/initiatives/mobile/Mobile_Guidance_v1.pdf.

20. M. Ali, S. U. Khan, and A. V. Vasilakos, Security in cloud computing: Opportunities and challenges. *Information Sciences* 305, 357–383 (2015).

21. M. A. Morsy, J. Grundy, and I. Müller, An analysis of cloud computing security problem. In: *Proceedings of APSEC 2010 Cloud Workshop*, APSEC, Sydney, Australia (2010).

Index

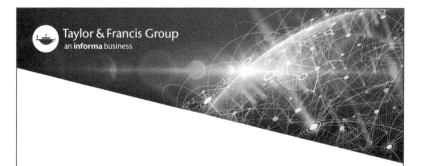